Building an Event-Driven Data Mesh

*Patterns for Designing and Building
Event-Driven Architectures*

Adam Bellemare

Beijing · Boston · Farnham · Sebastopol · Tokyo

Building an Event-Driven Data Mesh

by Adam Bellemare

Published by O'Reilly Media, Inc., 1005 Gravenstein Highway North, Sebastopol, CA 95472.

O'Reilly books may be purchased for educational, business, or sales promotional use. Online editions are also available for most titles (*https://oreilly.com*). For more information, contact our corporate/institutional sales department: 800-998-9938 or *corporate@oreilly.com*.

Acquisitions Editor: Melissa Duffield	**Indexer:** nSight, Inc.
Development Editor: Melissa Potter	**Interior Designer:** David Futato
Production Editors: Jonathon Owen and Beth Kelly	**Cover Designer:** Karen Montgomery
Copyeditor: Stephanie English	**Illustrator:** Kate Dullea
Proofreader: Penelope Perkins	

April 2023:   First Edition

Release History for the First Edition

2023-04-04:   First Release

See *https://oreilly.com/catalog/errata.csp?isbn=9781098127602* for release details.

978-1-098-12760-2

[LSI]

Table of Contents

Preface

Data mesh is a fundamental shift in the way we think about, create, share, and use data. We promote data to a first-class citizen by carefully curating and crafting it into *data products*, supported with the same level of care and commitment as any other business product. Consumers can discover and select the data products they need for their own use cases, relying upon the commitment of the data product producer to maintain and support it. At its heart, data mesh is as much about technological reorganization as it is about the renegotiation of social contracts, responsibilities, and expectations.

Back when I wrote *Building Event-Driven Microservices* (O'Reilly) I made reference to (and a bit vaguely defined) a *data communication layer*, very similar yet not nearly so well thought out as data mesh. The principles of the data communication layer were simple enough: treat data as a first-class citizen, make it reliable and trustworthy, and produce it through event streams so that you can power both operational and analytical applications.

The beauty of data mesh is that it's not a big-bang total revision of everything we know about data. In fact, it's really an affirmation of best practices, both social and technical, based on the collective hard work and experiences of countless people. It provides the framework necessary to discuss *how* to go about creating, communicating, and using data, acting as a *lingua franca* for the data world.

Zhamak Dehghani has done a phenomenal job in bringing data mesh to the world. I remember being blown away by her initial article in Martin Fowler's blog from 2019. She very eloquently described the problems that my team was facing at that very moment and identified the principles we would need to adopt for working toward a solution. Her work really influenced my thinking on the need to have a well-defined data communication layer to make sharing and using data reliable and easy. Dehghani's data mesh is precisely the social-technical framework we need to build a better data world.

Events and event streams play a critical role in a data mesh, as your business opportunities can only ever be solved as fast as your slowest data source. Classic analytical use cases, such as computing a monthly sales report, may be satisfied with a data product that updates just once a day. But many of your most important business use cases, such as fulfilling a sale, computing inventory, and ensuring prompt shipment, require real-time data. An event-driven data mesh provides the capabilities to power both operational and analytical use cases, in both real time and batch.

There is real value in adopting a data mesh. It streamlines discovery, consumption, processing, and application of data across your entire organization. But one of the best features of data mesh is that you can start applying it wherever you are today. It is not an all-or-nothing proposition. You can take the pieces, principles, and concepts that work for improving your situation, and leave the rest until you're ready to adopt those next.

I'm quite excited about data mesh. It provides us with a principled social and technological framework for building out our own data meshes, but just as importantly, the language to talk about and solve data problems with all of our colleagues. I hope you'll enjoy reading this book as much as I did writing it.

Conventions Used in This Book

The following typographical conventions are used in this book:

Italic

Indicates new terms, URLs, email addresses, filenames, and file extensions.

`Constant width`

Used for program listings, as well as within paragraphs to refer to program elements such as variable or function names, databases, data types, environment variables, statements, and keywords.

This element signifies a tip or suggestion.

This element signifies a general note.

This element indicates a warning or caution.

O'Reilly Online Learning

 For more than 40 years, *O'Reilly Media* has provided technology and business training, knowledge, and insight to help companies succeed.

Our unique network of experts and innovators share their knowledge and expertise through books, articles, and our online learning platform. O'Reilly's online learning platform gives you on-demand access to live training courses, in-depth learning paths, interactive coding environments, and a vast collection of text and video from O'Reilly and 200+ other publishers. For more information, visit *https://oreilly.com*.

How to Contact Us

Please address comments and questions concerning this book to the publisher:

O'Reilly Media, Inc.
1005 Gravenstein Highway North
Sebastopol, CA 95472
800-998-9938 (in the United States or Canada)
707-829-0515 (international or local)
707-829-0104 (fax)

We have a web page for this book, where we list errata, examples, and any additional information. You can access this page at *https://oreil.ly/build-data-mesh*.

Email *bookquestions@oreilly.com* to comment or ask technical questions about this book.

For news and information about our books and courses, visit *https://oreilly.com*.

Find us on LinkedIn: *https://linkedin.com/company/oreilly-media*

Follow us on Twitter: *https://twitter.com/oreillymedia*

Watch us on YouTube: *https://youtube.com/oreillymedia*

Acknowledgments

There are many people who I would like to thank for supporting, reviewing, and advising me while writing this book. I'd like to thank my development editors, Nicole Tache and Melissa Potter, who both provided a ton of great support and really helped keep me focused and accountable. I've also been fortunate enough to have two stellar production editors, Beth Kelly and Jonathon Owen. They really helped take a kludge of TODOs, mostly completed figures, and run on sentences and reshape it into something coherent and sensible. Thanks as well to Stephanie English who provided the copyediting as we moved from draft into production.

My reviewer and former Confluent colleague Hubert Daley provided initial thoughts and feedback that helped shape the rest of the book. Chris Ford, Head of Technology, Thoughtworks, provided critical feedback, helping me identify what worked and what didn't. Pramod Sadalage of Thoughtworks, Data Mesh leader for North America, similarly provided me a wealth of constructive criticisms and support. Thanks to each of you for taking the time to help me improve this book.

Thanks to my Confluent colleagues Ben Stopford, Andrew Sellers, Jack Vanlightly, Ian Robinson, and Travis Hoffman with whom I had many discussions on the merits, drawbacks, and implementation of data mesh. I greatly value your thoughts, comments, constructive criticisms, and helpful insights.

And finally, thanks to my family and friends who provided me with the emotional support and encouragement to keep on keeping on.

CHAPTER 1
Event-Driven Data Communication

The way that businesses relate to their data is changing rapidly. Gone are the days when all of a business's data would fit neatly into a single relational database. The big data revolution, started more than two decades ago, has since evolved, and it is no longer sufficient to store your massive data sets in a big data lake for batch analysis. Speed and interconnectivity have emerged as the next major competitive business requirements, again transforming the way that businesses create, store, access, and share their important data.

Data is the lifeblood of a business. But many of the ways that businesses create, share, and use data is haphazard and disjointed. Data mesh provides a comprehensive framework for revisiting these often dysfunctional relationships and provides a new way to think about, build, and share data across an organization, so that we can do helpful and useful things: better service for our customers, error-free reporting, actionable insights, and enabling truly data-driven processes.

To get an understanding of what we're trying to fix, we first need an idea of the main data problems facing a modern business.

First, big data systems, underpinning a company's business analytics engine, have exploded in size and complexity. There have been many attempts to address and reduce this complexity, but they all fall short of the mark.

Second, business operations for large companies have long since passed the point of being served by a single monolithic deployment. Multiservice deployments are the norm, including microservice and service-oriented architectures. The boundaries of these modular systems are seldomly easily defined, especially when many separate operational and analytical systems rely on read-only access to the same data sets. There is an opposing tension here: on one hand, colocating business functions in a single application provides consistent access to all data produced and stored in that system. On the other, these business functions may have absolutely no relation to one another aside from needing common read-only access to important business data.

And third, a problem common to both operational and analytical domains: the inability to access high-quality, well-documented, self-updating, and reliable data. The sheer volume of data that an organization deals with increases substantially year-over-year, fueling a need for better ways to sort, store, and use it. This pressure deals the final blow to the ideal of keeping everything in a single database and forces developers to split up monolithic applications into separate deployments with their own databases. Meanwhile, the big data teams struggle to keep up with the fragmentation and refactoring of these operational systems, as they remain solely responsible for obtaining their own data.

Data has historically been treated as a second-class citizen, as a form of exhaust or by-product emitted by business applications. This application-first thinking remains the major source of problems in today's computing environments, leading to ad hoc data pipelines, cobbled together data access mechanisms, and inconsistent sources of similar-yet-different truths. Data mesh addresses these shortcomings head-on, by fundamentally altering the relationships we have with our data. Instead of a secondary by-product, data, and the access to it, is promoted to a first-class citizen on par with any other business service.

Important business data needs to be readily and reliably available as building block primitives for your applications, regardless of the runtime, environment, or codebase of your application. We treat our data as a first-class citizen, complete with dedicated ownership, minimum quality guarantees, service-level agreements (SLAs), and scalable mechanisms for clean and reliable access. Event streams are the ideal mechanism for serving this data, providing a simple yet powerful way of reliably communicating important business data across an organization, enabling each consumer to access and use the data primitives they need.

In this chapter, we'll take a look at the forces that have shaped the operational and analytical tools and systems that we commonly use today and the problems that go along with them. The massive inefficiencies of contemporary data architectures provide us with rich learnings that we will apply to our event-driven solutions. This will set the stage for the next chapter, when we talk about data mesh as a whole.

What Is Data Mesh?

Data mesh was invented by Zhamak Dehghani (*https://oreil.ly/P-SQc*). It's a social and technological shift in the way that data is created, accessed, and shared across organizations. Data mesh provides a *lingua franca* for discussing the needs and responsibilities of different teams, domains, and services and how to they can work together to

---

make data a first-class citizen. This chapter explores the principles that form the basis of data mesh.

In my last book, *Building Event-Driven Microservices* (O'Reilly), I introduced the term *data communication layer*, touching on many of the same principles as data mesh: treat data as a first-class citizen, formalize the structure for communication between domains, publish data to event streams for general purpose usage, and make it easy to use for both the producers and consumers of data. And while I am fond of the data communication layer terminology, the reality is that I think the language and formalized principles of data mesh provide everything we need to talk about this problem *without* introducing another "data something something" paradigm.

Dehghani's book, *Data Mesh* (O'Reilly), showcases the theory and thought leadership of data mesh in great depth and detail, but remains necessarily agnostic of specific implementations.

In this book, we'll look at a practical implementation of data mesh that uses the event stream as the primary data product mode for interdomain data communications. We can be a bit more pragmatic and less intense on the theory and more concrete and specific on the implementation of an event-driven design. While I think that event streams are fundamentally the best option for interdomain communication, they do come with trade-offs, and I will, of course, cover these too, mentioning nonstreaming possibilities where they are best suited.

Data mesh is based on four main principles: domain ownership, data as a product, federated governance, and self-service platform. Together, these principles help us structure a way to communicate important business data across the entire organization. We'll evaluate these principles in more detail in the next chapter, but before we get there, let's take a look at *why* data mesh matters today.

An Event-Driven Data Mesh

The modern competitive requirements of big data in motion, combined with modern cloud computing, require a rethink of how businesses create, store, move, and use data. The foundation of this new data architecture is the event, the data quantum that represents real business activities, provided through a multitude of purpose-built event streams. Event streams provide the means for a central nervous system for enabling business units to access and use fundamental, self-updating data building blocks. These data building blocks join the ranks of containerization, infrastructure as a service (IaaS), continuous integration (CI) and continuous deployment (CD) pipelines, and monitoring solutions, the components on which modern cloud applications are built.

Event streams are not new. But many of the technological limitations underpinning previous event-driven architectures, such as limited scale, retention, and performance, have largely been alleviated. Modern multitenant event brokers complete with tiered storage can store an unbounded amount of data, removing the strict capacity restrictions that limited previous architectures. Producers write their important business domain data to an event stream, enabling others to couple on that stream and use the data building blocks for their own applications. Finally, consumer applications can in turn create their own event streams to share their own business facts with others, resulting in a standardized communications mesh for all to use.

Data mesh provides us with very useful concepts and language for building out this interconnected central nervous system. Figure 1-1 shows a basic example of what a data mesh could look like.

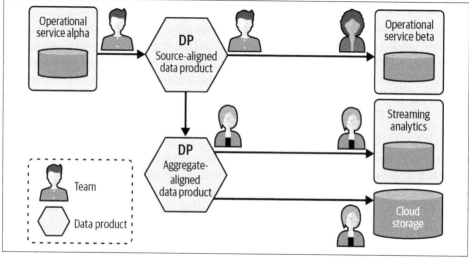

Figure 1-1. A very basic Hello Data Mesh implementation

The team that owns operational system Alpha selects some data from their service boundary, remodels it, and writes it to a *source-aligned data product*, which they also own (we'll cover data product alignments more in "The Three Data Product Alignment Types" on page 33). The team that owns operational system Beta reads data from this data product into its own service boundary, again remodeling it, transforming it, and storing only what they need.

Meanwhile, a third team connects to Alpha team's data product and uses it to compose their own *aggregate-aligned data product*. This same team then uses its aggregate-aligned data product to both power a streaming analytics use case and to write a batch of files to cloud storage, where data analysts will use it to compose reports and power existing batch-based analytics jobs.

This diagram represents just the tip of the data mesh iceberg, and there remain many areas to cover. But the gist of the event-driven data mesh is to make data readily available in real time to any consumers who need it.

Many of the problems that data mesh solves have existed for a very long time. We're now going to take a brief history tour to get a better understanding of *what* it is we're solving and *why* data mesh is a very relevant and powerful solution.

Using Data in the Operational Plane

Data tends to be created by an operational system *doing business things*. Eventually, that data tends to be pulled into the analytical plane for analysis and reporting purposes. In this section, we'll focus on some of the operational plane and the common challenges of sharing business data with other operational (and analytical) services.

The Data Monolith

Online transaction processing (OLTP) databases form the basis of much of today's operational computer services (let's call them "monoliths" for simplicity). Monolithic systems tend to play a big role in the operational plane, as consistent synchronous communication tends to be simpler to reason and develop against than asynchronous communication. Relational databases, such as PostgreSQL and MySQL, feature heavily in monolithic applications, providing atomicity, consistency, isolation, and durability (ACID) transactions and consistent state for the application.

Together, the application and database demonstrate the following *monolith data principles*:

The database is the source of truth
> The monolith relies on the underlying database to be the durable store of information for the application. Any new or updated records are first recorded into the database, making it the *definitive source of truth* for those entities.

Data is strongly consistent
> The monolith's data, when stored in a typical relational database, is strongly consistent. This provides the business logic with strong read-after-write consistency, and, thanks to transactions, it will not inadvertently access partially updated records.

Read-only data is readily available
> The data stored within the monolith's database can be readily accessed by any part of the monolith. Read-only access permissions ensure that there are no inadvertent alterations to the data.

Note that the database should be directly accessed only by the service that owns it, and not used as an integration point (*https://oreil.ly/SQ9Hb*).

These three principles form a binding force that make monolithic architectures powerful. Your application code has read-only access to the entire span of data stored in the monolith's database as a set of authoritative, consistent, and accessible data primitives. This foundation makes it easy to build new application functionality provided it's in the same application. But what if you need to build a new application?

The Difficulties of Communicating Data for Operational Concerns

A new application cannot rely on the same easy access to data primitives that it would have if it were built as part of the monolith. This would not be a problem if the new application had no need for any of the business data in the monolith. However, this is rarely the case, as businesses are effectively a set of overlapping domains, particularly the common core, with the same data serving multiple business requirements. For example, an ecommerce retailer may rely on its monolith to handle its orders, sales, and inventory, but requires a new application powered by a document-based database (or other database type) for plain-text search functionality. Figure 1-2 highlights the crux of the issue: how do we get the data from Ol' Reliable into the new document database to power search?

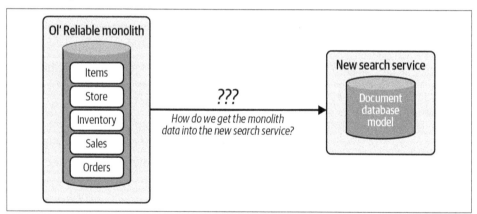

Figure 1-2. The new search service team must figure out how to get the data it needs out of the monolith and keep it up to date

This puts the new search service team in a bit of a predicament. The service needs access to the item, store, and inventory data in the monolith, but it also needs to model it all as a set of documents for the search engine. There are two common ways that teams attempt to resolve this. One is to replicate and transform the data to the search engine, in an attempt to preserve the three monolith data principles. The second is to use APIs to restructure the service boundaries of the source system, such that the same data isn't simply copied out—but served completely from a single system. Both can achieve some success, but are ultimately insufficient as a general solution. Let's take a look at these in more detail to see why.

Strategy 1: Replicate data between services

There are several mechanisms that fall under this strategy. The first and simplest is to just reach into the database and grab the data you need, when you need it. A slightly more structured approach is to periodically query the source database and dump the set of results into your new structure. While this gives you the benefit of selecting a different data store technology for your new service, there are a few major drawbacks:

Tight coupling with the source
> You remain coupled on the source database's internal model and rely on it exclusively to handle your query needs.

Performance load on the source
> Large data sets and complex queries can grind the database to a halt. This is especially true in the case of denormalizing data for analytical use cases, where multi-table and complex joins are common.

The second most common mechanism for the data replication strategy is a read-only replica of the source database. While this may help alleviate query performance issues, consumers still remain coupled on the internal model. And, unfortunately, each additional external coupling on the internal data model makes change more expensive, risky, and difficult for all involved members.

Coupling on the internal data model of a source system causes many problems. The source model will change in the course of normal business evolution, which often causes breakages in both the periodic queries and internal operations of all external consumers. Each coupled service will need to refactor its copy of the model to match what is available from the source, migrate data from the old model to the new model, and update its business code accordingly. There is a substantial amount of risk in each of these steps, as a failure to perform each one correctly can lead to misunderstandings in the meaning of the models, divergent copies of the data, and ultimately incorrect business results.

Data replication strategies become more difficult to maintain with each new independent source and each new required replica. This introduces a few new issues:

The original data set can be difficult to discover

It's not uncommon for a team to accidentally couple its service on a copy of the original data, rather than the original data itself. It can be difficult to discover what the original source of data is without resorting to informal knowledge networks.

Increase in point-to-point connections

Additionally, each new independent service may become its own authoritative source of data, increasing the number of point-to-point connections for interservice data replication.

Point-to-point replication of data between services introduces additional complexity, while simultaneously introducing tight coupling on the internal data model of the source. It is insufficient for building the modern data communications layer.

Strategy 2: Use APIs to avoid data replication needs

Directly coupled request-response microservices, also sometimes known as synchronous microservices, are another common approach to dealing with accessing remote data. Microservices can directly call the API of another service to exchange small amounts of information and perform work on each other's behalf.

For example, you may have one microservice that manages inventory-related operations, while you have other microservices dedicated to shipping and accounts. Each of these service's requests originate from the dedicated mobile frontend and web frontend microservices, which stitch together operations and return a seamless view to users, as shown in Figure 1-3.

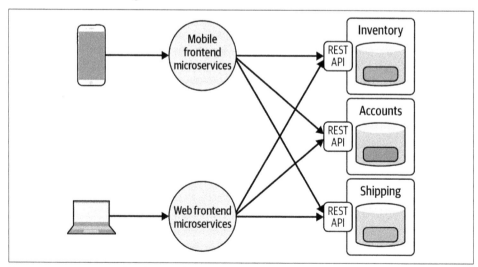

Figure 1-3. An example of a simple ecommerce microservice architecture

Synchronous microservices have many benefits:

- Purpose-built services serve the needs of the business domain.
- The owners have a high level of independence to use the tools, technologies, and models that work best for their needs.
- Teams also have more control over the boundaries of their domains, including control and decision making over how to expand them to help serve other clients' needs.

There are numerous books written on synchronous microservices, such as *Building Microservices* by Sam Newman (O'Reilly) and *Microservices Patterns* by Chris Richardson (Manning), that go into far more detail than I have space for, so I won't delve into them in much detail here.

The main downsides of this strategy are the same as with a single service:

- There is no easy and reliable mechanism for accessing data beyond the mechanisms provided in the microservices' API.
- Synchronous microservices are usually structured to offer up an API of *business operations*, not for serving reliable bulk data access to the underlying domain.
- Most teams resort to the same fallbacks as a single monolith does: reach into the database and pull out the data you need, when you need it, (see Figure 1-4).

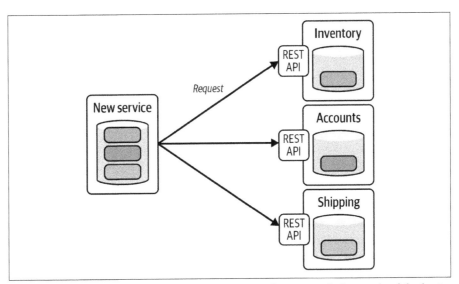

Figure 1-4. The microservice boundaries may not line up with the needs of the business problem

In this figure, the new service is reliant on the inventory, accounts, and shipping services just for access to the underlying business data—but not for the execution of any business logic. While this form of data access *can* be served via a synchronous API, it may not be suitable for all use cases. For example, large data sets, time-sensitive data, and complex models can prevent this type of access from becoming reality. In addition, there is the operational burden of providing the data access API and data serving performance on top of that of the base microservice functionality.

Operational systems lack a generalized solution for communicating important business data between services. This isn't something that's isolated to just operations. The big data domain, underpinning and powering analytics, reporting, machine learning, AI, and other business services, is a voracious consumer of full data sets from all across the business.

While domain boundary violations in the form of smash and grab data access are the foundation on which big data engineering has been built (I have been a part of such raids during the decade I have spent in this space), fortunately for us, it has provided us with rich insights that we can apply to make a better solution for all data users. But before we get to that, let's take a look at the big data domain requirements for accessing and using data and how this space evolved to where it is today.

The Analytical Plane: Data Warehouses and Data Lakes

Whereas operational concerns focus primarily on OLTP and server-to-server communication, analytical concerns are historically focused on answering questions about the overall performance of the business. Online analytical processing (OLAP) systems store data in a format more suitable to analytical queries, allowing data analysts to evaluate data on different dimensions. Data warehouses help answer questions such as "How many items did we sell last year?" and "What was our most popular item?" Answering these questions requires remodeling operational data into a model suitable for analytics, and also accounting for the vast amounts of data where the answers are ultimately found.

Getting data into a data warehouse has historically relied on a process known as Extract, Transform, and Load (ETL), as shown in Figure 1-5.

A periodically scheduled job extracts data from one or more source databases and transforms it into the data model required by the data warehouse. The data is then loaded into the data warehouse, where data analysts can run further queries and analyses. Data warehouses typically enforce well-defined schemas at write time, including column types, names, and nullability.

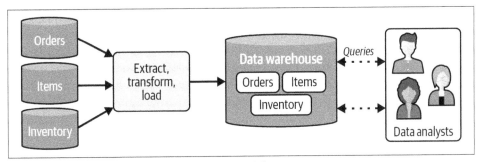

Figure 1-5. A typical data warehouse ETL workflow

Historically, data warehouses have proven to be successful at providing a means for analytical results. But the ever-increasing data and compute loads required larger disk drives and more powerful compute chips and ultimately ran into the physical limits of computer hardware. So instead of further scaling up, it became time to scale out.

The need for massive scale was plainly evident to Google, which published The Google File System (*https://oreil.ly/iakeU*) in October, 2003. This is the era that saw the birth of big data and caused a massive global rethink of how we create, store, process, and, ultimately, use data.

 Many modern data warehouses also offer high scalability, but it wasn't until the advent of the big data revolution that this became a reality. Historically, data warehouses were limited by the same factors as any other system operating on a single server.

Apache Hadoop (*https://oreil.ly/T0Hde*) quickly caught on as the definitive way to solve the scaling problems facing traditional OLAP systems. Because it's free and open source, it could be used by any company, anywhere, provided you could figure out how to manage the infrastructure requirements. It also provided a new way to compute analytics, one where you were no longer constrained to a proprietary system limited by the resources of a single computer.

Hadoop introduced the Hadoop Distributed File System (HDFS), a durable, fault-tolerant filesystem that made it possible to create, store, and process truly massive data sets spanning multiple commodity hardware nodes. While HDFS has now been largely supplanted by options such as Amazon S3 and Google Cloud Storage, it paved the way for a bold new idea: copy all of the data you need into a single logical location, regardless of size, and apply processing to clean up, sort out, and remodel data into the required format for deriving important business analytics.

Big data architecture introduced a significant shift in the mentality toward data. Not only did it address the capacity issues of existing OLAP systems, it introduced a new concept into the data world: it was not only acceptable, but *preferable*, to use unstructured or semi-structured data, instead of enforcing *schema on write* as in a data warehouse. In this new world of big data, you were free to write data with or without any schema or structure and resolve it all later at query time by applying a *schema on read*. Many data engineers were pleased to get rid of the schema on write requirement, as it made it easier to just get data into the ecosystem.

Consider Table 1-1, comparing the data structures and use cases between the relational database and MapReduce. MapReduce is an early Hadoop processing framework and is what you would use to read data, apply a schema (on read), perform transformations and aggregations, and produce the final result.

Table 1-1. A comparison of a relational database management system and Hadoop, circa 2009

	Traditional RDBMS	MapReduce
Data size	Gigabytes	Petabytes
Access	Interactive and batch	Batch
Updates	Read and write many times	Write once, read many times
Structure	Static schema	Dynamic schema
Integrity	High	Low
Scaling	Nonlinear	Linear

Note that this definitive guide from 2009 promotes MapReduce as a solution for handling *low integrity data* with a *dynamic schema*, emphasizing the notion that HDFS *should* be storing unstructured data with low integrity, with varying and possibly conflicting schemas to be resolved at runtime. It also points out that this data is *write once, read many times*, which is precisely the scenario in which you want a strong, consistent, enforced schema—providing ample opportunity for well-meaning but unconstrained users of the data to apply a read-time schema that misinterprets or invalidates the data.

A schema on write, including well-defined columns with types, defaults, nullability, and names, doesn't necessarily restrict downstream transformations in any way. It also doesn't force you to denormalize or join any data before writing.

A schema does provide you with a sanity check, ensuring that the data you're ingesting at least fits the most basic expectations of the downstream processors. Abandoning that sanity check pushes the detection of errors downstream, causing significant hardships for those trying to use the data.

In the early days of Hadoop, I don't think that I—or many others—appreciated just how the notion of schema on read would end up changing how data is collected, stored, and analyzed. We believed in and supported the idea that it was okay to grab data as you need it and figure it out after the fact, restructuring, cleaning, and enforcing schemas at a later date. This also made it very palatable for those considering migrating to Hadoop to alleviate their analytical constraints, because this move didn't constrain your write processes or bother you with strict rules of data ingestion—after all, you can just fix the data once it's copied over!

Unfortunately, the fundamental principle of *storing unstructured data to be used with schema on read* proved to be one of the costliest and most damaging tenets introduced by the big data revolution. Let's take a look at precisely how this negatively affects distributed data access and why well-defined schematized data is such an important tenet of data mesh.

The Organizational Impact of Schema on Read

Enforcing a schema at read time, instead of at write time, leads to a proliferation of what we call "bad data." The lack of write-time checks means that data written into HDFS may not adhere to the schemas that the readers are using in their existing work, as shown in Figure 1-6. Some bad data will cause consumers to halt processing, while other bad data may go silently undetected. While both of these are problematic, silent failures can be deadly and difficult to detect.

	A	B	C	D	E	F
	Record ID	Name (String not NULL)	Size (String not NULL)	Quantity (Int > 0)	Price (Float)	Adheres to Intended Schema
	1	"Adam Bellemare"	"Medium"	-3	$12.50	No
	2	"Mackenzie B. Dog"	"Small"	15	$22.37	Yes
	3	8675309	NULL	12	$98.75	No
	4	NULL	"Extra-Large"	100	%3CNull%3E	No
...		...	...	...	...	...
	100	"Julia Banderas"	"Tiny"	2	$12.50	Yes
				Number of Perfect Records:		77

Figure 1-6. Examples of bad data in a data set, discovered only at read time

To get a better understanding of the damaging influence of schema on read, let's take a look at three roles and their relationship to one another. While I am limited to my own personal experiences, I have been fortunate to talk with many other data people in my career, from different companies and lines of business. I can say with confidence that while responsibilities vary somewhat from organization to organization, this summary of roles is by and large universal to most contemporary organizations using big data:

The data analyst
> Charged with answering business questions, generating insights, and creating data-driven reports. Data analysts query the data sets provided to them by the data engineers.

The data engineer
> Charged with obtaining the important business data from systems around the organization and putting it into a usable format for the data analysts.

The application developer
> Charged with developing an application to solve business problems. That application's database is *also* the source of data required by the data analysts to do their job.

Historically, the most common way to adopt Hadoop was to establish a dedicated *data team* as a subset of, or fully separate from, the regular engineering team. The data engineer would reach into the application developer's database, grab the required data, and pull it out to put into HDFS. Data scientists would clean it up and restructure it (and possibly build machine learning models off of it), before passing it on to be used in analytics.

Finally, the data analysts would then query and process the captured data sets to produce answers to their analytical questions. This model led to many issues, however. Conversations between the data team and the application developers would be infrequent and usually revolve around ensuring the data team's query load did not affect the production serving capabilities.

There are three main problems with this separation of concerns and responsibilities. Let's take a look at them.

Problem 1: Violated data model boundaries

Data ingested into the analytics domain is coupled on the source's *internal data model* and results in direct coupling by all downstream users of that data. For simple, seldom-changing sources, this may not be much of a problem. But many models span multiple tables, are purpose-built for OLTP operations, and may become subject to substantial refactoring as business use cases change. Direct coupling on this internal model exposes all downstream users to these changes.

One example I have seen of a table modification that silently broke downstream jobs involved changing a field from boolean to long. The original version represented an answer to the question "Did the customer pay to promote this?" The updated version represented the budget ID of the newly expanded domain, linking this part of the model to the budget and its associated type (including the new trial type). The business had adopted a "try before you buy" model where it would reserve, say, several hundred dollars in advertising credits to showcase the effectiveness of promotion, without counting it in the total gross revenue.

The jobs ingesting this data to HDFS didn't miss a beat (no schema on write), but some of the downstream jobs started to report odd values. A majority of these were Python jobs, which easily evaluated the new long values as Booleans, and resulted in over-attribution of various user analytics. Unfortunately, because no jobs were actually broken, this problem wasn't detected until a customer started asking questions about abnormal results in their reports. This is just one example of many that I have encountered, where well-meaning, reasonable changes to a system's data model have unintended consequences on all of those who have coupled on it.

Problem 2: Lack of single ownership

Application developers are the domain experts and masters of the source data model, but their responsibility for communicating that data to other teams (such as the big data team) is usually nonexistent. Instead, their responsibilities usually end at the boundaries of their application and database.

Meanwhile, the data engineer is tasked with finding a way to get that data out of the application developer's database, in a timely manner, without negatively affecting the production system. The data engineer is dependent on the data sources, but often has little to no influence on what happens to the data sources, making their role very reactive. This production/data divide is a very real barrier in many organizations, and despite best-efforts, agreements, integration checks, and preventative tooling, breakages in data ingestion pipelines remain a common theme.

Finally, the data analyst, responsible for actually *using* the data to derive business value, remains two degrees of separation away from the domain expert (application developer), and three degrees separated if you have a layer of data scientists in there further munging the data. Both analysts and data scientists have to deal with whatever data the data engineers were able to extract, including resolving inconsistent data that doesn't match their existing read schemas.

Because data analysts often share their schemas with other data analysts, they also need to ensure that their resolved schemas don't break each other's work. This is increasingly difficult to do as an organization and its data grow, and, unfortunately, their resolution efforts remain limited to benefiting only other analysts. Operational use cases have to figure out their own way to get data.

Problem 3: Do-it-yourself and custom point-to-point data connections

While a data team in a small organization may consist of only a handful of members, larger organizations have data teams consisting of hundreds or thousands of members. For large data organizations, it's common to pull the same data sources into multiple different subdomains of the data platform, depending on use cases, team boundaries, and technology boundaries.

For example, sales data may be pulled into the analytics department, consumer reporting department, and accounts receivable department. Each subgroup typically independently creates, schedules, and executes ETL jobs to pull the data into its own subdomain, resulting in multiple independently managed copies of the source data, as shown in Figure 1-7.

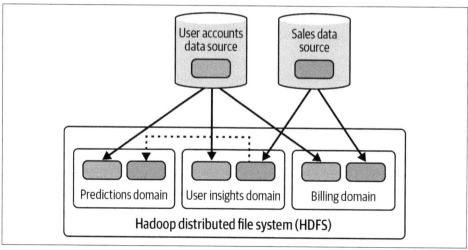

Figure 1-7. Three analytical domains, each grabbing data from where it can to get its work done

While purpose-built, point-to-point data connections let users access the data they need where they need it, it ends up causing a messy tangle. It can be difficult to tell who owns the ETL job, especially when users and teams share access credentials. Tracing lineage, freshness, and determining ownership of a data set can similarly be difficult, often leading to further proliferation of new ETL jobs. After all, if you're not sure the data is exactly what you need, you may as well just make your own job and your own copy for safety's sake.

Enforcing access controls on the source can help clear up who can access what data, but only from the primary source. But restricting data access can backfire. A lengthy or cumbersome process to gain access can result in people simply making copies from other less protected sources. In Figure 1-7, notice that the Predictions domain simply circumnavigates the source access controls by copying the sales data from the User insights domain.

But are these copies *really* the same data? Synchronization frequency, transformations, time zones, intermittent failures, and an incorrect environment (e.g., staging, not production) are just a few issues that can affect the integrity of your copied source. It's possible that you *think* you're getting the correct data, but you're not and you don't know it. For example, you copy one data set thinking it's synced to UTC-0 time, but it's actually synced to UTC-6. The format, partitioning, and ordering of data may appear identical, yet these hard-to-detect, undocumented differences still remain.

Custom point-to-point connections can be a challenge to maintain, cause a sprawl of data, and can result in many duplicate sync jobs that produce similar yet different data.

This disjointed model and responsibilities of data ownership and distribution lead to *bad data*, which is costly in terms of time, money, and missed opportunities. Let's take a look at the costs, before wrapping up with why data mesh purports to solve these issues.

Bad Data: The Costs of Inaction

Bad data typically goes undetected until it is applied to a schema. For example, you can't insert TEXT into an Int32 column in a database. By using schema on read, however, we effectively defer validating our data until the end of the data piping process. And while our *sources* may use a schema, there's no guarantee that our countless point-to-point pipelines have correctly captured the schema alongside the data. There have been many an Int32 captured as an String, or, at worst, an Object.

Bad data is costly to fix, and it's more costly the more widespread it is. Everyone who has accessed, used, copied, or processed the data may be affected and may require mitigating action on their part. The complexity is further increased by the fact that not every consumer will "fix" it in the same way. This can lead to divergent results that are divergent with others and can be a nightmare to detect, track down, and rectify.

Bad data is often inadvertently created by well-meaning individuals, simply because of the point-to-point, "reach in and grab it" nature of many data transfer tools. This has been further augmented by massive scale, where a team discovers that not only is their copy of the data set wrong, but that it's been wrong for several months, and the results of each downstream job computed using that data set are also wrong. These jobs may use hundreds or thousands of processing nodes, with 32x to 128x more in GB of RAM, churning through hundreds of TBs of data each night. This can easily amount to hundreds of thousands or millions of dollars just in processing costs to rerun all of the affected jobs.

Business decisions may also have been affected. I have been privy to the details of one scenario where a company had incorrectly billed its customers collectively by several million dollars, in some cases by too much, and in others by too little. The cause of this was actually quite innocent: a schema change compounded with a complex chain of "reach in and grab it" data ETLs resulted in some data interpretation issues when the schema was applied at read time. It was only when a customer noticed that their billing costs far exceeded their engagement costs that an investigation was started and the root problem discovered.

Data's increasing prominence in modern computing has led others to research the associated costs, especially regarding just how much bad data costs businesses. The results are staggeringly high.

In 2016, one report by IBM, as highlighted by the *Harvard Business Review* (HBR) (*https://oreil.ly/43SJw*) put an estimate of the financial impacts of bad data at 3.1 trillion US dollars, in the US alone. Though the original report is (frustratingly) no longer available, HBR has retained some of the more relevant numbers:

- 50%—the amount of time that knowledge workers waste hunting for data, finding and correcting errors, and searching for confirmatory sources for data they don't trust.
- 60%—the estimated fraction of time that data scientists spend cleaning and organizing data.

The problem of bad data has existed for a very long time. Data copies diverge as their original source changes. Copies get stale. Errors detected in one data set are not fixed in duplicate ones. Domain knowledge related to interpreting and understanding data remains incomplete, as does support from the owners of the original data.

Data mesh proposes to fix this issue by promoting data to a first-class citizen, a product like any other. A data product with a well-defined schema, domain documentation, standardized access mechanisms, and SLAs can substantially reduce the impact of bad data right at the source. Consumers, once coupled on the data product, may still make their own business logic mistakes—this is unavoidable. They will, however, seldom make inadvertent mistakes in merely trying to acquire, understand, and interpret the data they need to solve their business problems. Inaction is not a solution.

Can We Unify Analytical and Operational Workflows?

There's one more problem that sits at the heart of engineering—it's not just the data team that has these data access and quality problems. Every single OLTP application that needs data stored in another database has the same data access problems as the data team. How do you access important business data, locked away in another service, for operational concerns?

There have been several attempts at enabling better operational communication between services, including service-oriented architecture, enterprise service buses, and, of course, point-to-point request-response microservices. But in each of these architectures, the service's data is encapsulated within its own database and is out of reach to other services. In one way this is good—the internal model is sheltered, and you have a single source of truth. Applications provide operational APIs that other applications can call to do work on their behalf. However, these solutions don't resolve the fundamental issue of wholesale read-only access to definitive data sets to use as required for their own operational use cases.

A further complication is that many operational use cases nowadays depend on analytical results. Think machine learning, recommendation engines, AI, etc. Some use cases, such as producing a monthly report of top-selling products, can clearly be labeled as "analytical," to be derived from a periodically computed job.

Other use cases are not so clear cut. Consider an ecommerce retailer that wants to advertise shoes based on current inventory (operational), previous user purchases (analytical), and the user's real-time estimated shopping session intentions (analytical and operational). In practice, the boundary between operational and analytical is seldom neatly defined, and the exact same data set may be needed for a multitude of purposes—analytical, operational, or somewhere in between.

Both data analytics and conventional operational systems have substantial difficulty accessing data contained within other databases. These difficulties are further exacerbated by the increasing volume, velocity, and scale of data, while systems are simultaneously forced to scale outwards instead of upwards as compute limitations of individual services are reached. Most organizations' data communication strategies are based on yesterday's technology and fail to account for the offerings of modern cloud storage, computing, and software as a service (SaaS). These tools and technologies have changed the way that data can be modeled, stored, and communicated across an organization, which we will examine in more detail throughout the remainder of this book.

Rethinking Data with Data Mesh

The premise of the data mesh solution is simple. Publish important business data sets to dedicated, durable, and easily accessible data structures known as *data products*. The original creators of the data are responsible for modeling, evolution, quality, and support of the data, treating it with the same first-class care given to any other product in the organization.

Prospective consumers can explore, discover, and subscribe to the data products they need for their business use cases. The data products should be well-described, easy to interpret, and form the basis for a set of self-updating data primitives for powering both business services and analytics.

Event streams play the optimal role for the foundation of data products because they offer the immutable, appendable, durable, and replayable substrate for all consumers. These streams become a fundamental source of truth for operational, analytical, and all other forms of workloads across the organization.

This architecture is built by leveraging modern cloud computing and SaaS, as covered more in Chapter 5. A good engineering stack makes it easy to create and manage applications throughout their life cycle, including acquiring compute resources, providing scalability, logging, and monitoring capabilities. Event streams provide the modern engineering stack with the formalized and standardized access to the data it needs to get things done.

Let's revisit the *monolith data principles* from earlier in this chapter through the lens of this proposal. These three principles outline the major influences for colocating new business functionality within a monolith. How would a set of self-updating event streams relate to these principles?

The database is the source of truth → The event stream is the source of truth
> The owner of the data domain is now responsible for composing an external-facing model and writing it as a set of events to one (or more) event streams. In exchange, other services can no longer directly access and couple on the internal data model, and the producer is no longer responsible for serving tailored business tasks on behalf of the querying service, as is often the case in a microservices architecture. The event stream becomes the main point of coupling between systems. Downstream services consume events from the event stream, model it for their purposes, and store it in their own dedicated data stores.

Data is strongly consistent → Data is eventually consistent
> The event stream producer can retain strong read-after-write consistency for its own internal state, along with other database benefits such as local ACID transactions. Consumers of the event stream, however, are independent in their processing of events and modeling of state and thus rely on their own eventually

consistent view of the processed data. A consumer does not have write-access to the event stream, and so cannot modify the source of data. Consumer system designs must account for eventual consistency, and we will be exploring this subject in greater detail later in this book.

Read-only data is readily available (remains unchanged!)
Event streams provide the formalized mechanism for communicating data in a read-only, self-updating format, and consumers no longer need to create, manage, and maintain their own extraction mechanism. If a consumer application needs to retain state, then it does so using its own dedicated data store, completely independent of the producer's database.

Data mesh formalizes the ownership boundaries of data within an organization and standardizes the mechanisms of storage and communication. It also provides a reusable framework for producing, consuming, modeling, and using data, not only for current systems, but also for systems yet to be built.

Common Objections to an Event-Driven Data Mesh

There are several common objections that I have frequently encountered when discussing an event-driven data mesh . Though we will cover these situations in more detail throughout the book, I want to bring them up now to acknowledge that these objections exist, but that each one of them is manageable.

Producers Cannot Model Data for Everyone's Use Cases

This argument is actually true, though it misses the point. The main duty of the producer is to provide an accurate and reliable external public model of its domain data for consumer use. These data models need to expose only the parts of the domain that other teams *can* couple on; the remainder of their internal model remains off-limits. For example, an ecommerce domain would have independent sales, item, and inventory models and event streams, simply detailing the current properties and values of each sale, item, and inventory level, whereas a shipping company may have event streams for each shipment, truck, and driver.

These models are deliberately simple and focused on a single domain definition, resulting in tight, modular data building blocks that other systems can use to *build their own data models*. Consumers that ingest these events can restructure them as needed, including joining them with events from other streams or merging them with existing states, to derive a model that works for solving their business use cases. Consumers can also engage the producer teams to request that additional information be added to the public model or for clarification on certain fields and values.

Because the producer team owns the original data model, it is the most qualified to decide what aspects of the model should be exposed and allow others to couple on. In fact, there is no other team more qualified than the team that actually *creates the original source of data* to define what it means and how others should interpret what its fields, relationships, and values mean. This approach lets the data source owners abstract away their internal complexities, such as their highly normalized relational model or document store. Changes to the internal source model can be hidden from consumers that would otherwise have coupled directly on it, thereby reducing breakages and errors.

Making Multiple Copies of Data Is Bad

This objection, ironically, is implicitly in opposition of the first argument. Though just like the previous argument, it does have a grain of truth. Multiple copies of the same data set can and do inadvertently get out of sync, become stale, or otherwise provide a source of data that is in disagreement with the original source. However, our proposal is not to make copying data a free-for-all, but rather to make a formalized and well-supported process that establishes clear rules and responsibilities, embracing this reality rather than hiding from it.

There are three main subtypes of this argument.

There should only be a single master copy of the data, and all systems should reference it directly

This belief fails to account for the fact that big data analytics teams worldwide have already been violating this principle since the dawn of the big data movement (and really, OLAP in general) because their needs cannot be met by a single master copy, stored in a single database somewhere. It also fails to account for the various needs of other operational systems, which follow the same boundary-breaching data acquisition strategies. It's simply untenable.

Insufficiency of the source system to model its data for all business use cases is a prime reason why multiple copies of the same data set will eventually exist. One system may need to support ACID transactions in a relational model, whereas a second system must support a document store for geolocation and plain-text search. A third consumer may need to write these data sets to HDFS, to apply MapReduce style processing to yield results from the previous 364 copies of that data it made, cross-referenced to other annual data sets. All of these cannot be served from a single central database, if not just for the modeling, then for the impossibility of satisfactory performance for all use cases.

It's too computationally expensive to create, store, and update multiple copies of the same data

This argument is hyper-focused on the fact that moving and storing data costs money, and thus storing a copy of the same data is wasteful (disregarding factors such as remodeling and performance, of course). This argument fails to account for the inexpensiveness of cloud computing, particularly the exceptionally cheap storage and network costs of today's major cloud providers. It also fails to account for the developer hours necessary to build and support custom ETL pipelines, part of the multi-trillion dollar inefficiencies in creating, finding, and using data.

Optimizing for minimizing data transfer, application size, and disk usage are no longer as important as they once were for the majority of business applications. Instead, the priority should be on *minimizing developer efforts* for accessing data building blocks, with a focus on operational flexibility.

Managing information security policies across systems and distributed data sets is too hard

Formalizing access to data via data products allows you to apply user and service access controls. Encryption lets you secure all of your sensitive data to unauthorized consumers, so that only those with permission can read the sensitive data.

The self-service platform plays a big role in a data mesh architecture, as it enforces all the security policies, access controls, and encryption requirements. Infosec adherence becomes integrated into the normal workflows of data product producers and consumers, making it far easier to enforce and audit compliance.

Eventual Consistency Is Too Difficult to Manage

Data communicated through event streams does require consideration of and planning for eventual consistency. However, the complaint that eventual consistency is too difficult to manage is typically founded on a misunderstanding of how much of an impact it can have on business processes as a whole. We can properly define our system boundaries to account for eventual consistency between systems, while having access to strong consistency within a system. There's no getting around it—if a certain business process needs perfect consistency, then the creation and usage of the data must be within the same service boundary. But the majority of business processes *don't* need this, and for those that do, nothing we're proposing in this book precludes you from obtaining it. We'll be discussing how to handle eventual consistency in more detail in Chapter 10.

Summary

Existing data communication strategies fall flat in the face of real business requirements. Breaching a service's boundary by reaching in to grab its data is not a sustainable practice, but it is extremely common and often supports multiple critical systems and analytics workflows. Restructuring your systems into neat modular microservices does not solve the problem of data access; other parts of your business, such as the big data analytics and machine learning teams, will still require wholesale access to both current and historical data from domains across the organizations. One way or another, copies of data *will* be created, and we can either fight this or embrace this fact and work to make it better. In choosing the latter, we can use event streams to standardize and simplify the communication of data across the organization as self-updating single sources of truth.

Events form the basis of communication in event-driven architectures and fundamentally shape the space in which we solve our problems. Events, as delivered through event streams, form the building blocks for building asynchronous and reactive systems. These building blocks are primitives that are similar to synchronous APIs: other applications can discover them, couple on them, and use them to build their own services. Eventual consistency, consumer-specific models, read-only replicas, and stream materializations are just some of the concepts we'll explore in this book, along with the roles that modern cloud compute, storage, and networking resources have in this new data architecture.

The following chapters will dig deeper into building and using an event-driven data mesh. We'll explore how to design events, including state, action, and notification events, as well as patterns for producing and consuming them. This book covers handling events at scale, including multicluster and multiregion, best practices for privacy and regulatory compliance, as well as principles for handling eventual consistency and asynchronous communication. We'll explore the social and cultural changes necessary to accommodate an event-driven data mesh and look at some real-world case studies highlighting the successes and lessons learned by others.

Finally, we'll also look at the practical steps you can take to start building toward this in your own organization. One of the best things about this architecture is that it's modular and incremental, and you can start leveraging the benefits in one sector of your business at a time. While there are some initial investments, modern cloud compute and SaaS solutions have all but eliminated the barriers to entry, making it far easier to get started and test whether this is the right solution for you.

CHAPTER 2

Data Mesh

A helpful elevator pitch I often heard referred to data mesh as "microservices for data"—the same principles, but you're applying them to data instead of services. An organization using microservices will have a catalog to look up available services, including their APIs, SLAs, domain owners, security information, and access controls, along with any other organizational-specific information. The microservice catalog provides you with a view into the functions you have available to stitch together new business applications.

In both the microservice and data mesh worlds, common infrastructure services (e.g., Git, Kubernetes, containers, continuous integration, monitoring) provide self-service tooling that lets you focus on building useful business services instead of getting lost in the infrastructure and platforms. Data mesh draws a direct parallel to the microservices architecture—but with data sets, instead of services.

The benefits of a well-built data mesh include:

- Discovering trustworthy and reliable data, making it cheaper and faster to put it into use.
- Making it easier to publish new data sources, such that others can make use of them quickly and easily.
- Treating data as a first-class product, just like any other mission-critical product, including dedicated resourcing, well-defined responsibilities, SLAs, and product release cycles.
- Reducing and eventually eliminating unreliable, fragile, and expensive data pipelines and ETLs.

- Eliminating data inconsistencies between analytics and operational systems by using event streams as the single source of truth.

Data mesh relies on four interrelated principles. We'll investigate each of these principles in brief, along with the role that event-driven data plays in them. The following chapters will dig into a deeper discussion of the principles, the relationships between them, and specifics for building a data mesh powered by event streams.

Principle 1: Domain Ownership

Domain ownership is all about enforcing sovereignty over one's own domain, without having to seek approval or permission from others to change or modify it. This principle ensures a definitive answer to the question of "Who is in charge of this data set?" by unequivocally answering, "the domain owner." But with total ownership comes an important set of responsibilities: to export a selection of internal domain data in a mode suitable for use by those outside your domain boundaries.

In a data mesh, the owner of that data becomes responsible for making it readily available—it is no longer up to prospective users of the data to try to figure out the means to access it. For one, the team that owns the source data is the best qualified to determine what parts of the model should (and should not) be exposed to downstream consumers. Secondly, establishing data ownership at the source formalizes the boundaries of responsibility, simplifying the ownership issues that have plagued traditional centralized data teams.

But responsibility extends beyond modeling data for export to include handling on-call data issues, ensuring that the modes of access remain reliable, ensuring that evolution of the data model remains compatible with historical expectations (covered more in "Schema Evolution: Changing Your Schemas Through Time" on page 137), and ensuring that the agreed upon SLAs are met. This isn't simply a change in who models the data for export but rather a total shift in ultimate responsibility. Moving ownership of data modeling and availability to the producer is a fundamental shift away from the centralization common to today's data warehousing and data lake strategies. Instead of data engineers and data scientists trying to figure out how to get data from within a service's boundary (e.g., smash and grab into an ETL job), the owner of the source data must strive to make the necessary data available through a well-supported and reliable medium.

Domain-Driven Design in Brief

Domain-driven design (DDD), as created and articulated by Eric Evans in *Domain-Driven Design* (*https://oreil.ly/UVes7*) (Addison-Wesley), is a software design approach applied to data and domain modeling. It focuses on modeling the structure and language of the software model to match that of the business domain. Much like data mesh, it too provides us with a common language to discuss software and data models. We'll borrow from DDD's common language to start the discussion on how to share data between systems. Distinguishing between *data in here* and *data out there* is essential for navigating the social changes and delegation of responsibility necessary for data mesh to succeed.

To begin with, we have the *domain*, as in domain-driven design. A domain is the area of interest or concern over which a person or team has control, including all of the *entities*, *aggregates*, *business logic*, and *context* that compose it. The domain, in a nutshell, consists of the things that we concern ourselves with, in a specific area, as we try to build a solution for a problem.

Next is the *bounded context*. A bounded context is defined as the boundary within a domain where the domain model applies. In practice, a bounded context also contains what's known as a ubiquitous language, which describes every component within the boundary, including how it can be identified, its relations to other components, and how it's modeled.

> Ubiquitous language is ubiquitous only within the bounded context—in another bounded context, the same term may (and often does) mean something different. Subtly different meanings may cause confusion and inconsistent data interpretation and usage.

Entities are uniquely identifiable *things or items* that are defined within the domain. These are best thought of as *objects* with unique attributes that often change and evolve over time. For example, an ecommerce platform's entities include items for sale, coupons, deals, shipments, and warehouse-related matters like creating the package and managing inventory levels.

Finally, an *aggregate* is a cluster of entities that can be treated as a single unit. Further to our ecommerce example, aggregating the coupons, items, deals, shipping, and payment information forms the basis of an order. To compose this order aggregate, however, you need to apply domain-specific business logic to integrate each of the entities into the aggregate—the ordering and manner in which it's applied is a concern solely for the domain's aggregate owner.

Figure 2-1 shows a simplified automotive manufacturing domain, with a single bounded context containing entities, aggregates, and business logic. Each entity, aggregate, and process has a fully consistent meaning within the boundary, and any exposure of the inner data to the outside world is through the *anti-corruption layer*.

With these definitions, we can start discussing precisely what it is we're trying to do: publish important entities and aggregates from within a domain's bounded context for use in other domains. All data made accessible outside the domain will be through an anti-corruption layer, as we want to control what data is and isn't exposed to ensure that external parties do not couple directly on the internal model. This provides the domain owner with the ability to evolve and change the internal implementation without unduly affecting external data consumers.

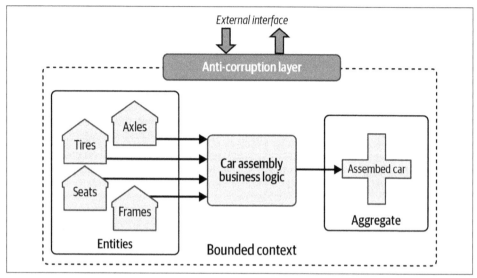

Figure 2-1. An example of an automotive manufacturing domain, including the anti-corruption layer

But how do we know what data to select and share outside our domain?

Selecting the Data to Expose from Your Domain

Deciding what data to expose from your domain can be a bit tricky. One of the best places to start is to identify the entities that are fundamental to your domain, as they are often good first candidates to evaluate. Given the ecommerce example of the previous section, we could expose data relating to the items available and the orders that have been created. Since this domain also maps to the physical world, it would be reasonable to also expose the current inventory to ensure that stock on hand is correctly displayed to our end users.

We would also likely expose select payment information as its own data set because this would provide important information for finance teams. We can link payments to orders via unique ID mappings, allowing downstream consumers to merge them together as they need, or simply use the data that is only relevant to their use cases.

However, the best way to determine which domain data is necessary for others to use is to simply *ask them*. Take a customer-focused approach and lean into the needs of those business processes that depend on your domain. And this brings us to the next data mesh principle.

Principle 2: Data as a Product

This principle elevates data to the status of first-class citizen, the same as any other product created by the organization. This is a complete reenvisioning of how data is created, stored, and communicated to other domains. By applying the same product rigor of existing production products, we can formalize how data is built and communicated across domains.

The domain owners are responsible for identifying, extracting, and modeling their data to present as a data product for external access. After all, who better than the domain model experts to construct the data for export? And like any other product, prospective consumers are identified and consulted to ensure that the data product is built to serve their needs. But a data product isn't just the data itself—it's also the code that builds it, the infrastructure that stores it, and the ports (or modes) by which you can access it, as shown in Figure 2-2.

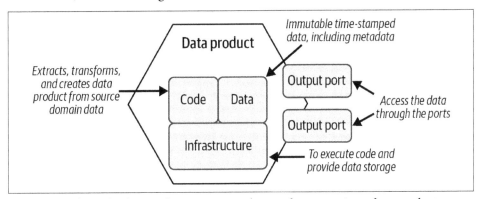

Figure 2-2. The code, data, infrastructure, and ports that comprise a data product

These four components are common to all data products. Every data product creator is going to need to identify and construct their data products with these in mind.

We'll *streamline* the creation and management of data products, much like we do with microservices, to reduce the overhead and toil of each data product owner. We want it to be easy to build and support data products without getting bogged down in the operational overhead. We'll cover self-service later in this chapter, but keep it in mind as we talk about serving data as a product.

There are four major factors to consider when building data products. Data products must provide immutable and time-stamped data, such that consumers obtain consistently reproducible results. Data products are multimodal, though some modes suit certain use cases better than others. Depending on the mode, you may end up needing to pull data via a query, or your data may be pushed to you via a subscription, affecting the kinds of use cases you can support. Finally, data products are constructed in alignment with the source domain, an aggregation, or the consumer domain, further affecting use case possibilities. Let's look at each one of these in turn.

 Creating a data product is a formal commitment by the domain owner to provide the time, resources, and know-how to make parts of their domain data usable to external customers. This includes providing a stable API, an SLA (e.g., do we get up at night to fix it?), and prioritizing and handling customer feature requests.

Data Products Provide Immutable and Time-Stamped Data

The data provided by a data product must be immutable and time-stamped. Consumers must obtain a consistent result when querying the data, regardless of when the query is executed. For example, a query executed today on a given date range and one executed in a month from now on that same date range must yield the same results. Similarly, two separate consumers reading the same data product must be able to obtain precisely the same data. Any modifications to that data need to be published as new, incremental changes to the data set.

These requirements are made a bit trickier to uphold when considering late-arriving data. How does the data product owner fold in data that is clearly late but that may still be essential to the data product? In consultation with consumers, one option is to forgo publishing the new data until a grace period has elapsed—say one-hour—after which all other late-arriving data is discarded. A second option is to simply drop the data on the floor and ignore it. While consistent, this may be problematic for some data product consumers who care more about accuracy than timeliness.

A third option, enabled by event streams, is to publish the late data as soon as it arrives. The late data is published as an event with the accurate but late timestamp of its occurrence. A stream consumer will see the event timestamps steadily increasing until they hit the late event, at which point they can choose their own course of action for handling it.

Immutable and time-stamped data unlocks the ability of multiple consumers to consistently and repeatedly use data products over time. As for late-arriving data, we'll take a look at this in more detail in Chapter 10.

Data Products Are Multimodal

There is no definitive "right way" to create a data product, nor is there a single expected form, format, or mode that it is expected to take. Data products are intrinsically multimodal, and precisely which modes *you* use for sharing data is open to negotiation. We'll return to this subject of mode selection in more detail in Chapter 4.

In the meantime, the same data product can be served up in a number of different formats and APIs. For example, a single data product may be:

- Produced to an event stream and updated as changes occur
- Composed into a set of Parquet files, updated daily to a cloud storage bucket
- Remain stored behind a REST API, provided to clients on demand

Figure 2-3 illustrates the composition of a multimodal data product. The data product code extracts the data from the operational database and composes it into a form of internal intermediate state. A secondary executable then converts the intermediate state into a format suitable for the output modes, such as events for an event stream or batch files for cloud storage.

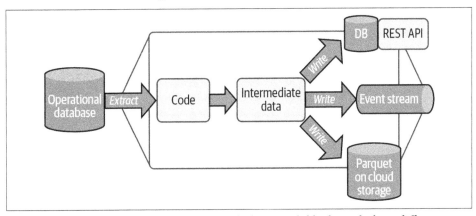

Figure 2-3. A multimodal data product, with data available through three different ports: a REST API, an event stream, and a cloud storage bucket

Batch-computed data products do have a place in a data mesh. After all, data warehousing and data lake architectures rely extensively on periodically computed batches of data to power their periodically executed jobs. The vast majority of analytical workloads have been built extensively on batch-computed data sources.

Most operational systems cannot rely on the ponderous frequency of batch-computed jobs, however. No one wants to wait 30 minutes for a batch of data to process to find out if their flight was actually booked. Event streams provide a substrate for rapidly changing data in motion and enable far quicker and more responsive applications, be they analytical or operational. They also provide the flexibility to aggregate the data into big batch files to power classic data analytics cases. We'll investigate these use cases more in Chapter 9. While batch data products will remain useful for batch-based analytical workloads, event streams form the overarching medium to power both event-driven operational and analytical workloads and support fast and effective data communication between domains.

Accessing a Data Product Via Push or Pull

There are two main ways in which users can access a data product: via a pull or a push mechanism. The pull mechanism is more familiar to most people—this is the type provided by a REST API, SQL, graph query language, or files stored in cloud storage. Data is stored behind some form of query-handling interface and, eventually, a consumer client will issue a query to *pull* that data into its domain.

Pull queries return all of the data that matches the query clause, which can be a significant amount. The consumer has to wait until the query completes and the data is returned before it can begin processing the data. Upon completion, the resultant batch of data needs to be written to its own output location, which, depending on the final record count, can also take some time. Pull-based data APIs lead to periodic querying and processing of large amounts of data in parallel: high throughput, but also high latency. The main issue with pull queries is that the only way you'll know if the updated data is available is to issue a query—and this can be quite expensive if you need to poll it every second.

 Ask your database administrator how comfortable they would be if you issued a tight-polling loop on a relational database (SQL API) to query it for new records. They'll probably feel uncomfortable once you start talking about polling frequencies in the single second count and suggest (or require) that you query less often.

In contrast, the *push* mechanism, as provided by the event stream, notifies downstream services when new data is available. A service need only subscribe to the event stream to be registered as a listener and be notified shortly after a new event is available for consumption. Consumers process events at their own rate, ideally keeping up with the rate of inflow to avoid falling behind.

Event streams tend to use very little overhead for managing consumer subscriptions, especially in contrast with pull APIs. There is low latency between when an event occurs and when the registered consumers are notified that there is an event for processing. And, if you want to serve both operational and analytical use cases, you're going to need data products with real-time performance. Pull-based query APIs are simply not well-suited for providing real-time access to up-to-date data product changes.

The reason that pull and push mechanisms matter is that *like begets like*. The more data products you serve via pull APIs, the more data products you'll have with pull APIs. The more data you serve with push-based event streams, the more data products you'll have using push-based event streams. The choices that you make in regard to how others can access your data product ripple across the organization, affecting more than just your immediate consumers.

In the next section, we'll take a look at the most common *types* of data products that you can build.

The Three Data Product Alignment Types

Data products can be aligned to the source domain, to an aggregate, or to the consumer domain. Let's take a look at each of them now.

Source-aligned data products

Source-aligned data products are aligned to the operational system of the source domain and are ideal candidates for powering both event-driven operational and analytical systems. For example, a source-aligned data product may emit sales facts containing detailed information about the items, prices, shipping, and payment information, as shown in Example 2-1.

Example 2-1. The data contents of a source-aligned sales event

```
Value: {
  sales_id: 8675309,
  item_ids: [4625382, 4625382, 4625382, 100900],
  total_usd: 89.12,
  datetime: "2022-11-12T03:51:19Z",
  shipping_address: "123 Fake Street, Springfield"
}
```

Aggregate-aligned data products

Aggregate-aligned data products provide an aggregation of multiple data points against specific business criteria—for example, an hourly aggregate of sales per store containing a set of sales IDs and dollar amounts, including the total quantity of sales and the total dollar amount. The data product owner is responsible for building the aggregation, but will need to consult with the intended consumers to ensure that they have a common understanding of the aggregate. The following shows the data contents of an aggregate-aligned daily sales event:

```
Value: {
  date: "2022-11-12",
  total_items_sold: 41292,
  total_items_value_usd: 1902712.22
}
```

Consumer-aligned data products

A consumer-aligned data product is highly customized and built to serve a specific use case for a single domain. For example, a consumer may mix in sales aggregates, inventory aggregates, and customer profile aggregates, enrich the data, and then process it through a set of complex business logic to get the data ready for further use within its domain. The following shows the data contents of a consumer-aligned event, composed to predict the value of a given consumer for advertisement targeting:

```
Value: {
  user_id: "UUID-123456789",
  predicted_item_ids_to_advertise: [4625382, 100901],
  cost_tolerance: "high",
  conversion_probability: 0.1233,
  estimated_spend_usd: 500.00,
  ad_bid_limit_usd: 9.75
}
```

These three data product alignments make trade-offs between the responsibilities of the owners and the consumers. On one end, source-aligned data products are fairly general purpose. Constructing them is relatively easy, and consumers can use them for a variety of purposes. However, consumers must apply their own business logic and transformations, and perform any remodeling to generate anything more specific to their needs.

Aggregate-aligned data products are the result of the domain owner applying business logic to internal domain data. While a simple version could include an aggregation of a source-aligned domain, aggregate-aligned data products often mix in data sourced from other data products. This is quite often in the name of usability: for example, we enrich the sales aggregates with store location, sales representative information, and product categories because these are the most common use cases of the data by our downstream consumers.

By taking the common consumer use cases and applying them to the source product, we avoid the risk of consumers incorrectly computing their own aggregates, while at the same time reducing the overall burden across the data product users. However, this does require that the data product owner have sufficient resources to support the data product improvement requests, which may not always be possible. This brings us back to our third type, the consumer-aligned data product.

Consumer-aligned data products are a recognition that a data product owner cannot possibly provide every consumer with all the data it needs. In fact, one of the most common reasons for creating a consumer-aligned data product is to mix data products from several distinct domains together, where no single data product owner could have provided it on their own. Consumer-aligned data products are highly focused on serving the specific domain needs of the consumer, be it for just one application or for several applications within their domain.

Consider an ecommerce shipping domain that needs sales data, payment data, inventory data, and warehouse data. Since this data crosses many domains and needs special business logic to correlate and remodel, the consumer creates a consumer-aligned data product focused on meeting these needs. Figure 2-4 shows these four domains providing source-aligned data products to the shipping domain's consumer-aligned data product (1).

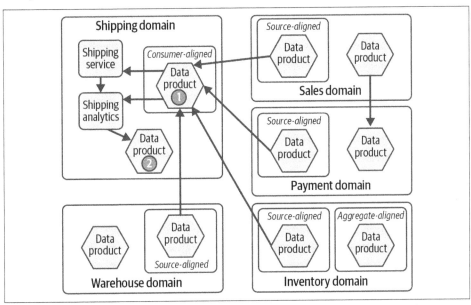

Figure 2-4. Consumer-aligned data product created using data products from four separate domains

The consumer-aligned data product, if powered by event streams, provides a real-time updated data product for products that the shipping domain can send out to customers, powering both the shipping service and the shipping analytics service. A second data product (2 in Figure 2-4) can be created from shipping analytics results, aggregated to highlight key performance indicators to monitor overall shipment domain health.

But data products are not simply for analytics. Event streams provide an optimal solution for driving both operational and analytical use cases.

Event-Driven Data Products as Inputs for Operational Systems

Data products may be used to serve both analytical and operational use cases, but suitability depends heavily on the modality of the data product and the latency tolerance of the operational consumers. The boundary between operational and analytical use cases gets blurrier the closer you get to real-time data. Fortunately for us, it doesn't really matter too much how the workload is defined—the important thing is that the performance objectives of the consumer are satisfied by the limitations of the data product's service level.

 Data mesh was originally conceived for the purposes of serving analytical data products between domains. But data products composed in real time and provided by event streams can satisfy both operational and analytical needs. Consider powering of operational systems to be an "off-label" application of data mesh, much like how some pharmaceutical drugs are used off-label for purposes other than what they were originally created for.

Event streams provide the optimum solution for this dual use case and we will explore them further in Chapter 3. A payments microservice can obtain a sales event from an event stream in milliseconds, whereas obtaining the data from a data product that writes hourly batches to cloud storage is simply far too slow. The closer to real time the data, the more suitable it is for operational use cases.

Promoting event-stream data products as a means of powering operational systems makes for a strong selling point for building internal organizational support for data mesh. Nonanalytical teams may be skeptical of the need to take on new responsibilities for formulating data products when they get nothing themselves out of the deal. However, promoting data product access through real-time event streams can serve as a strong incentive, as event streams also unlock operational event-driven services, not just analytics, all for the price of one data product.

Next, let's take a look at the role that governance plays in a data mesh.

Principle 3: Federated Governance

Creating data products requires that domain owners have a degree of autonomy in modeling, building, and delivering data to their consumers. However, by empowering them with autonomy and independence, you run the risk of a significant technological sprawl across data product implementations, making it more difficult for consumers to use the data products for their own ends. Federated governance focuses on finding an equilibrium between the needs of the consumers, the autonomy of the data product owners, the business compliance and security requirements, and global data product requirements.

Data product creators benefit from the freedom to compose it as they see fit, while data product consumers benefit from a simple and easy data access interface that matches other existing data products. Compliance and security requirements may prohibit autonomy and ease of consumption, while protecting the business from severe financial and legal repercussions. Federated governance is a balancing act. Finding the middle is no easy feat and requires participation and input from a whole host of people from across your organization.

Federated governance can be roughly broken down into two main tasks. The first is establishing cross-organization policies, including data product standards and data handling requirements, that apply to all users of the data mesh. The second is providing guidance on creating and using data products with self-service tools to make it easy to participate in the data mesh.

The governance team is a purpose-built team composed of individuals representing a cross-section of domains, technical requirements, and business use cases. Their job is not to dictate to others what can and cannot be done, but rather to discuss the problems inherent with a multidomain problem space, explore solutions, and try to find common ground for reducing the scope of potential sprawl.

For example, a federated governance body may decide that the organization should use PostgreSQL databases over MySQL databases in the implementation of data products—not because one is necessarily superior to the other, but because the organization has the technical expertise, familiarity, monitoring, and on-call playbooks to support one but not the other. Similarly, an organization may choose to use one programming language over another or one cloud service provider over another. The governance team seeks to reduce technological sprawl by selecting, supporting, and promoting just a few proven technologies for creating data products.

Building a data mesh with a wide range of technologies, languages, conventions, and APIs makes it difficult to use and support. A well-built data mesh is quite similar to a well-built microservice platform. The fewer technology choices you support, the easier it is to build support tooling and apply access controls, security measures, and data management policies. Finding the balance point between which technologies you'll provide first-class support for, and those which you will not, is one of most contentious points of federated governance. It requires a healthy and fact-based debate to be successful.

Let's dig into a few specific areas of concern for federated governance. Chapter 4 will cover each of these areas in much greater detail.

Specifying Data Product Language, Framework, and API Support

Which data product technologies and formats will you support? The previous MySQL/PostgreSQL example touched on this issue, but it goes beyond just databases. The most common technological choice of a company is usually which programming languages to support. It's only natural for a software developer to want to branch out and try new languages, frameworks, and technologies when it comes to implementing applications. But this comes at the incremental expense of requiring additional long-term support, such as monitoring integration, testing frameworks, and domain expertise. The types of data products, the data format, and the schema technologies used are just a few examples of the standards under the purview of federated governance.

Establishing Data Product Life Cycle Requirements

A data product has a life cycle just like any other product. Federated governance is responsible for outlining precisely how a data product owner goes about publishing it to the data mesh. Specifying the data product metadata to collect, determining quality and SLA classifications, and establishing the publishing process are only a few examples of the necessary life cycle requirements. A data product, much like a software application, will be created, updated, and eventually deprecated and deleted. It is important to streamline this process and ensure that every participant in the data mesh is aligned and shares the same expectations.

Establishing Data Handling and Infosec Policies

Data handling policies are varied and heavily influenced by regional laws, such as General Data Protection Regulation (GDPR) and the California Consumer Privacy Act (CCPA). A person's right to be forgotten by having all personally identifiable information (PII) scrubbed out or deleted from associated data is an important tenet for building and serving data products. Precisely how your organization achieves this is up to you, but include options such as crypto-shredding and default anonymization. We'll cover these subjects in more detail in Chapter 4.

Identifying and Standardizing Cross-Domain Polysemes

Domains often have different yet similar definitions for common business entities. Identifying and standardizing these across domains is an important step to ensuring interoperability of data products. One common example is the user entity: one domain may use an auto-incrementing `long` type as the unique identifier, whereas another may use a `string` UUID. Standardizing polysemes to use a common identifier is the responsibility of the federated governance team and makes using data products much simpler and less prone to user error.

Formalizing Self-Service Platform Requirements

The self-service tools that underpin the day-to-day functionality of data mesh are guided by the federated requirements. Relying on common tooling reduces the barriers for creating, publishing, discovering, and using data products. Federated governance is best suited for gathering requirements for the broad cross-cutting concerns such as monitoring, logging, access controls, compute services, and storage services. These requirements are codified and provided to the self-service platform team to build out the necessary tooling to support data mesh.

Now let's briefly take a look at the fourth and final data mesh principle before wrapping up this chapter.

Principle 4: Self-Service Platform

Self-service is the final principle underpinning data mesh. Precisely what it constitutes will vary from organization to organization, so instead of telling you what it should consist of, I think it's more helpful to illustrate the service needs of the participants. Their needs will help inform your own decisions about how to build your self-service platform. The three main user roles include:

Prospective consumers
> Consumers must be able to find the data products they need, subscribe as consumers, and extract/acquire the data into their own domains. They may in turn create their own data products from the data.

Data product creators
> These folks want to use the self-service platform for support in creating their data product. This includes self-service compute, storage, and processing, as well as a streamlined way to integrate it with their codebase, test it, and deploy it.

Data product owners

Owners must be able to manage their data products long term. This includes notifying existing consumers of upcoming changes, handling feature requests, issuing guidance on breaking changes, managing alerts and on-call rotations, and managing the data product life cycle, such as deprecation and deletion.

 The stricter your federated governance requirements around the modality of your data products, the easier it is to build the self-service platform. A self-service platform that enables just one or two data product formats with very opinionated processing frameworks is much easier to support than myriad options. This is a hard-learned lesson from the microservices world, and it's one that we would do well to apply to data mesh.

At a minimum, the precise makeup of the self-service will vary depending on your priorities, existing tools and frameworks, and culture. There is no one-size-fits-all solution, but there are a few things that we can take a closer look at to help you figure out what this could look like for you.

Discovering Data Products and Dependencies

Everyone participating in the data mesh needs to be able to easily browse, search, and find available data products. This includes, but is not limited to, the data product location, API, metadata, ownership, documentation, data samples, and links to existing applications that are already using it. A *data catalog* is a common tool for centralized lookup of available data products, with each data product owner responsible for updating and maintaining their records (more on this subject in Chapter 5).

Prospective consumers can make informed decisions about the suitability of the data product for solving their business needs. While a simple alphabetical list may be sufficient for discovery in a small data mesh, it quickly becomes untenable as your data product count increases. Search and filtering functionality become key, especially for identifying relevant data products by more complex querying of schemas and documentation.

You can make data product owners readily reachable by integrating email or instant messaging into the platform. With just a click of a button your prospective consumer could be forwarded to the relevant instant messaging channel and put into direct contact with the data product owner or on-call support specialist. Highly popular data products could even feature a collection of frequently asked questions as part of their data catalog metadata, sourced from these very conversations.

Finally, lineage tracking of data products' producers and consumers remains an important element of dependency tracking. A well-built self-service platform will provide not only current lineage of the entire data mesh but also snapshots of historical lineages. A data product owner can use lineage tracking to identify all consumers of their data product, communicating with them to identify any unmet or common needs or to inform them about upcoming changes to the data product. Data product consumers can similarly use lineage to identify where their data is coming from, to further validate their data product selections, or to exclude any upstream data products due to potential infosec or legal issues.

Data Product Management Controls

The self-service platform needs to standardize the management of the data product life cycle, as we outlined in "Establishing Data Product Life Cycle Requirements" on page 38. Creating data products requires not only the acquisition of compute and storage resources but also requisitioning a core repository, a deployment pipeline, monitoring integrations, and collection and display of metadata. Deprecating and removing data products requires notifying consumers, communicating expectations and migration strategies, and following established policies for data deletion and removal. Creating controls to manage data products requires integration with *each of these services* as well as ensuring compatibility among the data products published to the data mesh.

This is all to say that the data product management controls are difficult and expensive to do well across polyglot data product implementations. This also extends into the world of data policy application, such as legally required regulatory compliance. If you need to ensure your data products are free of PII, it's a lot easier to scan a set of data products created with a single data storage mode than it is to scan across a wide swath of relational, NoSQL, graph, time series, and event-stream data stores. The more types and languages you support, the more extensive your self-service tooling needs to be to ensure the correct application of data management policies across your data products.

The more options a self-service platform provides to data product owners, the more work the self-service platform team needs to do to ensure that the options fall in line with the governance policies, data security policies, and regulatory policies. For some organizations, this may simply mean that they'll leave it up to the data product owners to figure out, because the impact of a policy failure is low and they simply don't care too much. But many organizations do not have this luxury, and a policy breach can be an extremely costly and damaging scenario that must be avoided. Supporting a wide variety of data products increases the risk of a policy breach, while supporting only a few reduces the risk.

Data Product Access Controls

Self-service access control to data products is another area of concern. Registering for data product access should be easy for a consumer to do. A distinct set of credentials for each consumer enables permissions and access control at a per-consumer level, identification of dependencies, and, when combined with producer permissions, the ability to create a full dependency graph of who has access to what data. It's important to note that this data is obtained directly from real operational access controls—not as part of an opt-in solution that is almost always incomplete.

Access restrictions due to sensitive information should go through a more rigorous process of approval, in line with federated governance requirements. This allows for a paper trail for sensitive information access with the ability for infosec to audit consumer's adherence to data handling policies.

Compute and Storage Resources for Building and Using Data Products

Composing a data product can require additional compute and data storage resources beyond what is already available to the source domain. For example, an operational system may create and record a sale inside its database but be largely incapable of providing an aggregate-aligned data product of daily sales, split by salesperson, department, and promotional offers. Instead of tasking the domain owner with extending and supporting their own tooling to meet the data product composition needs, we provide them with a set of tools and options through a shared self-service platform.

Now, this part of the platform is *highly implementation-dependent* and will vary significantly depending on the tools and technologies you're already using. Since we're looking at building an event-driven data mesh, we need the ability to easily requisition an *event stream* (or *topic*) to write our events to. I'm a longtime user and contributor to Apache Kafka (*https://oreil.ly/2QA11*), which you may want to take a few minutes to familiarize yourself with if you haven't heard of it before. I suggest Confluent's "What is Kafka?" (*https://oreil.ly/qUJ8e*) to get you started.

There are a whole host of controls that users of the self-service data mesh may need access to. Users may need to specify the topic ownership via access controls, duration of record retention (infinite, for the majority of cases), and permission restrictions for who can and cannot read the data. Users must also be able to associate the Kafka topic with the data product metadata, so that it is easily discoverable and has well-documented schema and documentation.

Users also need to be able to requisition data processing resources so they can populate their data products. While there are many possible options for compute resources that can compose a data product, we may want to narrow it down to just a handful of technologies. As the single member of my governance team, I may decide to select the following technologies to help me build my data mesh:

Stream processing
> A native event-stream processor such as Kafka Streams or Apache Flink. Both provide a framework for handling data products provided through Kafka topics, including rich functionality such as stream-table and table-table joins.

Batch processing
> A big data processing framework that can handle large amounts of batch data, with some bonus points for also being able to handle some streaming use cases (e.g., Apache Spark, Apache Flink). These frameworks can make it easier to use data products provided by periodically updated batch data sets or those served via a mixture of batch data and event streams.

Stream ↔ batch data processing
> A tool to translate data from streams to batch data or vice versa. Kafka Connect is a prime example of this technology, where you can use a variety of connectors to put batch data into a Kafka topic for streaming use or take data from an event stream and write it into a batch data store.

Regardless of the sorts of processing framework options you choose to support, your self-service team will also be on the hook for maintaining and supporting them. We'll cover self-service capabilities in more detail in Chapter 5.

But your options are not limited to simply what you can support in-house. Cloud computing and SaaS can provide you with the building blocks you need to create your data mesh.

Providing Self-Service Through SaaS

SaaS solutions are changing the way that end users relate to their compute, storage, and processing resources. For a data mesh, they ideally provide easy-to-use services right out of the box for accessing data, transforming it in some way, and writing it back to a data storage location. Here are a few examples:

Confluent with Apache Kafka
> Offers Apache Kafka and supportive tooling as a service, including Kafka Connect and SQL-based stream processing. "Apache Kafka (*https://oreil.ly/2QA11*) is an open-source distributed event streaming platform used by thousands of companies for high-performance data pipelines, streaming analytics, data integration, and mission-critical applications."

StarTree with Apache Pinot
> A huge supporter of Dehghani's Data Mesh paradigm, StarTree offers Apache Pinot (*https://oreil.ly/SdrX9*) and supportive tooling as a service. Pinot is

described as "a realtime distributed OLAP datastore, which is used to deliver scalable real-time analytics with low latency."

Databricks with Apache Spark
Offers Apache Spark and supportive tooling as a service to streamline your use of Spark. "Apache Spark (*https://oreil.ly/pRTlL*) is a multilanguage engine for executing data engineering, data science, and machine learning on single-node machines or clusters."

One important part of each of these SaaS offerings is that they make it easy to acquire processing and storage resources for data, though only within the confines of their own services. They provide you with off-the-shelf building blocks to compose your own data mesh solution based on your teams' needs and capabilities. While you are certainly free to spin up and manage your own services, modern computing has pivoted strongly in favor of cloud-based services.

Unless you already have a robust compute, disk, and stream-processing platform available to build your data mesh with, you would do well to rely on SaaS solutions to kick-start your implementation. You'll be able to start getting immediate value out of your data products, and you can start working on figuring out what works well and what you'll need to change. Trying out a SaaS solution for a few months and finding it doesn't suit your needs is much better than building out the entire in-house platform first *and then* discovering that it doesn't meet your needs.

Keep your expenses and overhead low when you're starting out. You can always worry about optimizing for costs later, when you've found which technologies work best for your use cases. You'll likely need to use several technologies, especially if you're looking to support multiple data product modes. But at the very least, you're going to need a robust and reliable event broker, such as Apache Kafka, to serve your event-driven data products.

Summary

Data mesh covers a lot of ground. On one hand, it's a rigorous renegotiation of responsibilities and social norms in an organization. Domains and their teams become responsible for creating and publishing their own first-class data products, substantially reducing the scope of duties of the ubiquitous centralized data team. On the other hand, it's a streamlining of technical support for the definition, creation, modeling, and usage of data products via self-service capabilities.

Much like a parliament, a federated governance team, representing members, applications, products, and business use cases from across the organization, gathers to discuss, argue, fight, and legislate. Each member ensures the representation of their constituents with the goal of finding a balance between total domain autonomy and heavy-handed, top-down edicts.

Discovering the common ground will yield a landscape of desired languages, frameworks, tools, and technologies. The self-service platform team will need to focus their efforts toward creating a well-supported toolbox supporting common use cases and workflows. Meanwhile, the data product owners can start putting the platform tools to work by building and sharing their data products.

Figure 2-5 shows an overview of a basic event-driven data mesh. Domain owners can either write their data natively (1) or by using connectors (2) to the event streams (3) stored in the event broker. Domain owners may publish their data products and associated metadata to the discovery endpoint (4), allowing others to discover and use the data products for themselves.

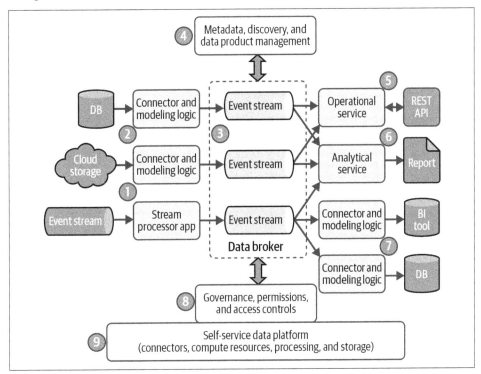

Figure 2-5. A birds'-eye view of an event-driven data mesh

Both operational (5) and analytical (6) services can natively source their data from the event-driven data products, selecting from source-aligned, aggregate-aligned, and consumer-aligned products as they see fit. Existing services that don't natively support event streaming can rely again on the self-service connectors (7) to consume, remodel, and insert data as required.

Finally, an organization-spanning governance (8) and self-service platform (9) underpin the common use cases of every data product. Governance focuses on security policies, roles, ownership, access controls, and lineage, while the self-service platform focuses on making it easy to find, use, and manage data products within the requirements of the organization.

Event streams play a pivotal role in data mesh because they provide a single unified mechanism of providing data for both real-time and batch processes, be they operational, analytical, or somewhere in between. Unlike periodically computed batch data sets, event streams can be used not only by analytical users, but by operational applications too. This choice greatly reduces the quantity of similar-yet-different data sets that can regularly cause problems and provides you with a common baseline for building all of your data-powered applications.

In the next chapter, we'll take a closer look at how to use event streams to build data products, including some fundamental event-stream properties, the relationship between the stream and the consumer, historical data, and composing state.

CHAPTER 3
Event Streams for Data Mesh

An event is published to an event stream for use by any interested subscribers. But what are the properties of an event stream and are they any different than a queue? Or a messaging system? What makes up an event, and how do we ensure we correctly compose reusable event streams? In this chapter, we'll take a good look at events and event streams, including requirements, differentiation from other similar architectures, and some of the modes of use that they unlock for our consumer services.

First, let's start with the event. An *event* is a well-defined record of an occurrence containing all of the information about what happened. Events are commonly based on business entities or on relationships between entities. For a simple automotive example, we could expect to see entity events detailing information about items, orders, and coupons. In terms of relationships between entities, you may expect to see events such as item_added_to_cart and coupon_applied_to_order.

We'll get more into precisely what events are, how they're structured, and the supporting technologies we'll need to use in a moment. First, it's important to understand a few key concepts about the role that event streams play in an event-driven data mesh.

Figure 3-1 shows an extension of the automotive domain bounded context from Figure 2-1. The internal implementation uses a relational database, with tables representing the components/entities required to compose an automobile. The anticorruption layer provides the REST API for operational use cases, such as requesting the assembly of a new automobile and modifications to existing inventory.

Additionally, the domain publishes two data products to event streams—one based on items and the other based on orders. Specialized business logic extracts and isolates the internal model from the data published to the event stream. Whatever you choose to expose via your anti-corruption layer becomes part of the public API, so be careful about what you add and how you add it.

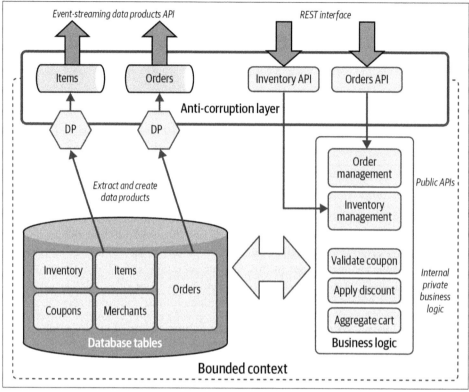

Figure 3-1. An ecommerce domain including an event-stream API for data products and a REST API for operational concerns

Note that the internal implementation need not be event-driven to extract or use event-driven data products. Chapter 8 covers integrating nonevent-driven systems with event-driven ones and the options you have for bridging the gap. You may also note that we're incorporating traditional request-response options alongside event streams. This is a very common pattern for systems of record that are not event-driven but need to provide well-formed data products for external consumers. We simply maintain the existing APIs and add on event-driven data products based on consumer needs and the existing data requirements.

Figure 3-2 shows an abstracted implementation of an event-driven automotive domain, complete with domain events specific to the internal operational of the system.

You may choose to expose certain domain events to the outside world, but you must be careful about about which ones you select to expose. We'll cover event design and selecting which events to expose (and which to conceal) more in Chapter 7. At this stage, just be aware that you don't need an event-driven system to produce event streams and that not all event types are suitable for production as a data product.

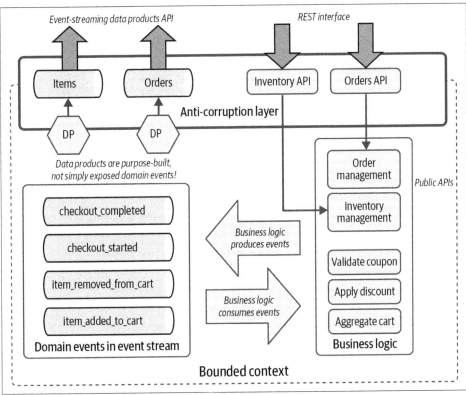

Figure 3-2. Data products are purpose-built for external usage and are meant to be coupled on. Domain events may not be suitable for data product purposes

For now, let's now take a closer look at events, records, and messages, as well as the relationship between an event stream and an event broker.

Events, Messages, and Records

An event is an occurrence in an application recorded into a *record* (the container holding the event data) and published to an event stream hosted by an event broker.

I generally avoid using the term *message* when discussing event streams and event-driven architectures because it's a term that has adopted different meanings to different people over time. In common parlance, we send a message *to* a person or *to* a specific private group—an intended recipient and not a posting (like a message board) for public general-purpose use. In contrast, data products are meant to be *broadcast and shared widely*, with the intention of letting others subscribe to and use them however they choose (much like a public post on channel-based social media). For clarity's sake, I'll use *event* or *record* instead of *message* for the remaining chapters of this book.

Each logical record is made up of three components:

The key
> The key is optional, but extremely useful. It contains a unique ID associated with the contents of the event, just like the primary key of a relational table. Data is almost always partitioned according to the key, such that all data of the same key goes to the same partition and consumer instance, allowing for vast amounts of data to be processed in parallel.

The value
> Contains the bulk of the data relating to the event. If the key can be thought of as the primary key of a row in a database table, then the value can be thought of as all of its column values. Every property and field recorded during the creation of the event should go in the value component. Values should always have a well-defined schema, whereas a key can contain a schema or a primitive.

The header (also known as "record properties")
> Contains metadata about the event itself, such as timestamps, tracking IDs, and other custom user-defined fields. Both the presence of a header and its format depend on what technologies you're using to create and communicate events. Headers are commonly composed of a simple key-value map appended to the key-value pair.

Figure 3-3 shows the structure of an event recording a sale of six items (in an array) purchased by user-id-6384291. The header contains both the timestamp that shows when the event was created as well as a custom_tracking_id specified by the event producer.

Figure 3-3. A sales event showing the purchase of six items

One final thing to note: *events are immutable*. You can never modify an event once it is published to the event stream. Instead, you create and publish a new event containing the necessary correction or update. Immutability is essential for ensuring that every consumer has access to precisely the same data set and can reproduce the same results of a computation at a later point in time.

What's an Event Stream? What Is It Not?

> The business facts are best presented as business Domain Events, can be stored and served as distributed logs of time-stamped events for any authorized consumer to access.
>
> —Zhamak Dehghani (*https://oreil.ly/P-SQc*)

Event streams are hosted on an *event broker*, with perhaps the most common option being Apache Kafka (a personal favorite of your author). The event broker, such as in the case of Kafka, provides a structure known as a *topic* that we can write our events to. It also handles everything from data replication and rebalancing to client connections and access controls. Publishers write events to the event stream hosted in the broker, while consumers subscribe to event streams and receive the events.

In its most basic form, an event stream is a time-stamped sequence of business facts pertaining to a domain. Events form the basis for communicating important business data between domains in a reliable and repeatable way, leading us to the following requirements:

Immutable
Events cannot be modified once written to the log. Only new events may be added.

Durable and replayable
Events are durable, such that they can be consumed immediately or in the future. Events can be replayed by new and existing consumers alike, provided the event broker has sufficient storage to host the historical data.

Scalability and indefinite storage
The event broker provides high availability, scalability, and indefinite retention, allowing the event stream to become the single source of truth for specific domain data.

Event streams rely on the *durable append-only log*, an immutable data structure that only permits appending of new data. Once written, data cannot be altered. The log is durable, such that consumers can consume the data as many times as they need. Events are not deleted once they are read, nor are they simply discarded in the case of an absence of consumers.

Figure 3-4 shows a durable append-only log with two partitions. New data is appended to the end of one of the two partitions. Each individual logical consumer is represented by a *consumer group* and is responsible for consuming the events and incrementing the offset pointer pertaining to its group. With sufficient processing power, a logical consumer can remain up to date with real-time data flows, while a new consumer beginning at an earlier offset will need to process all of the events to catch up to current time.

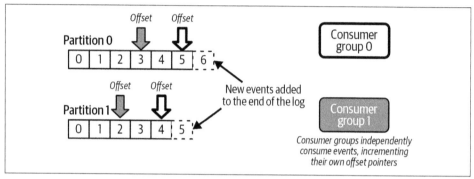

Figure 3-4. A durable append-only log with two partitions and two individual consumer groups

Unfortunately, due to a long and often messy history, event brokering has been often confused with *ephemeral messaging* and *queuing*. Each of these three options is different, and neither ephemeral message-passing nor queues are suitable for building an event-driven data mesh. Let's take a quick look at why.

Ephemeral Message-Passing

A *channel* is an ephemeral substrate for communicating a message between one producer and one or more subscribers. Messages are not stored for any significant length of time, nor are they written to durable storage by the broker. In the case of a system failure or a lack of subscribers on the channel, the messages are simply discarded, providing at-most-once delivery. NATS.io (*https://nats.io*) is an example of this form of implementation.

Figure 3-5 shows a single producer sending messages to the ephemeral channel within the event broker. The ephemeral messages are then passed on to the currently subscribed consumers. In this figure, Consumer 0 obtains messages 7 and 8, but Consumer 1 does not because it is newly subscribed and has no access to historical data. Instead, Consumer 1 will receive only message 9 and any subsequent messages.

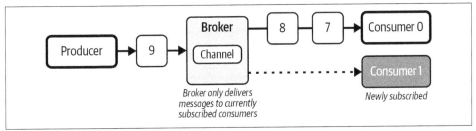

Figure 3-5. An ephemeral message-passing broker forwarding messages

Ephemeral communication lend itself well to simplicity, low overhead (no disk!), and ease of use. It facilitates a message-passing architecture, though the lack of reliability guarantees may limit its usefulness. It may or may not be highly available, depending on your deployment.

Message-passing architectures facilitate point-to-point communication between systems that don't necessarily need at-least-once delivery and can tolerate some data loss. As an example, the online dating application Tinder uses NATS to notify users of updates (*https://oreil.ly/rTZrp*). If the message is not received, not a big deal—a missed push notification to the user only has a minor (though negative) effect on the user experience.

Ephemeral message-passing brokers lack the necessary indefinite retention, durability, and replayability of events that we need to build event-driven data products. Message-passing architectures are useful for event-driven communication between systems for current operational purposes but are completely unsuited for providing the means to communicate data products.

Queuing

A *queue* is a durable sequence of stored events or messages awaiting processing. One of the more common use cases is that of a *work queue*, where the producer publishes "work to do" events. A subscriber dequeues an event, processes it, and signals to the queue broker that the work is complete, whereby the broker then deletes the event. Figure 3-6 shows two subscribers consuming events from a queue. Note that the queue predominantly contains events currently being processed and those yet to be processed. Already processed events are deleted after they have been consumed and marked as processed by the consumer.

Processing order may or may not be guaranteed in a queue. While you can enforce processing order by allowing only a single consumer instance per partition (or queue), this can significantly limit throughput. It is fairly common to have multiple subscribers that asynchronously (and competitively (*https://oreil.ly/JQgyB*)) select, process, and acknowledge events on a first-come, first-served basis. Additionally, latency and network partitioning may result in competitive subscribers processing the same events multiple times.

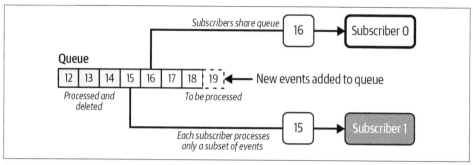

Figure 3-6. A queue with two subscribers each processing a subset of events

Historically, queue brokers have required a maximum retention time for events stored in the queue. If events are not processed within a certain time frame, they are marked as dead, are no longer delivered to the subscribers, and are subsequently deleted. Similar to ephemeral communications, time-based retention and non-replayable data has influenced the (incorrect) idea that brokers cannot be used to retain data indefinitely.

Event-driven data products need replayability and *each* consumer must get *all* of the events in *precisely the same order* that they were published.

Modern queue brokers tend to support both replayability and infinite retention of events via the adoption of the durable append-only log, which we will cover more in the next section. For example, both Solace (*https://oreil.ly/Tuphg*) and RabbitMQ Streams (*https://oreil.ly/40BK5*) allow for individual consumers to replay queue events. However, these systems struggle to support the strict ordering semantics, indefinite replayability, and scalability requirements of a modern data mesh.

Queues are best used at the individual application level to act as a *buffer*, either for input events or for interprocess communications. They are very useful at ensuring that each event is processed by only one consumer, but are not suitable as a conduit for communicating complete data sets as event-driven data products.

In the next section, we'll take a look at how consumers can use events provided by the event stream.

Consuming and Using Event-Driven Data Products

Event streams enable event-driven business logic. Upon consuming the event, the consumer application can update its state, execute logic, contact other systems, and produce its own events, just to name a few possibilities. Consumers subscribing to more than one event stream execute business logic specific to that stream, integrating the data into its application space.

State events form a critical component for composing the majority of event-driven data products. Let's take a look at these more closely.

State Events and Event-Carried State Transfer

A *state event* contains the entire *public state* of a specific business entity at the time the event was created. Think of a state event like a row in a database table—it contains all of the data relating to that entity that you, as the data product owner, would want to expose to the outside world. It does not contain any state that is private to the source domain.

Any changes to the row would simply result in a new event with a full copy of the now-updated data, including everything that hasn't changed, appended to an immutable event stream. This model is quite powerful, and it forms the basis of the event-driven data mesh through a pattern known as *event-carried state transfer* (ECST).

As the name suggests, events carry state about the entity and permit the transfer of asynchronous, eventually consistent state to the consumers of the data. Each consumer can re-create the state through a process known as *materialization* (see the next section), where a read-only model of the state can be re-created and processed by any consumer who needs it.

Your event definitions can change and evolve over time, as we'll discuss more in Chapter 6. Upon adding a new field to an event, the data product owner will need to decide whether to republish updated state events containing the new field or t include it only for new events going forward. In a relational database table, this would be akin to adding a new column and then running a migration job to populate that column for every single row in the table.

Chapter 7 covers both *state* and *action* event types in much more detail, including a discussion of the variations of each, trade-offs, and when each are best used. In the meantime, let's stick with the state model for now, as it forms the basis of the majority of event-driven data mesh communications.

Materializing Events

Materialization is the process of consuming an event and merging it into your own local data store. If a record with the same primary key already exists in that store, it is usually simply overwritten, though you may choose to implement more complex merging logic if you choose.

In practice, consumers don't usually need to store the entire event contents, but only the subset of data relevant to its domain. This substantially reduces the amount of data stored and processed, and helps keep the footprint of the consumer service small.

Figure 3-7 shows a consumer materializing the item event stream into its own state store. The consumer has decided to keep only the most recent record and to discard the older values for a given item. In this example, item key = 123 has been updated by the change of type from hat to helmet, as represented by the event at offset 2. Upon consumption, the consumer commonly evicts the previous materialized value for that key (offset 0) by overwriting the data in the database with the newest values. In some cases, you may want to keep a list of previous entries for a given key, a subject we'll cover more in "Slowly Changing Dimensions" on page 193.

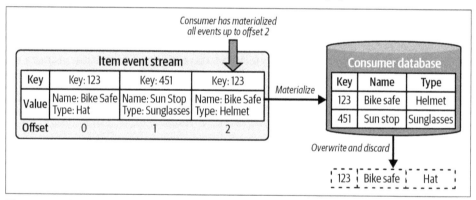

Figure 3-7. A consumer materializing the item event stream into its local database

Thanks to materialization, consumers can also execute logic based on changes from one event to another, since they retain the "current" state in memory and obtain the "new" state from the event stream. They can infer changes to any field within the event, which provides them with exceptional flexibility in how they use and process the event data.

Up next: materialization's fancier and often more complex cousin, aggregation.

Aggregating Events

An *aggregation* is an entity composed by merging multiple state events together. An aggregation could be as simple as a running sum but could also entail using multiple event types to build a more complex result. Figure 3-8 shows two instances of a single consumer application processing two partitions from a single event stream.

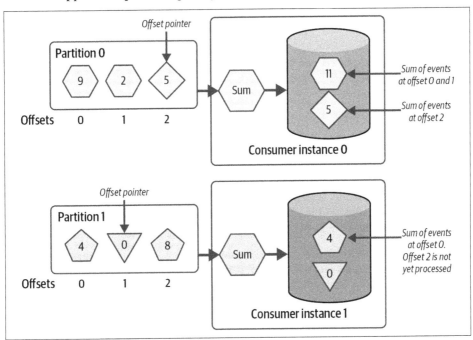

Figure 3-8. Aggregating state local to each consumer instance. The key is represented by the shape of the event.

Consumer instance 0 has processed all of the events in its assigned partition 0 and is awaiting new incoming events. The database within its boundary shows the current SUM aggregations that it has computed. Meanwhile, Consumer instance 1 is still processing historical data from its assigned partition 1 and is catching up to the current head event.

One of the major advantages of event-driven data products is that they make it very easy for you, as a consumer, to build your own aggregates. Instead of relying on the data product owner to build your aggregates for you, you can simply ingest the data into your own domain and aggregate it according to your own needs. If your derived data product is "just" an aggregation, you could consider republishing it to the data mesh as an aggregate-aligned data product (recall "The Three Data Product Alignment Types" on page 33). Alternatively, you may choose to make a consumer-aligned data product if you end up building an aggregation with more complex business logic that joins and mixes multiple input streams.

While this strategy does require extra work on your part, it also provides you with substantial *operational freedom*: you can simply change your computation and replay the event stream to rebuild the results instead of relying on the upstream data product owner to redefine and re-create the aggregate for you.

However, building your own aggregates brings the risk that a peer in another domain may be computing the same aggregate, with logic that doesn't match yours. As your data mesh evolves, expect to see aggregations in consumer domains moved upstream to become formal aggregate data products, reducing the risk of similar-yet-different and duplicate aggregates.

Operations, Analytics, and Limited Resources

Renegotiating team responsibilities is part of implementing a data mesh. But one of the risks is that this renegotiation can become untenable for those holding new responsibilities, especially if they lack sufficient resources. For example, a very popular source domain may find itself responsible for creating a large number of different kinds of data products but be unable to dedicate sufficient resources to the efforts.

The reality is that we live in a world with multiple competing requirements. While data mesh can prescribe clean and neat boundaries about who *should* be responsible for creating, building, and maintaining a data product, the reality is often quite a bit messier. Operational concerns tend to take precedence over creating new data products *unless those data products also serve operational use cases*. For example, the sales data product of "Source-aligned data products" on page 33 illustrates operational concerns—a sale has occurred, the data is published in an event, and consumers will now react to it to fulfill it. At the same time, this data product can also be used to compute analytical results, such as the daily sales aggregate-aligned data product in "Aggregate-aligned data products" on page 33.

Building your own aggregates from source-aligned and other aggregate-aligned data products is an essential escape hatch to the problem of insufficient resources. Source-aligned data products are fairly easy to create in comparison to aggregates, and the fact that they can be tailored to support operational use cases tends to give them a much higher priority in the responsibility queue of the data domain owner. When resources are tight, focus on creating general-purpose source-aligned data products that can be used by many different teams.

There remains a popular though incorrect notion that event streams are incapable of storing data indefinitely. And that even if you *could* do it, you shouldn't, because they're not built for that purpose. This mentality is an extremely outdated viewpoint, often based on the historical limitations of messaging systems, queues, and nascent event brokers. In the next section, we'll evaluate the role of event streams from the lens of data through time, the Kappa and Lambda architectures, and the modern way to think about event streams.

The Kappa Architecture

The *Kappa architecture* posits the use of an event stream as the source of both current and historical data. Consumers who want a complete picture of the data simply set their offset to the beginning of the stream and consume all of the data in sequence, eventually reaching the real-time head of the stream. This architecture is in contrast to the Lambda architecture, which posits two separate storage layers, one for historical data and one for near real-time data. We'll come back to Lambda in a bit.

The Kappa architecture was first presented in 2014 by Jay Kreps (*https://oreil.ly/oHgGP*), cocreator of Apache Kafka and cofounder of Confluent. The Kappa architecture has only relatively recently become feasible, in large part due to technical advances in modern event brokers.

Indefinite retention provided by tiered storage is now the norm for modern event brokers, making it easy and affordable to store as much data as you need in the stream. Deletion of old records through compaction keeps the size of streams built for ECST to a minimum, in line with the scope of the actual data domain. Figure 3-9 shows the end-to-end workflow in a Kappa architecture. The producer (1) writes events as they occur into the event stream (2), and each consumer is responsible for processing that data, including storing it in its own internal state store (3).

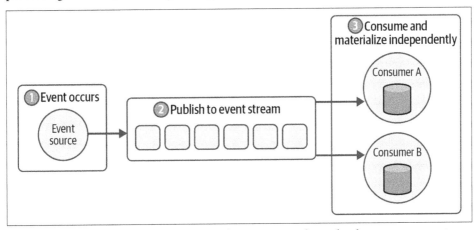

Figure 3-9. In the Kappa architecture, each consumer independently consumes events and builds its own state

Of course there are some trade-offs with the Kappa architecture. For example, you must build your service's state by processing the entire history of events. For extremely large data sets, particularly if there is an insufficient partition count, you could be looking at many hours. New and existing applications that need to build or rebuild their state will need to account for that with historical data processing time.

Consumer applications can rely on maintaining their own snapshots of materialized state to bootstrap loading their application. In the event of an outage or a failure, a restarted application can simply load its own personal snapshot, complete with offset tracking history, and resume processing from precisely where it left off. The application remains responsible for building and loading its own snapshots, though this functionality comes out of the box with leading stream-processing technologies such as Apache Kafka Streams, Apache Flink, and Apache Spark.

The Kappa architecture is key to building decoupled event-driven services (and microservices) and provides your applications' builders with unparalleled flexibility for application development. The business logic for consuming, transforming, storing, and reacting to state changes is completely within the consumer's control. Modern cloud service providers offer easy access for requisitioning storage space, memory, compute, network I/O, and durability to help build and use data products.

Example 3-1 shows a Kafka Streams application with two KTables, which is just a stream materialized into a table using ECST. Next, the inventory KTable and the sales KTable are joined using a nonwindowed INNER join to create a KTable of denormalized and enriched item inventory. Stream-processing frameworks make it very easy to handle event streams, build up internal state using ECST, and merge and join data from various data products, in just a few lines of code.

Example 3-1. Showcasing joins with Kafka Streams

```
StreamsBuilder builder = new StreamsBuilder();
//Materialized state of the "inventory" stream
KTable inventory = builder.table("inventory")
//Materialized state of the "items" stream
KTable sales = builder.table("items")

//Join events on primary key and apply custom business logic
//Note that inventory and items need to be keyed on the same itemId
KTable enrichedItemInventory = inventory.join(items, ...)
```

Something similar can be accomplished in SQL code using Apache Flink. In Example 3-2, Inventory and Items are materialized tables based on the associated Kafka topics. An Enriched_Item_Inventory table is created by INNER joining on the item_id (primary key) of the two tables.

Example 3-2. Showcasing joins with Flink SQL

```
CREATE TABLE Inventory (
  item_id VARCHAR,
  quantity BIGINT,
  timestamp TIMESTAMP(3),
  PRIMARY KEY (item_id) ENFORCED,
) WITH (
  'connector' = 'kafka',
  'topic' = 'inventory',
  'properties.bootstrap.servers' = 'localhost:9092',
  'properties.group.id' = 'my_app_group_id',
  'format' = 'avro',
  'scan.startup.mode' = 'earliest-offset'
);

CREATE TABLE Items (
  item_id VARCHAR PRIMARY KEY,
  name VARCHAR,
  description VARCHAR,
  brand VARCHAR,
  timestamp TIMESTAMP(3),
  PRIMARY KEY (item_id) ENFORCED,
) WITH (
  'connector' = 'kafka',
  'topic' = 'items',
  'properties.bootstrap.servers' = 'localhost:9092',
  'properties.group.id' = 'my_app_group_id',
  'format' = 'avro',
  'scan.startup.mode' = 'earliest-offset'
);

CREATE TABLE Enriched_Item_Inventory AS
  SELECT *
  FROM INVENTORY
  INNER JOIN ITEMS
  ON ITEMS.item_id = INVENTORY.item_id;
```

The Flink SQL code is concise, clean, and powerful. You can write extremely useful data transformations quickly and easily, leveraging the Kappa architecture with little heavy lifting on your part. Kafka Streams and Flink are among the most popular stream-processing frameworks, and either one is a good choice if you're looking for a full-featured, event-driven framework. For the sake of brevity, I won't cover each of the possible options and frameworks but I do encourage you to familiarize yourself with your options before selecting one for your use cases.

Kappa architecture is the best way to build and use event-stream data products. It is simple and effective, allowing consumers to use a single data product API for acquiring both historical and real-time data. Despite Kappa's clear advantages, you will likely encounter recommendations to use the Lambda architecture, based on the now-false assumption that an event stream cannot indefinitely retain data. Let's now take a look at exactly what the Lambda architecture is and why it falls short of Kappa.

The Lambda Architecture and Why It Doesn't Work for Data Mesh

The *Lambda architecture* is a composite of offline historical batch data and online event-streamed data. In this architecture, consumers obtain their data from these two sources and must recombine it into a consistent model within their own domain. There are two main versions of this architecture, and we'll look at each in turn.

In the first version, the batch data layer comprises the results of some sort of computation made by the domain owner, such as a materialization or aggregation. At startup time, the consumer loads the batch layer data into its context, then switches over to the event-streaming layer to read and process events.

Figure 3-10 shows a simplified implementation of the Lambda architecture. The producer writes a new event (1) to both the event stream (2) and the batch data layer (3). Note that the batch data store does *not* source its data from the event stream but directly incorporates the new data (1) into its database. The serving layer (4) contains two periodically updated materialized views of the batch data. In this case, one view is for consumer A and the other view is for consumer B.

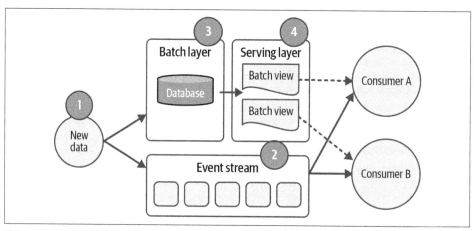

Figure 3-10. Lambda architecture, with data written to both batch and the event stream

Why two materialized views? Consider two consumers with different yet similar requirements. One consumer needs an hourly net sales aggregation, split up by sales area, while the other needs daily gross sales, excluding seasonal items. Without access to the full history of events, the two consumers remain beholden to the Lambda batch owner to maintain, compute, and provide the historical results to them.

You may also notice another problem with this approach—the consumers each require their own business logic requirements to be computed and maintained by the serving layer's owner! This leads to a shared responsibility model where the consumers do not have full ownership of their business logic. If they need to change their business logic, it must then be changed at the producer side during the composition of the batch data *and* at the consumer side for merging in the event-stream data.

In the second version of Lambda architecture, the batch data layer is simply a long-term store for events maintained *outside* of the event broker, as shown in Figure 3-11.

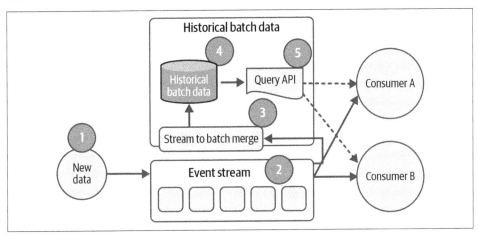

Figure 3-11. Lambda batch store built from event stream

In this version, new data (1) is written to the event stream (2) and eventually copied (3) into the batch data store (4). The batch store applies no special business logic and is simply a secondary store for immutable, incrementing events, exposed via a queryable API (5) for consumers (6). Each consumer is responsible for side-loading/bootstrapping the events they need from the batch data store into their own context, building up their own state as they go. Once they build up their current state, they then switch over to the real-time event stream (2).

This places the business logic related to the interpretation and modeling of events squarely within the domain of each consumer. The producer is no longer required to support any custom, precomputed views for the consumer, greatly simplifying operational concerns.

Now, you may think this Lambda variation is a bit odd—why use a second state store if you're just going to store raw events? Remember when I mentioned the tendency of designs to assume it's not possible to store events in a broker indefinitely? Lambda architecture is based on the notion that it's simply not possible to store a comprehensive history of events in an event broker.

However, modern event brokers, in conjunction with cheap disk and cheap cloud storage, have made indefinite retention a reality. And though once promising, the Lambda architecture has proven to be more complicated and difficult to implement than many originally thought. Let's look at some of the main issues that make Lambda architecture fiendishly difficult to use at scale:

The producer must maintain two code paths
One path handles the insertion of data into the batch data store and one constructs events to publish to the event stream. Atomic commits for both the event stream and the batch data store are not readily available, so you run the very real risk of duplicate or missing data. Reading the data from the batch may give you different results than reading from the stream.

The consumer must maintain two code paths
Just as the producer must maintain two code paths for publishing data, the consumer must maintain two code paths for resolving data. Both the stream and the batch representations of the data need to be consistent, which is hard to do in practice, especially over a long period of time as data changes and evolves.

A batch data-sourced consumer and a stream-sourced consumer may not converge on the same result
You have one consumer running since day 0. It has never loaded any data from the batch data store. Its internal state has been constructed solely by consuming and aggregating the event stream. You start a second consumer, which is an identical copy of the first, but it bootstraps its state from the batch data store. Once they're both up to date with the latest offset, you pause the inputs of new data. Are their states identical? The answer should be a resounding "Yes!", but unfortunately, in practice, it is usually a sad "No." Resolving consistent state from multiple sources with multiple code paths tends to be very complex in practice.

The batch data store and stream data models must evolve in sync
As the source domain model evolves, the representation of the data in the event streams usually changes too—but so too does the format of the batch store. The producer must ensure that what it writes to the event stream is fully consistent with the model in the batch serving layer. And through all of this, a historical consumer reading mostly from batch and a real-time consumer who only ever reads from the event stream must end up with copies of identical data. If this sounds like it's difficult to do well, you're right. I've seldom seen it used with success.

Merging multiple Lambda-based data products is difficult
The final nail in the coffin of the Lambda architecture is due to the difficulty of *merging multiple Lambda data products*. Each Lambda data product maintains its own rules pertaining to event-stream retention, when the event data is folded

into batch, how the events are folded into batch, and the period of duplicate data overlap between the batch and stream. The result is a *seam* between the batch and the stream data, and each data product has its own *seam* with its own nuances that rarely line up with the seams of another data product.

Reconciling seams proves to be extremely difficult. Each consumer application must reconcile not only every batch-to-batch relationship but also every batch-to-stream and stream-to-stream relationship, too. Two Lambda data products result in four unique relationships to manage, while three Lambda data products result in eight(!) (2*2*2) unique relationships that must be interpreted and reconciled. Each additional Lambda source increased the complexity exponentially.

To be blunt, I've never seen widespread successful use of Lambda-based data products, simply because it is too difficult to resolve more than a single Lambda source. While Lambda architectures *can* work in certain circumstances for limited application, in practice they're simply insufficient for the purposes of a data mesh. Instead, stick to using a Kappa architecture for the majority of your data product production and usage.

Supporting the Requirements for Kappa Architecture

Modern-day event brokers, combined with cheap and efficient cloud storage, let us store events for as long as they remain relevant to the business. For example, a user account entity event created 10 years ago would remain in the stream indefinitely, until perhaps there comes a day that the user is deleted or the account is purged for inactivity. Otherwise, a new consumer reading from the beginning of the account stream would see that account, regardless of how much time has elapsed.

Managing precisely what data is kept in a stream, how long it's kept, and when it's deleted depends on four things: infinite event retention, infinite storage, compaction, and deletions. Let's take a look at each one:

Indefinite event retention
> Your event broker should let you keep events in your stream indefinitely, just as you would expect to store data in a relational database for as long as it remains relevant to the business. Many event brokers do not let you do this, enforcing a time-based maximum for data retention. Those event brokers are entirely unsuitable for our purposes in building an event-driven data mesh.

Infinite storage
> Retaining events indefinitely also requires having sufficient storage space. Tiered storage is a common approach to this problem, where the event broker offloads older segments to slower and cheaper "cold" storage, keeping the most recent "hot" data in memory for fast service. Offloading and management of the

underlying data storage is entirely transparent to the clients, allowing us to use just the single event broker streaming protocol.

Compaction

Compaction is the deletion of older events for a given key provided a *newer event of the same key* exists in the stream partition. Compaction is essential for keeping the size of the event stream proportional to the key space of the entity domain. The event broker periodically scans the event stream, identifies the events to remove, and purges them from the stream.

 Event brokers with compaction support typically allow you to select a minimum period of time (*compaction lag time*) where events will not be compacted. This provides your consumers with a time period where they can consume and process *all* events, such that all state transitions are available. Apache Kafka uses 24 hours as the default compaction lag, but in practice it's common to tweak compaction lag on a per use case basis.

Deletions

ECST also requires the ability to *delete* data of a specific key from a stream partition. A *tombstone* is a record containing the key of the entity to be deleted and a null-value for the body. A tombstone tells the consumer that the entity with that key has been deleted, and any data associated with it can (and usually should) now be deleted from their state store. A tombstone record can be compacted like any other record, although the tombstone itself is also deleted.

Figure 3-12 shows an example of event-stream compaction. The event broker iterates through the log of events, keeping a list of keys that it has encountered. It marks any older records that have a newer record with the same key for deletion. Since there is an event with K=20 at offset 4 (newer), the compactor can delete all earlier events of K=20, such as the event at offset 1. Meanwhile, K=10 at offset 2 is a tombstone event, so both it and the event at offset 0 are deleted. All remaining events retain their offsets.

The compaction lag time is commonly set to several days (or weeks), meaning that events younger than the lag time won't be compacted. One common reason for setting it longer than a 24-hour default is to account for nonessential services that may crash over the weekend. The operations team can wait until the next business day to fix the crashed service and bring it back up, without worrying about missing uncompacted events.

Precisely how and when compaction occurs is specific to the event broker.

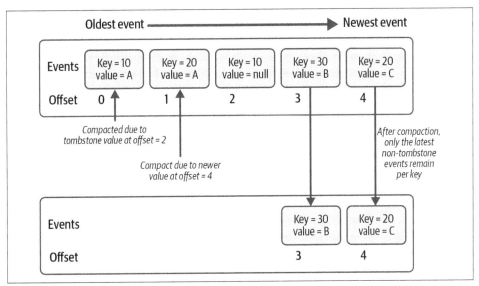

Figure 3-12. Compacting older events of the same key due to updated values or tombstones

Selecting an Event Broker

Selecting a suitable event broker that supports the Kappa architecture pattern is essential for creating a self-service data mesh. Both ephemeral message-passing and queues are insufficient to underpin a data mesh—you will need to ensure your event broker supports event streams in the form of durable append-only logs.

To select a broker, you need to focus on the essential requirements and make your own informed decision. These include:

Unlimited durable data capacity
 You must be able to store all pertinent events for as long as they are relevant. For most data products, you'll need to store them indefinitely. Data product consumers must be able to access and replay the events whenever they want.

Scalability
 Though scalability is largely a given in the era of cloud computing, you need to ensure that your event broker can scale up to extremely high throughputs and number of clients. Additionally, the event broker must be able to serve the stored data with high performance, as data products follow a write-one, read-many-times access pattern.

Support tooling

Schema registries, access controls, metadata cataloging systems, and governance and lineage systems all play an important role in building a data mesh. We'll cover these in more detail in Chapter 5, but it's important that you consider what options you have available based on your event broker choice.

Broker as a service deployments

By using cloud services, you can bypass managing your own event broker deployments and all the overhead that comes with it. If you're focused on building a data mesh, not having to manage your own infrastructure can be a big time and money saver. The event broker will often come as part of a larger platform providing support tools, so ensure that you investigate the full platform offering.

Retention period

The final but deal-breaking criterion is that of *retention*. How long can you keep the events in your event stream? A data product must be available in its entirety upon demand by any consumer, so any event broker that limits retention is unsuitable for use in a data mesh. Table 3-1 compares retention periods of several popular event brokers. You'll note that only Kafka and Pulsar provide the ability to store events indefinitely.

Table 3-1. Maximum event retention periods of popular event brokers

Broker name	Retention period
Kafka	Unlimited (*https://oreil.ly/VoyXU*)
Pulsar	Unlimited (*https://oreil.ly/qigVS*)
Amazon Kinesis	365 days (*https://oreil.ly/ID_Ed*)
Microsoft Event Hubs Premium	90 days (*https://oreil.ly/xOiHt*)
Google Pub/Sub	31 days (*https://oreil.ly/bSzPz*)

Apache Kafka is my current preferred choice for an event broker due to its dominance in the streaming industry, the excellent supporting software and tools, and the wide base of user knowledge. I am also biased in my selection, as I have been working with Kafka since 2014, have contributed to its codebase, and have also worked at Confluent with its cocreators.

The most popular projects also tend to have the most community-built tools and contributions. Schema registries, code generators, processing frameworks, operational system integrations, and data catalog integrations are just a few of the necessary dependencies to consider. KIP-405 for Apache Kafka (*https://oreil.ly/eYsOD*) provides an excellent example of some large players in the community coming together to collaborate on building tiered storage support directly into Kafka, making indefinite topic retention and scalable storage both cheaper and more reliable.

Technology will continue to change with time, and new options will certainly come into existence. Thus it's important to note that should AWS, Microsoft, or Google choose to support indefinite retention in their event brokers, they too may become viable candidates for supporting an event-driven data mesh.

The event broker you choose is a critical component for the success of your data mesh. Choose a safe, reliable, and extensively tested option for building the foundations of your data mesh.

Summary

Event streams form the best option for serving the majority of data products because they offer a real-time, immutable, durable, replayable, and scalable way to serve data. Their real-time interface can power both operational and analytical use cases. Queues and ephemeral message systems are often misconstrued as equivalent to an event stream. This is not the case, as covered in this chapter.

Materialization and aggregation are two common operations for event-stream consumers. These operations enable consumers to generate their own eventually consistent state by storing event-driven data within their own boundaries. Accessing a replayable source of historical data is another significant data product requirement. Event streams have typically been seen as unsuitable for maintaining data indefinitely, partially due to historical limitations in technology and partially due to preconceived notions that events should only ever be ephemeral or short-lived. This chapter addressed these issues and discussed both historical and modern options for dealing with event streams. The Kappa architecture enables the event stream to be a single source of both current and historic data and is far easier to use in practice than the older and less useful Lambda architecture.

Finally, I have also outlined the requirements and considerations for selecting an event broker. The reality is that there are only a few options at the moment, though there is room for improvement as event-driven architectures continue to increase in popularity. A data mesh can be challenging enough to implement, so ensure you select a popular and well-supported technology. You'll find it easier to hire talent to help build your data mesh, as well as leverage SaaS solutions and open source projects to increase your productivity.

In the next chapter, we're going to take a look at governance. If we're planning to publish data for others to use and consume, we're going to need some standards, security, and a degree of oversight and control.

CHAPTER 4

Federated Governance

Data mesh architectures are inherently decentralized, and significant responsibility is delegated to the data product owners. A data mesh also benefits from a degree of centralization in the form of data product compatibility and common self-service tooling. Differing opinions, preferences, business requirements, legal constraints, technologies, and technical debt are just a few of the many factors that influence how we work together.

Federated governance allows us to sort out the decisions that should remain at the local level from those that must be made globally, for all domains. To quote Dehghani (*https://oreil.ly/toG45*), "Ultimately global decisions have one purpose, creating interoperability and a compounding network effect through discovery and composition of data products." We need to figure out, enforce, and support the common building blocks and modes of operating to make data mesh work for everyone.

Founding a *federated governance team* is one of the first steps toward discovering common ground to work toward mutually beneficial solutions. Precisely what your governance team will do will vary based on your own business needs, but there are several common duties that we'll cover in this chapter.

Federated governance is about finding an appropriate balance between individual autonomy and top-down centralized control, between the delegation of responsibilities and the creation of overarching rules and guidelines for consistency and order. Like any form of effective government, we need participation, representation, debate, and collaborative action to actually get stuff done.

Creating a charter is an important first step in founding a federated governance team. This outlines duties and responsibilities of the group, such as establishing standards for data product formats, quality levels, interoperability, security, and supported technologies. It also lays out producer, consumer, and manager responsibilities, as well as any other social and technical aspects.

Federated governance is primarily focused on several main areas:

Data concerns
> Pertains to how data is created and used within an organization. Specifically, data product types, metadata, schemas, support, discoverability, lineage, quality, and interoperability.

Technology concerns
> Includes programming languages, frameworks, and processes that you'd like to incorporate into your data mesh. Assessing your existing technologies for suitability, as well as vetting new options, remains a key component of federated governance.

Legal, business, and security concerns
> Pertains to regulatory compliance and security issues, such as handling financial, personally identifiable, and other forms of sensitive data. Business-level requirements may also factor in, such as internal data security, access policies, and retention requirements.

Self-service platform concerns
> Makes it easy for your users to do the right thing. Users need a reliable self-service platform to build and use data products. Streamlining tooling, reducing friction, and making it easy for everyone to *get things done* is at the bedrock of data mesh. A self-service platform provides an opportunity to apply regulatory and security policies at the source, providing insight into how data flows through the organization.

Each of these areas relates to one another and offers a helpful lens through which to view the priorities for your governance team. Keep these four areas in mind as we go through the remainder of the chapter, because each section will touch on one of more of these main concerns.

But first—who gets to govern?

Forming a Federated Governance Team

A governance team requires a *mandate* to be effective in its work. A mandate includes two main components. The first is an *institutional* component, where the "higher-ups" endorse the data mesh and the governance team, providing members with some degree of authority, ownership, and responsibility. The second component is a *social* component, where those who are meant to use the data mesh appreciate its importance and buy into it. An absence of either component will likely result in a failed initiative.

The governance team is composed of people from across the organization who act as representatives of the teams, products, technologies, and processes pertaining to building and supporting a well-defined data mesh. As representatives of their peers, each member brings forward ideas, requirements, and concerns from their problem space and works together to come up with satisfactory solutions.

Finding representatives is often as simple as asking for a volunteer to represent the team for a fixed period of time (say three months), though they must be well-versed in the challenges that the team is facing. Senior technical people often get "volunteered" (selected) for this role, as they usually have the best understanding of team needs, the problem space, and historical contexts, such as past attempts at reform. There are often fairly important technical reasons why past efforts at reformation may have failed, and this historical context often helps guide the discussion in finding a way to a new successful resolution.

The size of the federated governance team will vary with the organization's size, but should be limited to a size that would make for an effective one-hour meeting. With too small of a group, you may find you lack sufficient representation, alienating teammates and damaging trust and support. With too large of a group, you may find that people start to feel like their input doesn't really matter or that someone else in the group will make the difficult choices. Finding the optimal size of the federated governance team is, perhaps ironically, up to the federated governance team. Start small, and feel free to pull in more members when you hit representation boundaries.

 Collect anonymous feedback on how the group thinks it's doing, as well as feedback from teammates and stakeholders outside of the group. This will help the group have more effective meetings, find appropriate boundaries for the areas of governance, and dial in on an effective group size and charter.

Once you have an initial body, you can start implementing standards to streamline the data mesh experience.

Implementing Standards

The federated governance team is responsible for coming up with a set of data product and technology standards. Think about the technologies your organization must support as a physical toolbox with limited space. If you want to add new tools to the toolbox, you'll need to make sure there's room and that there aren't other suitable tools that can do the job just as well. Imposing a reasonable limit on the toolbox ensures that technological sprawl is kept in check and that only tools that offer a substantial improvement are added.

Establishing barriers to entry for new tools, languages, standards, and technologies is *essential* for reducing sprawl, fencing out marginal options, and protecting against flavor-of-the-week implementations. Keeping your toolbox small and lean makes it far easier to provide first-class support for each tool in your self-service data mesh platform.

Standards should be introduced by *proposal*, with a detailed explanation of why the new option is better than what's already in the toolbox. A new option may cover a sorely needed use case for which there is nothing in the toolbox. Or the new option may be categorically better than something already in use. The proposer must craft a story and provide examples as to why their recommendation is a good one and what effects it'll have on tool and option selection.

It's very important to *trial* a proposed standard or technology before adding it to your first-class sanctioned toolbox. Ensure that the trial highlights the importance of the technology, how it is better than something that already exists, and what trade-offs it imposes given the current tools and support.

Be careful that trial systems don't get promoted into production on a "temporary" (but actually permanent) basis. It's important to test new technologies and frameworks in systems outside the critical path so that you can rewrite or abandon them without causing business delays.

Let's go through some of the main standards that your governance team will need to establish.

Supporting Multimodal Data Product Types

As introduced back in "Data Products Are Multimodal" on page 31, your federated governance team will need to decide what data product types and ports you *do* and *do not* support. Event streams form the core data product type covered in this book, but

---

you may also choose to support others, such as batch-computed Parquet files in a cloud data store, as we'll discuss more in Chapter 9.

Supporting multiple data product types provides additional options to data product owners, but comes at the expense of significantly more complexity for both governance and self-service tools. It's important to understand the opportunity cost and the amount of work required to support each data product type.

For example, you'll need to ensure that infosec, encryption, access controls, data product interoperability, and self-service data platform integrations are all accounted for. There can be a substantial amount of work adding a new data product type, and if the return on that investment is marginal, it may make more sense to simply serve the data product using an existing (if somewhat suboptimal) type instead.

If you believe that support for a new data product type is merited, then you should create a proposal and present it for consideration at the federated governance meeting. We'll investigate proposals more in "2. Drafting Proposals" on page 85.

The goal here isn't to constrain data product owners but to ensure that the tools that are made available are supported, meet governance requirements, are easy to use, and cover the necessary business use cases. Do not add new tools to the toolbox for the sake of variety or novelty, especially when there are existing and well-supported ways to provide sufficient access and usage.

Supporting Data Product Schemas

Schema frameworks are effectively programming languages for data. Much as you compose an application with code, you compose a data product schema with its own code. Precisely what that code looks like and which options are the best for you to choose are covered in more detail in Chapter 6. For now, consider how many, and what kind of, schemas and formats you may support. The two most common considerations include:

Event schemas
> Apache Avro, Protocol Buffers (Protobuf), and JSON Schema tend to be the most common formats for events. Each of these has its own trade-offs, in particular regarding type enforcement, schema evolution capabilities, default values, enumerations, and documentation.

File formats
> Batch files written to a cloud storage bucket have traditionally followed big data file conventions, including CSV, JSON, Avro, Protocol Buffers, Parquet, and ORC—to name a few. Additionally, consider the newer open source technologies that sit on top of these basic file formats, such as Apache Iceberg (*https://oreil.ly/NPxSx*), Apache Hudi (*https://oreil.ly/HGv8f*), and Delta Lake (*https://delta.io*). Each of these provides higher-level filesystem-type features, such as hidden

partitioning, transactions, and compaction and can make using batch-hosted data products easier to use, at the expense of tighter coupling to the technology.

It's best to standardize on just one event schema framework or file format for each data product type. For example, Avro for streams and Parquet for batch-computed files kept in your data lake. Only expand to support other formats if it's absolutely essential. Single formats greatly simplify tooling and the consumer experience while keeping complexity and risk low.

 If you must support multiple file formats or event schemas, ensure that data product owners can find easy-to-follow instructions on *which one* they should use and why. A failure to do so will introduce friction when neighboring teams end up implementing their data products with completely different schema frameworks, making consumption and use more difficult for their common consumers.

Next, let's look at some of the programming language questions and concerns.

Supporting Programming Languages and Frameworks

One common approach to producing data products is to use a language already in use within the source domain. The team would already be well-versed in it, which simplifies both creation and support of the data product. Another option is to select a language (or tool) in use in another part of the organization, perhaps because it is much more suited to the creation of the data product. We'll look into the specifics of bootstrapping existing data into event-driven data products in Chapter 8.

Sometimes developers use data product creation as an opportunity to try out a new esoteric language, regardless of whether it's officially supported. This puts that developer on the hook for all support and maintenance well into the future and will put the product at risk should no one else learn the language. In time, the developer who built the data product will likely move on to new projects or job opportunities, further increasing risk.

It is important to only implement data products in languages that are well-used or otherwise officially supported by your organization. If you think a language has merit to be used more widely, then you would do well to create a proposal (see "2. Drafting Proposals" on page 85) and discuss it with the federated governance team.

Deciding which languages (and frameworks) to support for building data products is based largely on the same criteria as building any other service. Such factors include:

Social factors

Is it a well-known technology? Are our developers familiar with it? Are there other people in the industry using it, and have they shown success with it? Will people want to work with it? Will it be appealing for new hires and can we find people with these skills in the market?

Technology factors

Does it solve our problems in a simple and effective way? Is it a proven technology that will continue to be updated and improved for years to come?

Integration factors

Is it easy to support? Does it integrate well with our existing development, test, build, and deploy pipelines? Can you get linters, debuggers, memory analyzers, testing tools, and other productivity enhancement tools that integrate with it?

Event broker clients

Does your event broker have high-performance clients written in the language of your choice? Will you be able to produce and consume events fast enough?

Supportive tooling

Does your language and framework work well with your event schemas (Chapter 6)? Do they support code generators? Can you generate test events to test your data product inputs and outputs?

Deciding which languages to support, and how extensively to support them, will be up to your organization and governance team. Choose languages that your organization is familiar with and that have event-broker support.

Metadata Standards and Requirements

A good data mesh requires well-defined metadata for each data product. Data mesh users should be able to discover and identify the data products that they need for their business use cases. A data product owner must provide all required metadata during registration of the data product to be allowed to publish the data product to the mesh. Enforcing metadata requirements is essential for ensuring that only well-defined and well-supported data products are made available to others, lest we repeat the mistakes of previous data strategies as discussed in "Bad Data: The Costs of Inaction" on page 17.

There are several fields that are essential for a healthy data mesh. In this section, we'll cover each of them and provide you with some basic examples for your own governance team to consider.

Domain and owner

First up is ownership. Who owns the data product? And where is it from? This metadata includes the domain namespace and the name of the data product owner. The name of the data product owner is an individual person, who represents the data product from that domain.

Tiered service levels

A data product requires support and uptime guarantees. But to what degree? If the data product encounters a failure, what is the appropriate course of action? Many companies already organize their applications into a tiered system, with the highest tier having 24-hour on-call rotations and the lowest tier having simple best-effort support. You should apply the same tier system to data products and offer the same support and guarantees as you would any other service or product of the same tier. The following is an example of a four-tier system:

Tier 1

> Data products that are critical to the operation of your business, where an outage or failure will result in significant impact to either the customer or to the business's finances. Data products that power real-time operational applications often fall into this category.

Tier 2

> Data products that are important to the business but are less critical than Tier 1. A failure in this tier may cause a degraded customer experience but does not completely prevent customers from interacting with your system. Data products in this tier also often power real-time operational applications.

Tier 3

> Data products that may affect background tasks and operations in the business, but are likely not visible to consumers nor impact them significantly. However, a failure in this tier may still require intervention should the data product be powering time-sensitive use cases.

Tier 4

> Data products that have the largest time window for recovery. It is not essential to have an on-call rotation to support these data products; they can wait until the next business day to resolve.

Uptime and availability are not the only considerations of a data product's service level. You will also need to monitor your data products to ensure they're meeting their SLAs, something that we'll cover in a bit more depth in "Monitoring and Alerting" on page 122.

Data quality classifications

The quality of the data provided by the data product should also be categorized, similar to the approach of the SLA tier system. One choice is to leverage the medallion classifications of *bronze*, *silver*, and *gold* commonly used in data lake architectures. Let's look at each classification:

Bronze

Unstructured and raw data that is untransformed from the original source format. May be strongly coupled on the internal data model of the source system, and may also contain fields that need to be sanitized or scrubbed. May also include data that is well-structured and defined, but for which quality is intermittent or the data owners simply cannot provide a higher guarantee.

Silver

Well-structured data with strong typing and typically sanitized and standardized. Usually denormalized to be sufficiently useful as is, with the most common foreign-key relationships having been joined and resolved to provide ease of use to consumers. Type-checking and constraints have been applied to ensure a minimum data quality (e.g., 99.99% of events pass quality checks). The context of the event is clearly defined and documented, as are the type checks and constraints. If a consumer wants to impose their own further, tighter constraints on the data, they would do best to communicate with the data product owner to evaluate options.

Gold

The highest level of quality. Often referred to as "authoritative," data products with the gold level of quality are meant to be relied on without reservation. Data products are rigorously tested and monitored, with type-checking and constraints exceeding that of the silver quality level (e.g., 99.9999% of events pass quality checks). Gold data products are often more complex, built up by significant aggregations and transformations that offer significant value, and would be quite difficult for consumers to replicate on their own.

 Data quality classification is separate from the data product alignments (source-aligned, aggregate-aligned, and consumer-aligned), and is concerned only with data quality.

You are free to select alternative classification models as you see fit. The important part is that your data mesh users must be able to easily understand and apply the modeling to their own data products, preserving a common understanding between producers and consumers of the data.

Privacy, financial, and custom tagging

In conjunction with security and financial information representatives, the governance team can come up with tags to apply to data products to help automate specialized treatment. For example, you may choose to include a tiered system for security classifications similar to that of SLAs. You may also choose to use tags that pertain to the type of data included within the event stream, such as financial, PII, or region-based tags.

Supporting tags on data products makes it easier to apply governance rules because they can be applied on a per-tag basis. For example, a consumer seeking to use a data product with a financial tag will need to prove their compliance with their organization's financial data handling requirements. Tags also enable easier auditing of data usage on a per-consumer basis.

Upstream metadata dependencies

Upstream services and data products each have their own SLAs, data quality levels, and other guarantees. Any service or data product that relies on upstream services or data products must take these dependencies into account when specifying their own guarantees. For example, a service cannot offer Tier 1 support when it depends on data products with Tier 4 guarantees. We'll touch more on lineage later in this chapter in "Data Product Lineage" on page 92.

As part of your governance requirements, you may choose to establish minimum upstream requirements for data quality and SLAs to power your production applications, be they operational, analytical, service, or data product. One common convention is to allow only services that have Tier 1 or Tier 2 SLA guarantees in production.

Upstream data quality requirements are not quite as strict—it's entirely possible that you can power a Tier 1 gold data product with a Tier 1 bronze data product. In fact, this is usually how bronze data is transformed into a high-quality gold-layer data product.

You can enforce upstream checks during the creation of a data product, as we'll explore more in Chapter 5.

Metadata wrap-up example

Figure 4-1 shows an example of what a user may see when looking up information about a data product. While we're going to explore metadata cataloging more in Chapter 5, for the moment you can think of it as a read-only database where you can look up the available data products and their properties.

The data product name, domain, and user are all mandatory pieces of metadata created at time of publishing. A description field is also included to describe context and disambiguate the data product from other similar ones. Metadata about the service, quality, and security levels are also present, as are tags describing PII, financial, and regional information.

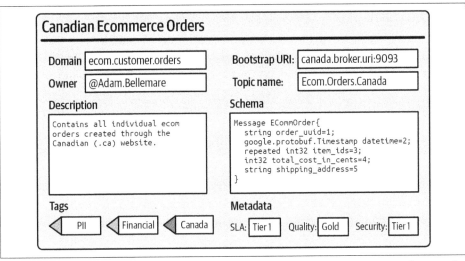

Figure 4-1. An example of data product metadata you may expect to see as a data mesh user

The schema field in the metadata is pulled in from the schema registry, which is a component that stores and manages schemas for event streams and is an essential piece of the self-service data platform. We'll cover this in more detail in "The Schema Registry" on page 99. The broker name and topic name are also pulled in to provide the digital address of the data product.

Metadata helps us make informed decisions about what data products are available for our use cases. Compatibility between data products is essential in enabling us to merge data from different sources and is the subject of the next section.

Ensuring Cross-Domain Data Product Compatibility and Interoperability

There are many factors that make up aggregating, merging, and comparing data products between domains. As part of the data concerns outlined at the beginning of this chapter, interoperability and ease of use remain two of the major concerns of federated governance. Rules and guidelines about common entities, time zones, aggregation boundaries, and the technical details of event mappings, partitions, and stream sizes all fall under the governance team's purview. Let's take a look at these areas now.

Defining and Using Common Entities

One of the first important steps is to define the minimal entities that are used across many areas of your business. Let's take a look at an example first.

An ecommerce company defines a common Item entity containing two fields: long id and long upc_code. Data product owners are expected to use the Item entity in any data product that references their ecommerce items, be it Order, Inventory entry, or Return. Each of these related entities uses a common and standardized version of Item, removing the need for consumers to interpret similar-yet-different representations of the same data.

Common entities do not preclude you from adding more information about that entity to your data product. You are free to extend your data products to include other information about Item, such as size and color in the case of a clothing item or weight and serving_size in the case of a food item. Think of a common entity as an attachment point between data products in other domains and as an extendable base for the entity's data model.

Event Stream Keying and Partitioning

Interoperability of event-streaming data products is affected by the partition count of the stream, the key of the event, and the partition assignment algorithm (see Chapter 3). An event stream contains one or more partitions, and each event is assigned to a partition based on the partition assignment algorithm, the event key, and the number of partitions. Here are some useful interoperability tips:

Partition count
> Joining and aggregating data products from multiple streams can be made much less computationally intensive if the event partition counts are the same size. While event-stream processors like Kafka Streams and Flink can automatically repartition event streams as needed, it requires more processing power and can incur higher costs. Try using a T-shirt sizing approach to standardize partition counts, such as x-small=1, small=4, medium=8, large=16, x-large=32, xx-large=64, jumbo=256. As part of your self-service platform (which we'll cover in the next chapter), you can provide the data mesh users with instructions for choosing partition count based on the key space, volume of events, and consumer reprocessing needs.

 If you're building a data product keyed on a common entity, check the partition count of other data products also keyed on that entity—if they're all using the same partition count, you would do well to use it, too.

Event key

The event key is best served by using a primitive value, such as a `string`, `int`, or `long`. The common entity's unique ID is your best choice for interoperability.

Partition assignment algorithm

This algorithm takes the event key as an input and returns the partition ID to write the event to. Event producer clients of different programming languages and frameworks may use incompatible algorithms, resulting in event streams that are not cross-compatible, despite using the same event key and the same partition count. While using a single framework like Kafka Streams will ensure that your partition assignment is consistent, you will need to do a bit of research to evaluate other frameworks as part of your self-service platform.

Be careful about hot partitions where a disproportionate number of events are assigned to a single partition. For example, 99% of all events may be assigned to a single partition, while the remaining partitions get only 1% of the data. While this is usually due to an extremely narrow key space, it can also be due to an unsuitable partition assignment algorithm.

It's important to think about keying and partitioning for compatibility from the start, since many of the data products you create will stick around for a while. Changing partitions is possible, but it often requires rewriting the data to a new event stream and migrating the consumers. Stick to using T-shirt sizes, come up with some recommendations for selecting partition counts based on consumers' needs (e.g., reprocessing, parallelization), and define a common partition assignment algorithm based on your available client frameworks.

Time and Time Zones

Data products may be associated with a window or period of time. For example, an aggregate-aligned data product may represent data over a period of time, such as an hourly or a daily aggregation. As part of a standard of ensuring interoperability, establish a primary time zone such as UTC-0 for all time-based data products. Consumers will have a far simpler experience combining different time-based data products if they do not have to contend with converting time zones and dealing with daylight saving time.

Where applicable, you should include the aggregation period and time zone-related information as part of the data product's metadata. This information will help your consumers decide what further processing, if any, they need to do to merge it in with their other data products.

Now that we've covered ways of providing data product compatibility, it's time to get into a bit more of the social side. How do we make effective decisions about our data mesh standards and requirements?

What Does a Governance Meeting Look Like?

Covering the entirety of an effective meeting is beyond the scope of this book, but there are a few pointers that should help you get started. First, ensure that you follow best practices common to all technical meetings. Second, send out an invite well ahead of time and provide an agenda for the meeting. Third, ensure that you have a chairperson and someone to take notes and record action items, and ensure that everyone knows what needs to be done for the next meeting. It's common to rotate responsibilities and duties to ensure equal representation.

It's very important to get the people who work on operational systems into the same meeting room with those who work on analytical systems. You may be surprised, or possibly just disappointed, at how seldom this happens. The isolation of "data teams" from "engineering teams" has long plagued the IT space, as we touched on in "Bad Data: The Costs of Inaction" on page 17.

 As with any meeting, people with a strong personality or a loud voice may try to dominate the conversation. Ensure that you have a chairperson to conduct the meeting and ensure that everyone has a chance to speak uninterrupted. If the meeting gets heated and starts to be unproductive, take a 5-minute recess or adjourn for the day.

You should expect to meet frequently during the starting stages of your data mesh transformation. You will have many things to discuss, solve, support, and standardize. As time goes on, you can expect to meet less frequently.

But what are the main tasks that the governance team should focus on? Let's go through five main areas and discuss how they pertain to data mesh.

1. Identifying Existing Problems

The first task of the governance team is to identify where the problems are. Your team should be composed of individuals from across the organization with a good view of the technological and data landscape. A grassroots, bottom-up approach to reporting problems and issues tends to work best. Ask your colleagues to identify the areas that they're having problems in, the barriers and obstructions they're facing, and what it is that they would like to be able to do—either in terms of business requirements or simplifying operational complexity.

Have everyone list their main problems and issues using cards or sticky notes. Then you can cluster similar issues together, such that you can find the areas of improvement that may have the biggest impact.

Identifying problems is the first step forward in improving the data mesh for everyone. Common issues may include a lack of self-service tooling, inconsistent data in existing products, and a lack of policies regarding duplicate data, infosec, PII, and financial information. Once the problems are identified, you can prioritize which ones are the most important and dedicate resources toward solving them.

2. Drafting Proposals

The next step is to create a proposal that frames the problem, explains why it is important to solve, articulates challenges and opportunities, and identifies a possible solution. A proposal is much like a *bill* as introduced in the houses, senates, and parliaments of many democratic systems. It proposes changes, provides details, and specifies scope, all packaged up in a single debatable unit.

It's not just the governance team that can create proposals for review—*anyone* in the organization can create one. In fact, you'll get the best results by following up with the folks who have identified the problems—they usually have some idea about how to make things better and just need someone to organize and promote the necessary work. Proposals should be focused on solving specifically identified problems that have a real-world impact to users of the data mesh.

Some examples of proposals could include:

- Introduce field-level encryption to restrict access to some sensitive information in a data product
- Implement regulations for handling data products spanning multiple cloud deployments
- Add custom tagging to data product metadata to improve search functionality
- Add namespacing to data products to enable security access at a namespace level
- Introduce a centralized authentication and authorization service to unify identity management from across each cloud service in the self-service platform

Although proposals can cover a wide area of concerns, the majority of the time they should lead to an improvement in the self-service tools and platforms available to data mesh users. Mandating a new process is all fine and dandy, but if it's not baked into the tools and services that data mesh users use every day, there's a good chance it won't be followed or used.

Proposals should illustrate what a successful resolution of the problem looks like. Prototyping a solution to showcase precisely *how* it will work keeps ideas anchored in the practical realm instead of the theoretical. Devise experiments, run trials, assign research, investigate options, and prototype technological solutions before rolling them out for general usage.

3. Reviewing Proposals

The federated governance team reviews the proposals to determine the viability of the solution and the required implementation resources. How you review these proposals will vary from team to team, especially as remote work, time zones, and other distribution factors are taken into consideration. One option that works well is to have members of the federated governance team individually review the proposals, making any notes or marking any concerns, before getting together in a larger group. If you can get everyone into a room, digital or physical, you may find it easier to ask questions, debate options, and come up with a unified plan. You could also meet asynchronously, and decide to get together only if there is sufficient disagreement or confusion.

 Keep reviews open and inclusive. Invite individuals from across your organization that you think could help by providing additional context and information. You may need to explicitly seek out and invite them as most people tend to be pretty busy. Ensure that you do not rely on the same people to review every proposal, lest you give the idea that no one else is welcome to contribute to federated governance.

The main goal of the review should be to validate the proposed solution, vet any prototypes, identify any missed considerations, and assess the boundaries of the work involved. The review may result in the proposal being rejected—either sent back to the creator for additional work or declined outright due to other insurmountable issues. An accepted review will require a final step—planning and executing the implementation work.

4. Implementing Proposals

An accepted proposal must next be converted to detailed work items. Break up the proposal into incremental steps to build, test, deploy, and validate your data mesh changes. Use your existing work ticket system to detail each work item, including a description of work to be done, what success looks like, and an estimate of how much time and effort it'll take to complete.

Implementing a proposal is identical to the process of implementing features for any other product. While you may be able to avoid having a self-service data platform product manager at the start of your data mesh journey, you'll come to find that it's an essential role for getting things done.

You're also going to need to get someone to do the work! Depending on your organization, you may have chosen to assign one or more people to implementing data mesh platform tickets. Alternatively, you may request that the proposal creator provide the people-hours to get the work done, given that they are likely to be the most familiar with the solution.

However you choose to get the work implemented, focus on getting iterative improvements into use in a reasonable time frame. Like any other product, your data mesh itself needs to help your colleagues solve their data access, usage, and publishing problems. If you fail to build confidence in your data mesh platform, people will simply not use it and will instead resort to their own ad hoc data access mechanisms. In this case, your data mesh will be nothing but a waste of time.

5. Archiving Proposals

Keep all of your accepted and rejected proposals, along with notes (or recorded videos) about their discussion in a commonly accessible location such as a cloud file drive. People should be able to look up the proposals to see their status, as well as which ones have been accepted or rejected, and why. Transparency is essential because it provides a record as to why a technology or decision was or was not adopted.

Archived proposals also remove some operating complexity. You can search the existing proposals to see if something similar has already been proposed before, and, if so, what the results were. The original rationale for not adopting something may no longer apply, making it worth revisiting with a new proposal.

In the next section, we'll take a look at security and access controls. Both of these are essential for establishing a reliable framework of ownership and security and also for protecting against unauthorized access and accidental modification of each other's data products.

Data Security and Access Policies

Your data mesh's security and access practices depend heavily on the legal and business requirements of your business. For example, a bank will have far higher security and access control requirements than an anonymous message board website. Since this is a large field of study, we're going to assume you're following "good security practices," and instead focus on a few important concepts and techniques specific to making and using event-driven data products.

Defense in depth should be your guiding principle when dealing with security and access controls. There is no one single thing that will keep your data secure from unauthorized use, be it from a well-meaning but unauthorized colleague or from an external intruder. Limiting access by default, mandatory authentication of users and services, and securing and encrypting private, financial, and other sensitive information each help reduce the blast radius and mitigate fallout.

Identity management is a foundational component of data security, as all of the user and service permissions will be tied back to it. We'll look at this subject more in the next chapter in "Service and User Identities" on page 110. For now, let's investigate a few of the most important security principles that your governance team may choose to implement and support in your data mesh.

Disable Data Product Access by Default

Data products should only be available for use by registered consumers. If you're not registered as a consumer of the data product, you can't read it. While this principle introduces a hurdle, compared with allowing a data product to be read-only to anyone who may want it, it forces users and services to register as explicit consumers. We need to know *who* is reading *what*, so that any changes and requests can be effectively communicated both upstream and down.

Consider End-to-End Encryption

Depending on infosec requirements, you may need to encrypt your data product data prior to publishing it to the event broker. The data remains encrypted in the event broker, preventing any unauthorized backdoor access to the data on disk. A registered consumer with the assigned decryption keys can consume and decrypt the data locally for its own use.

Streamlining data encryption and decryption is a function of the self-service platform. However, it's up to the governance team to determine the requirements and supported use cases.

End-to-end encryption is often required for handling sensitive data. Encrypting data at the producer side provides extra security during the network communications and data storage of the event and ensures that the cloud provider of the event broker cannot somehow read (or leak) the unencrypted data. Additionally, end-to-end encryption acts as defense in depth—it is possible that someone may gain access to read your event data, but without the decryption keys, will not be able to decode and use the original data.

Figure 4-2 showcases a producer and a consumer client using end-to-end encryption. The producer has encrypted the data before writing to the event stream and has published the key to a key management service (KMS). A consumer that wants to read the data product must obtain access to the decryption keys from the KMS and then apply them to each event read from the stream.

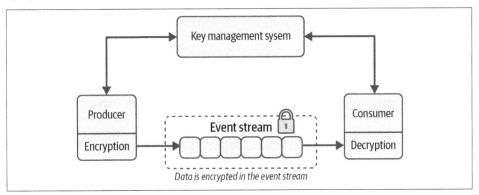

Figure 4-2. End-to-end encryption at work in a data product served as an event stream

A KMS provides you with a mechanism for safely creating, sharing, storing, and rotating your keys. While you can get started without any formal self-service data platform support, you're most likely going to need to invest in streamlining this process if you end up using a lot of encryption.

You may not always need to encrypt the entire event—sometimes encrypting just the sensitive fields is more than enough. Let's take a look.

Field-Level Encryption

Field-level encryption offers the ability for a data product owner to encrypt specific fields, so that only select consumers can access the data. Personally identifiable, account, and financial information are common use cases for field-level encryption. For example, when modeling a bank transfer, you may use field-level encryption on the user and account fields, but leave the amount and datetime fields unencrypted. Consumers with decryption permissions can access the decrypted information to settle account balances, while an analytical system without decryption permissions can still track how much money is moving around during a period of time, all from the same data product. Table 4-1 shows the encryption of the email, user, and account fields of an event.

Table 4-1. Using field-level encryption to partially encrypt an event

Field name	Original event	Partially encrypted event
email	adam@bellemare.com	n2ZI@p987NhB4.LOP
user	abellemare	9ajkpZp2kH
account	VD8675309	OPlwW81Mx
amount	$777.77	$777.77
datetime	2022-02-22:22:22:22	2022-02-22:22:22:22

You may also choose to use format-preserving encryption to maintain the format of the event data. In this case, we used format-preserving encryption for the `email`, `user`, and `account` fields—the same alphanumeric characters, spacing, and character count of the original fields, but without exposing any of the PII to users without decryption permissions.

 One of the advantages of using field-level encryption is that it permits finer-grained access controls for consumers. Your consumers can request decryption keys only for the data they need, instead of for the entire payload, reducing the potential for inadvertently leaked information.

Format-preserving encryption is particularly useful for applying encryption to data after the fact because you don't need to renegotiate the schemas with downstream consumers. In contrast, using nonformat preserving encryption often results in malformation, such as converting a `long` bank account ID into a 64-character `string` or encrypting a complex nested object into an array of hashed bytes.

Encryption of sensitive data, whether end-to-end or field-level, can also help us with another significant governance requirement: the right to be forgotten and have our data deleted.

Data Privacy, the Right to Be Forgotten, and Crypto-Shredding

General Data Protection Regulation (GDPR) (*https://oreil.ly/mW7fs*) is (among other things) a law requiring the careful handling, storage, and deletion of data. It is an excellent example of a legal constraint that your organization may need to adhere to in order to stay on the right side of the law. And if you're looking to create a data mesh of useful data products, it's very likely you're going to end up dealing with personal, account, and financial information that may require you to take extra steps and precautions to secure.

Article 17 of the GDPR (*https://oreil.ly/d3620*) requires that individuals have the ability to request that all of their personal data be deleted, without undue delay. At first glance this stipulation may appear to be directly in opposition to the tenets of a data mesh: publishing well-defined data products for other teams and services to use as they see fit. Event-driven data products may seem to further exacerbate the issue, as consumers read the data into their own local data stores and caches.

Crypto-shredding (*https://oreil.ly/HtQOC*) is a technique you can use to ensure that data is made unusable by overwriting or deleting the encryption keys. In short, you allow the end user full control over when they want to delete their keys, making their data cryptographically unavailable once the keys are deleted. You can use crypto-shredding with any form of encryption, including end-to-end and field-level.

Meanwhile, the consumers of the encrypted data products simply contact the central KMS and request access to the decryption keys. Provided the consumer has the correct permissions, the decryption keys are passed back to them and they can then decrypt and process the data as needed.

Why do it this way? Can't we simply sort through the data in the data product and just delete it outright? Wouldn't that be far safer?

Deleting data product data remains a reasonable choice; however, there are several complications that make encryption and crypto-shredding an important consideration:

Large amounts of data
> Large amounts of data may be stored in backups, tape drives, cold cloud storage, and other expensive and slow-to-access mediums. It can be very expensive and extremely time-consuming to read in all of the historical data, selectively delete records, and then write it back to storage. Crypto-shredding enables you to avoid having to search through every single piece of old data in your organization.

Partially encrypted data is still useful
> Deleting just a user's PII is often sufficient for meeting the GDPR Article 17 requirements. The remaining data in the event may still be of use for certain consumer use cases, like building up analytical aggregations. We can leave the remaining data in place and still obtain limited benefit from it.

Data across multiple systems
> Deleting the decryption keys simultaneously invalidates all data access across all consumer services. We don't need to worry about when the data is deleted, especially for systems that are slow to delete their data.

Further defense in depth

> Crypto-shredding provides an additional layer of security for preventing data security incidents. Leaking encrypted data is far less damaging than leaking unencrypted data and helps reduce both the risk and the impact of a data security breach.

Crypto-shredding doesn't protect you from consumers who negligently store decrypted data or the decryption keys. You can counter this by ensuring that consumers have clear and simple infosec policies to follow, such as retaining the decryption keys for only 10 minutes, prior to deleting them and having to request them from the KMS again. You can also use the access-control list to keep track of which services request access for data decryption, so that your infosec team can audit them for compliance.

The rules and regulations for securing and handling data are a major component of the governance team's responsibilities. These concerns are fundamental to the viability and survival of an organization and cannot be left up to individual data product owners to implement ad hoc. Ensure that you and your federated governance team have a solid understanding of the legal and business requirements for handling your data so that you can guide the security requirements of the self-service data platform.

The next related component is data product lineage. While access controls and encryption help with meeting legal data handling requirements, it's important to know all of the upstream and downstream dependencies of a data product. Let's take a closer look at lineage to see how it can improve our data mesh.

Data Product Lineage

Lineage allows us to track which services are reading and writing a data product, including if the consumer client is actively reading the stream. Basic read/write permissions, along with client identities, provide us with a pretty good picture that we can use to track dependencies and lineage. We can determine which systems and users do or do not have access to sensitive data, as well as the routes and paths that data takes as it travels from one client and product to the next.

For an event-driven data mesh backed by open source Apache Kafka, the access controls are established at the event broker itself. Many SaaS providers also provide higher-order functionality in the form of role-based access controls (RBAC), letting you compose roles based on rules and personas. In either case, permissions are essential for keeping track of and constructing lineages.

There are two main types of data lineage to consider for your own implementations. The first is *topology-based lineage*, which shows dependencies between services and data products at a point in time. The second is *record-based lineage*, which tracks the propagation of a record through services. Let's take a look at each in turn.

Topology-Based Lineage

Topology-based lineage shows the dependencies between data products and their consumers as a graph, with arrows pointing from the data product to the registered consumers. New data products show up as nodes on the graph, as do data product consumers. The graph may show which clients are actively consuming events, at what rate, if they're up to date, or if they're replaying historical data. It's also possible to add service and data product information and metadata to the topology, providing an alternate mode of discovery for your prospective data mesh users.

Topology-based lineage is relatively easy to obtain given that permissions and client identities are already essential for infosec and are frankly just good practices all around. You could even build your own by dumping your client identities and permissions into a file and reconstructing them into a graph using the graph framework of your choice.

A significant majority of lineage tools today focus on topology-based lineage, usually with an attractive and interactive graph that you can click on to see additional information, such as upstream and downstream dependencies. While many can give you only the topology *as it is right now*, others have started rolling out *point-in-time lineage*, where you can examine and download the lineage at a specific point in time.

Topology-based lineage is useful for tracking which consumers have accessed which data products. In the event of erroneous data in a product, you can also detect which downstream consumers may have been affected so that compensatory actions can begin. Finally, a data product owner can simply consult the lineage graph to see who is consuming its data products to coordinate with them on upcoming changes.

Record-Based Lineage

Record-based lineage focuses on tracking a single record through its history, recording everywhere it goes, which systems process it, and any derivative events that it may be related to. Record-based lineage should provide an auditor with a comprehensive history of the event's life cycle, such that further investigation is possible. Record-based lineage is far more complex to implement because there are many corner cases to consider. Record-based lineage can be used in conjunction with topology-based lineage, though it tends to be the less commonly implemented of the two.

One simple implementation option is to record an event's progress through its journey from data product to consumer. At each stage of its journey, a unique service ID, processing time, and any other necessary metadata is attached to the record, usually in the header. However, record-based lineage tends to be much more difficult to achieve at scale, as there are several major complicating factors:

Multiple consumers of the same events
> A record can be consumed by many different users, resulting in multiple copies of the same event, each with its own lineage.

Not all consumers emit events
> Some consumers do not emit events and may instead serve up access to data via a REST API. They would need to take additional steps to create a log of which records they have ingested and ensure that the data is made available for query.

Aggregating and joining events
> An aggregation can be composed of a large number of events, making it impractical to track all of the records associated with its composition. The same is true for joins, though in practice joins tend to only span a small quantity of events.

Complex transformations
> Consumers can have fairly complex use cases where input events simply do not map easily to outputs.

An alternative to storing record lineage in the record is to instead use an external database. Each service must report to the endpoint the events that it has consumed, processed, and emitted. This option does make it easier to track record usage when multiple services have consumed and used the data product, including those where new events are not emitted after use.

However, it does not solve the issues relating to joins, aggregations, and complex transformations, leaving a potential gap in record-level lineage. Furthermore, you will also need to invest in client tooling that automatically reports each record's status to the central service, including accounting for scaling, outages, and client language support.

It's important that you consider *why* you want lineage and what problems it's meant to help solve. There is no one-size-fits-all solution to lineage. A bank will have far greater lineage requirements than a store that sells socks, so you'll need to ensure that your governance team has a good idea about its own organization's true requirements. There are lineage solutions that can conceivably solve the issues that we've discussed in this section, but they require time and effort to accomplish—time and effort that may be best spent elsewhere.

If you don't have a good understanding of what problems your lineage solution is meant to solve, you run the risk of building something completely irrelevant. You must figure out what audits you need and what the risks to your systems are, and then come up with a detailed proposal for how a lineage solution can help you meet your needs.

Summary

Federated governance covers a large territory.

Data mesh requires a governance team to help bring order to the varied technologies, domains, data models, and use cases of the organization. Governing is an intensely social commitment to work together with your peers and come up with effective solutions for the hurdles of implementing data mesh. As part of the governance team, you'll focus on identifying common standards, frameworks, languages, and tools to help support data mesh use cases.

The governance team works together with technical domain experts to identify areas of improvement in the self-service platform. If you want everyone in your organization to adhere to data encryption policies, it's far easier to ensure that they're integrated into the data product platform by default and not left up to each team to implement for themselves. Similarly, the governance team makes sure that those who use the data mesh are heard, their complaints are addressed, and success stories are shared and exemplified.

Federated governance is also about tracking data usage, ensuring it adheres to legal requirements and good infosec practices. You will need strong access controls to ensure you know which systems and people have access to which data, but you'll need to balance it against making sure that your teams can get access to most data when they need it. Data may also need to be encrypted, either partially or fully, and may also need to be archived indefinitely, again depending on your data handling requirements.

Finally, governance is also about providing direction for the implementation of the self-service platform. The governance team, in conjunction with its technical experts, should codify and streamline the self-service platform functionality, such that it's easy for users to do *the right thing* and hard for them to do *the wrong thing*. We'll take a look at this more in the next chapter.

CHAPTER 5

Self-Service Data Platform

A self-service data platform makes it easy to discover, use, publish, manage, and secure data and data products for all mesh users. We've already introduced some of the components that go into making this platform: the event broker for serving event streams, a metadata store for tracking essential metadata, and access controls for managing data product access. In this chapter, we'll cover the features of a self-service platform beginning with minimalism and ending with ideal.

There are a few important overarching questions yet to be addressed: How do prospective consumers discover available data products? Once discovered, how do they plug them into their existing applications and analytics? How do they build new applications on top of the data products? Similarly, what does the workflow for a data product publisher look like? How do they go about managing their data products and actually communicating with their customers? The self-service platform must provide a streamlined solution for each of these questions.

The self-service data platform consists partially of components that are already in use in your organization and partially of components that you'll need to build or buy. For example, you may already have a metadata catalog that tracks important data sets that you can also use for tracking data product metadata. You may be deploying applications using Docker images, running them on Kubernetes, and monitoring them with a cloud-based monitoring service. But you may be lacking the stream-processing frameworks, connector systems, and workflow standardization to get a data mesh up and running. Precisely what you have and what you're lacking will vary from what others have, so it's best to focus on the central needs to identify what to work on.

At its core, the data mesh self-service platform is simply *glue code* that binds together the individual components and subplatforms that your organization uses. It streamlines the processes your teams, people, and services use to make data mesh into a reality. While I realize that this description may be a bit amorphous, the reality is that every organization's data mesh is heavily influenced by the existing systems, processes, governance, people, teams, and technologies already at play. Your self-service platform will be unique to your organization, but it will share some common themes that we'll cover in this chapter: identity, discovery, authentication, authorization, management, communication, and computation.

In this chapter, we'll cover all of the important features that a data mesh self-service platform *should* have—and we're going to be very pragmatic about it. The most important thing about building a data mesh is that you get short-term benefit to test, try, and reiterate what works and what doesn't. For this purpose, we're going to split up our approach to data mesh into a three-level maturity model that focuses on iteratively building and improving self-service functions while still deriving real business value.

The Self-Service Platform Maturity Model

There are three main maturity levels for the self-service platform.

A colleague of mine has often referred to building the self-service platform as "building the airplane while you're flying it," and for good reason: as with most things in the software space, we want to get this up and running as a minimum project so we can start getting value from it:

Level 1: The minimal viable platform (MVP)
> Defines the minimum required investment to have a passably functional platform. This model will help you obtain immediate value from available data products while also providing an opportunity to garner feedback and plan iterative improvements.

Level 2: The expanded platform (EP)
> Defines a much more robust and production-capable self-service platform, remediating many of the shortcomings of the MVP. Data mesh user operations are far more streamlined and integrated into the platform, such that room for manual error is substantially reduced.

Level 3: The mature platform (MP)
> Defines the fully developed and integrated platform. Users can easily discover, publish, manage, evolve, and remove data products. Data products can effortlessly power both operational and analytical applications.

These maturity levels are not gospel, and you don't need to accomplish everything at one level before you move to the next. The construction and evolution of your own platform will look similar to what's outlined in this chapter, but will vary according to your starting position, the needs of your business, and your unique governance requirements.

In the following sections, we'll take a look at each of these levels in greater detail. We'll evaluate the platform levels, identify strengths and shortcomings, and discuss how to incrementally resolve the deficiencies.

As you source feedback and observe use cases, you'll discover the areas that need more investment that will lead you from one level to the next. Focus on getting incremental value, and ensure that the features you're adding are indeed solving the use case problems that people have. A data mesh self-service platform needs to be only as complicated as you make it—so what's the minimum that you can get away with? Let's find out.

Level 1: The Minimal Viable Platform

The MVP is meant to act as a starting point for your data mesh journey. The MVP is not an ideal implementation by any means—it contains just enough functionality to implement the core data mesh principles and provides a quick and dirty yet strong base for your users to gain practical experience.

The four main components in the MVP include an event broker, a schema registry, a metadata catalog, and a connector service. Event broker selection was covered in "Selecting an Event Broker" on page 67, and for the purposes of this chapter we're going to consider using Kafka as our broker of choice.

Let's take a look at the remaining three components in turn.

The Schema Registry

An event schema definition details the names, types, ranges, mandatory fields, default values, and documentation of an event, much like a table schema details the data for a relational database table. Chapter 6 will cover schemas in far more detail, but for the purposes of this chapter, you can think of a schema as a strongly typed data definition that gives both the producer and the consumer of the data a common protocol. Example 5-1 shows a simplified `Person` Protobuf schema (*https://oreil.ly/y-TRW*) that details the `id`, `name`, and `height` of a `Person` object, published to an event stream.

Example 5-1. Simplified `Person` Protobuf schema definition

```
message Person {
  int32 id = 1;
  string name = 2;
  int32 height = 3;
}
```

The schema registry is a repository of event schema definitions that maps each schema to the event stream that it belongs to. It acts as a gatekeeping component by preventing events that do not adhere to the registered schema from entering an event stream, ensuring strict data quality. It also provides users an API to look up an event stream's schemas as part of the process for choosing the data product best suited for their use. We'll cover the schema registry more thoroughly in "The Role of the Schema Registry" on page 143. For now it's sufficient to think of the schema registry as both a gatekeeping component and one that provides an easy way to look up the event-stream data product schema.

Confluent provides a commonly used and simple to integrate open source schema registry (*https://oreil.ly/oIUsZ*) for Kafka that provides all of this functionality out of the box. As we discussed back in "Selecting an Event Broker" on page 67, easy and free access to community-built tools and services makes implementing and maintaining a data mesh much easier, versus building and maintaining your own tools in house.

Next, let's look at the metadata catalog.

An Extremely Basic Metadata Catalog

The metadata catalog of our MVP platform is a simple cloud-based spreadsheet. Registering a data product is as simple as filling in the metadata of your event stream and schema. Write permissions are restricted to data product owners and remain read-only for everyone else in the organization. Alternatively, only team leads can have access to modifying the spreadsheet, to avoid accidental mutations or deletions.

Table 5-1 shows an example of what a minimal basic spreadsheet could look like.

Table 5-1. An extremely basic metadata spreadsheet with headers

Name	Topic	Bootstrap URI	Owner	SLA	Quality	Schema URI	Description
Sales	gold_sales	k1.brk.kek:9093	@bondolabs	Tier 1	Gold	../gold_sales	Canonical sales data, including sanitized payment types
Orders	gold_orders	k1.brk.kek:9093	@smahmood	Tier 1	Gold	../gold_orders	Canonical orders data, excluding PII
Page views	page_views	x3.brk.uwu:9093	@vsalamanca	Tier 3	Bronze	../page_views	Page view metrics piped in from Google Analytics

Name indicates the data product name, while the combination of topic and bootstrap Uniform Resource Identifier (URI) indicates how you could go about connecting to the event stream, served by a Kafka broker. The owner indicates the Slack handle (or email address) to communicate with the data product owner. SLA and Quality are just two examples of the kinds of metadata made mandatory by the governance team, as discussed previously in "Metadata Standards and Requirements" on page 77. Schema URI provides a link to the schema registry API that produces a human readable page of the schema for that event stream. Finally, description offers a human readable string of text describing the data product and explaining any context that may otherwise be missing from the metadata.

A spreadsheet is a very easy and simple way to get started with communicating what data products are available, where they're located, their format, and who owns them. You could also choose to use something like a relational database, but given that at this stage of the product there's no need for a programmatic API, a shared spreadsheet tends to be the absolute quickest way to get started.

Next, let's take a look at the last component: connectors.

Connectors

Connectors allow you to easily *source* data from a database and write it into an event stream. They also allow you to *sink* data, reading it from an event stream and writing into a destination database. Individual connectors typically run on top of a distributed connector framework, offering scalability, redundancy, and resource isolation. The connect framework generally comes as an add-on component for the event broker, such as Kafka and Kafka Connect (*https://oreil.ly/XjvYZ*).

Connectors provide a rudimentary way to construct data products by enabling you to extract data from a source database, transform it, and sink it to an event stream. Kafka offers a whole host of connectors, enabling you to source data from MySQL, Postgres, Oracle, MongoDB, Microsoft SQL Server, and DynamoDB (just to name a few). Similar to source connectors, matching sink connectors provide an easy way to take data in the event stream and write it to the database of your choice. You can also write your own custom connectors to connect to less common or legacy systems that don't have readily available connectors.

Transformations are an essential part of selecting and modeling a data product and in the subsequent, more mature platforms in this chapter we will evaluate some more powerful options. But for our MVP, we can look at using the built-in transformation components to remodel and select just the data we want from our source. Kafka's single message transforms (*https://oreil.ly/7wddi*) allow you to chain together out-of-the-box transformations to filter, modify, and transform your data with minimal effort. Just as with custom connector code, you can also implement your own custom transformations if none of the existing ones suit your needs.

We're going to talk more about bootstrapping data from existing systems using connectors later in Chapter 8. For now, let's wrap up this MVP.

Level 1 Wrap-Up: How Does It Work?

Figure 5-1 illustrates the four main components of the MVP along with a basic registration and usage workflow.

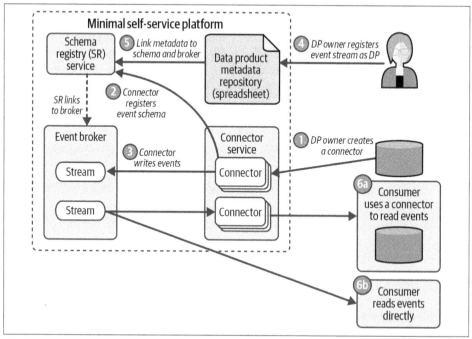

Figure 5-1. The minimal viable self-service platform for powering an event-driven data mesh

The data product owner creates a source connector (1) and grants it read permissions to a specific table in their team's database. The connector starts up, reads the table schema, and automatically creates a schema (2) to register with the schema registry. Next, the connector incrementally reads the source table rows and converts it automatically into events that match the registered schema. The events are then written into the event stream associated with that table (3).

The data product owner can then choose to register the event stream as a data product (4). Using their write-access permissions, they add the governance-required metadata to the spreadsheet, tag themselves as the owner of that product, and complete any other mandatory fields. They also link the metadata in the spreadsheet to the URL of the schema stored in the event broker (5). The schema registry is used not only for serializing and deserializing events but also for data discovery purposes for human users by answering the question "What is the format of data in this event stream?"

Finally, a prospective consumer can discover what data products are available in the metadata spreadsheet and choose those necessary for their use case. Then they can either create a new sink connector to write the data into their own database (6a), or they can simply consume the data natively using a stream-processing framework like Kafka Streams or Flink (6b).

The MVP self-service data platform makes it easy to get started with the practice of data mesh without over-investing in tools, systems, or processes that you may not need. You can begin practicing publishing data products, and arguing and negotiating roles and responsibilities, metadata requirements, service levels, connection interfaces, and schema types. You'll get a taste for the social changes that data mesh brings as well as identify the people and teams that are amenable to change and those who are going to have a much more difficult time with it.

The most important thing when getting started with a self-service platform is to internalize and practice the principle that "You aren't gonna need it" (*https://oreil.ly/ DRZcT*). Build new functionality as you need it, guided by the pain points you and your teammates are experiencing. Express the issues you encounter to the federated governance team so that together, you can come to a decision about the next set of features and improvements to make to the self-service platform.

> Focus on resolving a selection of major pain points when building out your data mesh MVP. Then you can evangelize the successful pain point resolution as a way to build trust in your data mesh platform and gather feedback from others who may have their own adjoining pain points.

There are some deficiencies with the MVP that we will look at solving in the next section. First, since registration is a voluntary process, it's possible that the metadata spreadsheet doesn't accurately represent what's available. Second, there are no permissions—anyone can read or write to any event stream, which is bad practice. Third, you can't really tell who is using your data products. And fourth, there is no enforcement of security or data quality standards. We'll look at resolving each of these issues with further evolution of the self-service platform to Level 2 and Level 3.

Level 2: The Expanded Platform

The expanded platform (EP) addresses a number of the shortcomings of the MVP, such as a lack of user and service identity, a lack of permissions, and a fairly low-effort data catalog that doesn't necessarily reflect reality.

It's best to think about the EP as focused on two main outcomes. The first is to make it easy for data product owners and prospective data product consumers to use the data mesh. For data product owners, this means making it possible for them to publish their event streams as data products, while for consumers it means making it easy for them to find data products, register as consumers, and set up any connectors they may need to pipe the data into their own service space.

The second main outcome is to implement basic service identity and controls. At a minimum, services need unique identities for the assignment of permissions. Though seemingly simple, we also must consider that the self-service platform will typically span many subplatform components—code repositories, event brokers, and compute resources, just to name three common inclusions.

The components and features of the extended platform include:

- Full-featured metadata catalog
- Data product management service and UI
- Service and user identities
- Basic access controls
- Stream processing for building data products

 Start talking to your infrastructure and platform engineering people. You're going to need to figure out how to leverage existing systems and tools for usage in the data mesh self-service platform. Your engineering team likely already has a process for building, Dockerizing, testing, deploying, and monitoring applications. Don't reinvent the wheel—copy what they already have to build and deploy data products and tweak it as needed.

First, let's take a look at improving that shared spreadsheet "data catalog" with something a bit more robust and useful.

Full-Featured Metadata Catalog

The first order of business is to replace the spreadsheet with a proper data catalog.

There are many options available for you to choose from. Popular open source software (OSS) projects include Apache Atlas (*https://oreil.ly/U_AlO*) and Amundsen (*https://oreil.ly/2d42w*), just to name two that I have successfully used in data mesh implementations. While you could also model and build your own data catalog using a relational database, these off-the-shelf, dedicated data catalog products include their own discovery UIs, well-formed APIs, and publishing, searching, and modeling functions.

Some important features of a full-feature metadata catalog include:

Metadata modeling
Aside from data product metadata, you can create metadata for people, teams, applications, event brokers, and connectors. You can also create metadata models for the relationships between these elements, resulting in a traversable graph of relationships.

Search functionality
A data catalog may also provide search functionality for you to query the metadata entries. Depending on the data catalog you select, you may have availability to SQL or SQL-like querying capabilities in addition to basic string matching. Search functionality is an essential component in making the platform self-service, so ensure you have evaluated the catalog's capabilities before investing in it.

Dependency identification through graph traversal
Identifying upstream and downstream dependencies via graph traversal is important for validating the integrity of your data mesh. For example, you could validate that all upstream data products and services meet a minimum service tier when adding a new dependent data product or consumer application, such that you don't violate your own SLA. Similarly, you could use this same graph functionality to identify all existing consumers of your data, so that you could then notify them of upcoming changes.

Data catalogs have a tendency to be chronically out of date, usually because they're treated like documentation—updated later, after the fact, if someone remembers to do it. It's essential for a data catalog to be part of the operational workflow for creating, discovering, and using data products, updated automatically as new products are created, removed, and subscribed to.

Once you have selected a new full-featured data catalog, your next step is to ensure that it's properly integrated into your data product management workflow. You can measure how successful you are in integrating your data catalog by the amount of manual interaction required to keep it up to date, with zero manual interactions being an indicator of success. Your data catalog should be populated and altered only via the confines of the data product management service. We'll look at this in more detail in the next section.

The Data Product Management Service and UI

The UI in the MVP is nonexistent. The data mesh user has to create their data products, manually add them to the spreadsheet, and hope that others have followed the same rules. It's likely that someone will forgo filling out the mandatory metadata, accidentally delete someone else's entry, or simply not register the data product formally. After all, you can still use the data even if it's not in the spreadsheet!

The easiest way to get a data product UI is to use a data catalog that already contains a UI and search elements. Bonus points if it also contains a way to set fine-grained permissions so that the majority of users have only read-only permissions (more on that in the next section). However, if you decide to craft your own UI, you're going to need to think about how your consumers can browse and search available data products as well as manage their own. The basic operations that it must support include:

Browse data products

Users will need to browse through existing data products to see what's available. Figure 5-2 shows a sample of what the UI could look like, including the name, a description, and some metadata-related information. Clicking on a data product would provide you with more information about the product.

Browse stream data products

Name	Description	Domain	
Customer orders–Canada	Orders originating from Canada	ecom.customer.orders	View
Customer orders	Orders originating from USA	ecom.customer.orders	View
Item inventory	Global item inventory	ecom.inventory	View

Figure 5-2. A data product browsing UI, including domain information, registered consumer list, and metadata

View data product information

Each data product should have a detailed page that showcases the full range of data, including owners, description, schema, digital location, and any other information your governance team deems relevant. Figure 5-3 shows information that you could expect to see when viewing a data product. Note that there are some buttons that enable self-service actions, including messaging existing consumers, messaging the data product owner, and requesting registration as a consumer.

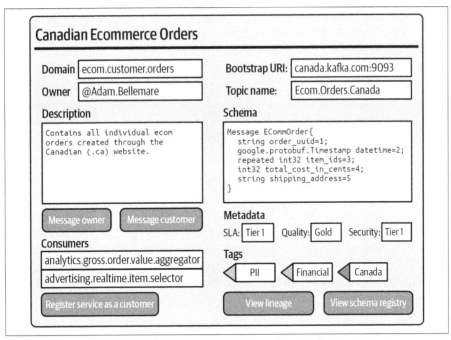

Figure 5-3. Data product information viewable to data mesh users

Search portal

The search engine enables queries of metadata, schemas, descriptions, and documentation. Figure 5-4 shows a sample search interface where the user specifies both keywords and fields to search. You may also choose to expose the search API for your data catalog directly as a lower-effort option—just provide some query examples to ensure that your consumers can figure out how to use it.

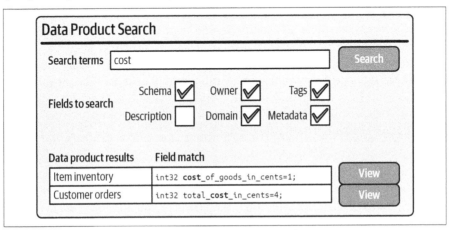

Figure 5-4. A search UI for searching through data products

The ability to self-register as a new consumer is a good acid test for self-service capabilities because it requires integration between the user's identity, application service accounts, and event-stream read/write access controls.

Data product management remains a second major requirement of a self-service platform. Users must be able to identify streams that they could publish, register them as data products, and deprecate any data products that are no longer needed:

Identify candidate data products

The system must provide the user with a list of event streams that they *could* register. Semantically, these are streams that fall within the domains that the user belongs to or otherwise has some form of jurisdiction over. One simple option is to allow only the user who created the event stream to register it as a data product. A more advanced option consists of integration with the event broker's user and organization accounts (covered next in "Service and User Identities" on page 110), such that only users belonging to the team or group that own the stream can manage it.

Register a data product

Once the data product owner identifies an event stream they want to publish as a data product, they can ideally click a big Register button to start the registration process. They should then be prompted for the mandatory metadata as specified by federated governance, such as Name, Owner, SLA, Quality, and Description. Additional properties should automatically be pulled in, such as the underlying stream name, event broker address, schema, and metadata pertaining to permissions and access controls.

Deprecate and deregister a data product

Eventually a data product may need to be removed. Deprecation would lock the data product down so that only existing consumers could continue to use it, while simultaneously marking it as deprecated and concealing it from search results. The data product owner is then responsible for providing a deprecation plan for its current users, including a migration plan and a timeline for when the work must be completed. You should ensure that only deprecated data products with zero existing registered consumers can be deleted, to prevent accidental deletion of system-critical data products.

Figure 5-5 is an example of what a management UI may look like. Starting from the top, you can see both the domain and user logged into the console. Under the "Unregistered streams" header are possible candidates for publishing as a data product—there is currently only one, the stream named Ecom.Orders.USA. These streams are shown to only the active user because they're associated with the ownership of this stream. Finally, the two currently registered data products are shown under the "Registered data products" header, including all of the mandatory metadata as well as several controls for viewing, updating, and deprecating them.

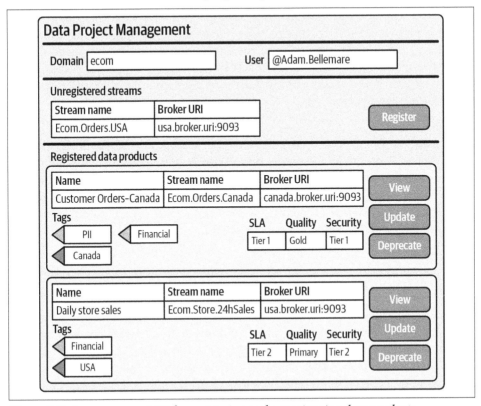

Figure 5-5. A management UI for registering and unregistering data products

The data product management UI provides the main hub for browsing, discovering, managing, registering, deprecating, and removing data products in the data mesh. A word of advice when building out your data management service—begin by focusing on data product consumer needs, such as discovery, because both current and prospective consumers will make up the largest segment of self-service platform users. If your process for registering data products remains a bit hacky, that's okay, as you'll be far more often using and discovering them than you will be publishing new ones.

In the next section we'll answer: how do we know who owns a data product? Or what service may be requesting access?

Service and User Identities

Identification is an important component for managing and tracking access to data in a data mesh. For a data product, it's important to know who the owner is and which services are using it. Similarly, it's also important to know the upstream dependencies of the data product itself. Identity forms the foundation of data product ownership as well as streamlining publishing controls, access requests, and dependency tracking, as we shall see later in this section. But first, here are a few concepts that we'll be revisiting in the next few sections:

Principal

A principal is a unique string that identifies a user or a service. For example, Google uses an email address as the service account principal (*https://oreil.ly/ Ywsit*), whereas a Secure Sockets Layer (SSL) certificate principal following RFC1779 (*https://oreil.ly/u5thv*) looks like `CN=CommonName,O=Organization, L=Location,ST=State,C=Country`. Regardless of the format, uniqueness and association with the service or user is essential.

User account

A user account represents a human user. These types of accounts are commonly used to log into systems and access resources assigned to the user.

Organization account

An account representing an organization. For example, GitHub provides organization accounts (*https://oreil.ly/MicMJ*) as a means of assigning ownership of projects, repositories, and packages to a group instead of an individual user. Both Confluent Cloud (*https://oreil.ly/SR9Ll*) and Google Cloud (*https://oreil.ly/ cmICP*) also have their own versions of organization accounts, allowing for additional organization of users, services, and other resources.

Service account

An account created specifically to represent a service. Applications use service accounts to access resources, connect to APIs, and access event streams. Each data product is assigned a service account for both the application that creates the data product and the event stream that stores the data.

Creating a self-service platform requires facing the challenge of unifying multiple service accounts and user accounts from the underlying subplatforms.

Figure 5-6 shows a sample of just three subplatforms that you may choose to use in building your data mesh: GitHub/GitLab, Google Cloud, and Confluent Cloud. Each of these has its own set of user accounts and organization accounts as well as service accounts for both Google and Confluent. The result is that each service (cloud or otherwise) ends up with its own set of accounts for users and services as well as similar yet different ways of managing resources, permissions, and memberships.

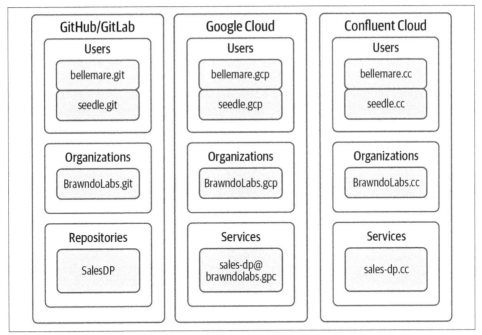

Figure 5-6. Managing separate accounts and resources for each subplatform in the data mesh is a challenging affair

The `Sales` data product resides in the `SalesDP` repository as part of the `BrawndoLabs` organization. The project is then compiled and deployed within Google Cloud using, for example, the Kubernetes platform. The Kubernetes pod that hosts the data product application code runs under the `sales-dp@brawndolabs.gcp` Kubernetes-specific service account (*https://oreil.ly/5GC6y*). Additionally, the code within the `Sales` data product needs to have its own set of credentials to access the `sales-dp.cc` Confluent Cloud service account so that it can successfully write data to its event stream.

 One of the most challenging parts of building a data mesh is integrating the various identity mechanisms, user accounts, service accounts, and organizations into an streamlined self-service solution. The more technologies, platforms, and service types you try to support, the more complex and challenging your experience will be.

For the EP solution, ensure that you have created and are using user accounts, service accounts, and organizations. Services should have a 1:1 mapping to a service account. Users should be mapped to organizations that allow them appropriate access to only the data products and services that they are involved with. Let's take a look at what basic access controls entail.

Basic Access Controls

Access controls are predicated on the implementation of service and user identities within your data mesh. Just as each subplatform has its own concept and boundary for its identities, so too does each platform have its own means of controlling access and granting permissions. Figure 5-7 shows a small sample set of the types of user and service access controls you'll have to account for, in continuation of the GitHub/GitLab, Google Cloud (GCP), and Confluent Cloud example.

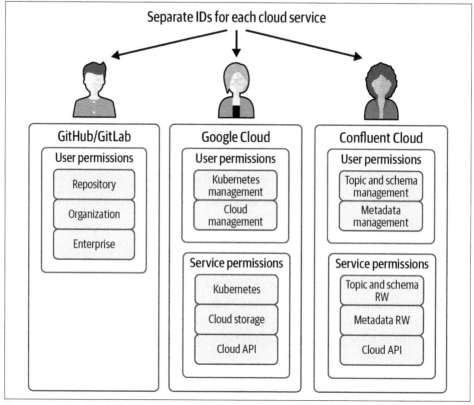

Figure 5-7. Each subplatform has its own set of permissions related to its own user and service identities

Access keys are a common way to grant permissions to both user and service accounts. An administrator generates an access key and secret key that effectively act as a username and a password, fulfilling the identity needs.

Next, the administrator grants permissions for each access key assigned to a service account, within its respective platform. In the case of the GitHub, GCP, and Confluent Cloud example, a user needs to be granted access to push commits to GitHub and compile and deploy it into a Kubernetes application in GCP. Meanwhile, the service accounts associated with the application need certain Kubernetes and GCP API permissions to run the application, as well as Confluent Cloud permissions to create the topic, write the events, update the schema, and update any other metadata.

While it may be a bit tedious to have a human involved in assigning and managing service accounts and permissions, at this stage of the data mesh evolution it's still your best option. You should aim to keep your processes flexible, with low overhead. For example, simply open up a work ticket, assign it to the administrator, and then give them a friendly heads up in your company's channel-based instant messaging application.

```
Hi Seedle!

Can you please add the following Kafka permissions to our microservice?

service name: ShippableOrdersResolver

topic name: Shopping.Orders.v1
permissions: read, describe

topic name: Shopping.Payments.v2
permissions: read, describe

topic name: Sales.ShippableOrders.v1
permissions: write, describe

Thanks!
```

A ticket will give you a minimum amount of auditing as to who requested the permissions, who granted them, and when this occurred. You also get to dodge the problem of having to fully automate the orchestration of permission management between all the subplatforms within your self-service platform. That can wait until later, when you have a better understanding of your data mesh technology stack and user needs.

But now, let's get back to talking about these secret keys. While *you* can save them locally to your own system for personal usage (security risks aside), it's unfortunately not quite so easy for containerized applications. Instead, we can store the keys in a purpose-built secrets store—for example AWS KMS (*https://oreil.ly/sCdZb*), Google KMS (*https://oreil.ly/S1cER*), or any other key management store that suits your cloud provider requirements.

Once your keys are generated and safely stored in a KMS, the next step is to integrate them with your containerized applications. One common mode is to inject the secrets into your containers at runtime, such that no other system can see or view them. However, this requires careful setup and configuration and runs the risk of inadvertently leaking secrets.

There are many security risks to using secrets as your main mode of authentication and access control, especially when it comes to storing them and properly restricting access. I recommend you pick up a book on modern services security to learn about the new best practices, as they are all far beyond the scope of this book.

Access keys are just one way of managing permissions; we'll explore a more robust option in Level 3. Since permissions are so closely linked to identity, it is difficult to get a simple view of the end-to-end permissions when crossing multiple sub-platforms and services. I won't paint a rosy picture of this step—it is difficult to orchestrate and streamline the permissions and identities of multiple platforms together into a single unified identity system.

You can let users freely register their services as event-stream consumers without requiring security checks, unless the stream contains PII, financial, or other sensitive data. If permissions are required, you can either have the consumer issue a work request ticket (human-in-the-loop) or have them run through an explicit terms-and-conditions acknowledgment before access is granted. Consult with your governance team about how you should proceed.

Stream Processing for Building Data Products

For the MVP, we relied on connectors to do the bulk of the processing work for simple stream transformations—things like masking sensitive information or converting data from one format to another. But the reality is that you're going to need more powerful stream processors to build full-featured, event-driven data products. For example, you'll need to be able to maintain state and aggregate events to build aggregate-aligned data products (see "The Three Data Product Alignment Types" on page 33). You'll also need to join streams together to make up consumer-aligned data products, as data often comes from disparate parts of the business and needs to be reconciled for many use cases.

Popular stream-processing frameworks include Kafka Streams, Apache Flink, and Apache Spark Structured Streaming, to name a few. Each of these provide a wide range of higher-order stream-processing functionality to build, use, and consume event-driven data products and will be entirely suitable for your own data mesh needs. Aside from figuring out the tech you want to use, you're also going to need to figure out how to run it and integrate it with your own application operations. Your choice really comes down to "Do I manage it on my own?" or "Do I rely on a cloud service provider to manage it for me?" The most important part is to make it easy for your teammates to create, run, and manage code to build and use data products, regardless of your technology choice.

You do not necessarily need to use a stream-processing framework to build an event-driven data product—a basic event-producing application can work just fine. However, without an event-driven processing framework, you will likely find it more difficult to *use* event-stream data products, for tasks such as joining streams together and building up complex event-driven state machines.

Running your own technology in house (or in your own cloud) is fairly self-explanatory. There is an absolute metric ton of information on this topic, so I'll leave it up to you to figure out how you'd host a stream-processing framework on your own. However, you should really look into cloud service providers to see what they offer and how they can reduce your efforts to get a data mesh up and running. Cloud service providers play an increasingly significant role in modern architectures, with the most significant contributions revolving around reducing toil and overhead for getting things done.

Stream processors can be both quite powerful and complex to run. As an example, Apache Spark Notebook has been a common way to perform big data analytics work for many years now; analysts simply write the code into a notebook and deploy it as is—just like a containerized application. One of the earliest value propositions undertaken by Databricks (founded by the creators of Apache Spark) was to reduce the toil of managing a Spark cluster and deploying the data processing applications. Instead, the focus is on making it easy for users to write, test, deploy, and monitor notebooks—the very same properties that we want in our own event-driven data mesh.

In the event-driven world, we run into a number of other issues: not only do we need the stream-processing framework, we also need to run the event broker that hosts and serves all of the streams. A cloud service provider like Confluent not only eliminates all of the stream-processing overhead, but also takes care of all of the event broker and data storage scaling, as well as provides a data catalog, managed connectors, identity management, and access controls.

Hosted stream processing lets you create persistent streaming queries that restructure, join, aggregate, and remodel events, letting you create new data products from other streams. You simply write the code, kick off the job, and the cloud service takes care of the rest—scaling it up and down as the load changes and restoring it in the case of a fault or exception.

There are, of course, many other cloud service providers that offer a wide range of alternative technologies and features. You'll need to figure out which ones work best for you based on your own organization's needs.

Cloud computing jump-starts your journey into data mesh. Instead of focusing on hosting, monitoring, and tuning commonly used technology, you simply outsource it all and focus on deriving value from the data itself, building the data products, and learning to use the cloud platform. You'll get feedback on what works and what doesn't far sooner, and you can switch technology selections if you find your initial choices unsuitable, without having invested heavily in infrastructure and operations. Your main goal should be to *try things out* to find what works before overinvesting. You can always optimize later; at this point, you're trying to find what works and what doesn't. Cloud computing makes this a far easier task.

That's it for Level 2. Let's take a look at what we covered and how it's all supposed to work together.

Level 2 Wrap-Up: How Does It Work?

The EP seeks to address the deficits of the MVP pertaining to service and user identity. It also provides the means for improved data product management and discovery, based on a full-featured data catalog.

The centralized data product management service and UI form the basis of the user-facing controls. Users can discover published data products, view metadata, and decide which data products they need for their own service's use cases. The management service stitches together the event broker, metadata catalog, schema registry, and subplatforms into a self-service experience. The self-service UI exemplifies the consumer-focused aspect of building a data mesh: make it easy for users to find and use data products.

However, the code and compute power that create data products remain outside the scope of what we've covered so far. We've alluded to using services like GitHub, Confluent Cloud, and Kubernetes to store code, host event streams, and provide general-purpose compute, respectively. But we haven't integrated these into our full-fledged self-service platform yet.

The self-service platform is also far from fully automated. Humans remain involved in the day-to-day servicing of platform requests. Administrators manually manage roles, accounts, and permissions for both services and humans.

Getting to Level 3 is fairly difficult, and like all things data mesh, should only be attempted if you're finding that the pain points of Level 2 exceed the investment costs of the self-service platform. In the next section, we'll investigate the features of the fully mature platform.

Level 3: The Mature Platform

The mature platform (MP) is the culmination of stitching together identities, services, processes, and data products into a cohesive set of streamlined operations. It leans heavily on implementing identities, access controls, and workflows spanning multiple services, platforms, and technologies. The MP focuses on reducing the manual steps and repetitive overhead encountered in the earlier self-service platforms and on hardening and streamlining a select set of data mesh operations for daily operations.

For example, creating a data product consumer application using Kafka Streams may be a primary use case for your business. So you streamline the creation of the Git repo, the Docker container and repository storage, the Kubernetes task, the testing, compilation, and deployment pipeline, as well as the monitoring, permission assignment, and service ownership rights—all in a single button from the self-service UI. If this sounds like a lot of work, well…it is! But as your data mesh needs grow, so too will your need to streamline its use by investing in new functionality.

The MP is a target more than an actual destination. If you find that your simpler platform with less automation and streamlining works fine, then great! Keep on using it until you find it's not meeting your needs. Stitching together multiple services, cross-platform identity management, teams, people, and systems into a centralized control panel is pretty tough. Remember, there are entire cloud service providers who have spent a ton of time trying to get this right. If you find it challenging, there's a good reason for it.

 You're most likely going to need to use an Infrastructure as Code solution like Terraform to help manage the infrastructure components of your data mesh. Terraform is one of the leading infrastructure management solutions and can integrate "stitching" operations between many cloud providers, SaaS solutions, and platforms.

Efficiency is your largest gain from implementing the features of the mature platform. It'll be far easier for your average user to create, publish, manage, and consume data products. You will encounter far fewer incidents and outages, data quality issues, and end user-affecting data discrepancies. You can expect to see a substantial reduction in the overhead for finding and using data, as discussed earlier in "Bad Data: The Costs of Inaction" on page 17.

The components and features of the MP include:

- Authentication, identification, and access management
- Integration with existing application delivery processes
- Programmatic data product management API
- Monitoring and alerting
- Multiregion and multicloud data products

First, let's take a look at standardizing identity and access management across the self-service platform.

Authentication, Identification, and Access Management

Authentication and identification and access management (IAM) is an extensive area in its own right, and we won't be able to do it full justice in the confines of this chapter. Much of the work regarding authentication and IAM is related to stitching together the various identities, roles, and permissions across each of the major infrastructural components in your platform. For example, Kubernetes, Apache Kafka, and GitHub/GitLab each offer their own identity management system, but only within the confines of their own service. Given that our data products consist of code, data, and infrastructure, we're going to need to find a way (like using Terraform) to bridge the gaps and stitch together a unified identity experience.

But what is authentication, and what is authorization? Think about when you check into a hotel. The front desk staff *authenticates* you by asking for your ID or your booking code to make sure you are who you say you are. Next, they *authorize* you to access your room by giving you a key card—the card works on only that room and will expire when it's time for you to check out. Both authorization and authentication are essential for stitching together a data mesh, and these requirements are best fulfilled using standard frameworks like OAuth2 and the accompanying OpenID Connect (OIDC).

Fortunately, the roots of this problem have largely been solved over time. There are best practices that we can follow and existing technologies that provide a good place to start building your self-service platform.

OAuth2 (*https://oauth.net/2*) is one of the leading industry protocols for authorization. As described in the original Internet Engineering Task Force (IETF) specification (*https://oreil.ly/o8IAW*), "The OAuth 2.0 authorization framework enables a third-party application to obtain limited access to an HTTP service, either on behalf of a resource owner by orchestrating an approval interaction between the resource owner and the HTTP service, or by allowing the third-party application to obtain access on its own behalf."

Kubernetes, GitHub, GitLab, and Apache Kafka each integrate and support OAuth2, so you'll be able to go quite a long way in unifying your authentication and authorization controls. OAuth2 is a fairly common standard, so you'll most likely find it easy to extend into the other cloud services and platforms that you're already using.

An OAuth2 service provides authorization through the use of access tokens (*https://oreil.ly/EWXaa*). When one application wants to talk to another application, it first makes a request to the OAuth2 server for an access token. The requesting application identifies itself to the OAuth2 server and, depending on business rules and permissions, may obtain a bearer token (*https://oreil.ly/QKtVG*). The requesting application can then take that bearer token and present it to the original application it initially wanted to connect to.

OIDC (*https://oreil.ly/yXkok*) works hand-in-hand with OAuth2, making it possible to enable data sharing between applications without directly sharing user and service credentials. OIDC extends OAuth2 by focusing primarily on authentication rather than authorization. Once an account is authenticated using OIDC, it then uses OAuth2 specifications for authorization. OAuth2 helps alleviate the major issues inherent in dealing with multiple different services and frameworks in your data mesh and allows you to stitch together a cohesive experience.

There are several major benefits of uniting under OAuth2. Your self-service users will be able to:

- Declare and manage user and service accounts in a single place
- Rely on the OAuth2 standards and tools to integrate with your cloud service provider platforms and applications
- Manage most permissions and access controls from a single location
- Enforce authentication and authorization as a mandatory step for building and using data products

There are other technologies you could use to achieve similar ends; this is just one option. For example, Security Assertion Markup Language (SAML) 1.0 (*https://oreil.ly/xS1kW*) was released in 2002 and remains a commonly used alternative. In any case, the end goal remains the same: unify and streamline identity management and access controls among people, systems, and data products.

Next, let's take a look at how we want to be able to deliver and deploy data products.

Integration with Existing Application Delivery Processes

There's a pretty good chance that you already have some sort of existing application development and deployment pipeline. A useful and sustainable self-service data platform should reuse as much of this existing pipeline as possible. A data product is quite similar to any other application, is particularly similar to microservices, and especially similar to event-driven microservices. In fact, if you were to look at them side by side, you would probably have a hard time defining the difference between an event-driven data product and an event-driven microservice: both use code, compute resources, and memory, and bundle up their results as data served out into event streams.

Because you're likely to be making a number of data products, you'll be running into the same sort of overhead that one runs into when using microservices—the microservice tax. Each new data product will need a Git repository and a build pipeline, plus a way to containerize the compiled application, deploy it to compute resources (such as via Kubernetes), scale it, monitor it, and update it.

However you have chosen to build your existing application delivery process, you'll need to evaluate how to leverage it to deploy your data products. If you have a monolithic tech stack with only a handful of custom-built and deployed services, you'll likely find this to be quite challenging. However, if you're already running multiple services with a relatively well-formed deployment and management process, you're likely to find this much easier.

In "Stream Processing for Building Data Products" on page 114 we looked at some options for building and using data products using stream-processing frameworks, and, in particular, we looked at using cloud services instead of hosting your own solutions. If you chose to follow the cloud route, you'll likely be able to leverage their recommended best practices for delivering data product applications into production. You'll find that many of the cloud providers make it easy to manage and deploy the "code container" of their choice, be it Docker images, Notebooks, or persistent queries. Regardless of where you may be, my advice to you remains the same: try to find a cloud service provider that can offer you an easy way to build, test, store, deploy, and run your data product code.

Programmatic Data Product Management API

The data product management UI is expanded to provide a programmatic API that integrates with your identity authentication and authorization service. The goal of this feature is to provide an API for automated management of data products, including publishing, updating, deprecating, and deleting. This API will likely be just an expansion of the API powering the self-service UI, extended to provide API access to whatever tools and services may choose to integrate with it. Outside of direct user-facing use cases, other candidates for API usage include deployment pipelines, monitoring systems, and auditing use cases.

Let's avoid the painstaking details of an in-depth API spec and focus on the *areas* that we need to support with this API:

Identity management
   Streamlining the creation and management of both human user and service account identities is essential for coordinating the assignment of resources and permissions for all candidate data products.

Resource creation
   All the resources required for creating a candidate data product can be created in the form of an application. Resources include a service identity, a code repo, build and deployment pipelines, Kubernetes resources, Kafka topics, schema reg-

istry subjects, and monitoring resources. The candidate data product will need to be assigned a data product owner with relevant access permissions.

Permissions management
A human owner (or a team of owners) needs to be assigned as the owner upon creating a candidate data product. The owner will have full control over the data product operations, including publishing, granting read permissions for, updating, deprecating, and deleting the data product. Permission management may also require integration with infosec reviews and controls to ensure that data policies are followed.

Publishing, deprecating, and deleting a data product
The three main stages of a data product's life cycle include publishing as a formal data product for others to use, deprecation to prevent new users from using it, and deletion to remove all possible usage of the data. The federated governance team will need to specify the requirements for moving between these states, including if reversal of steps is possible (deletion → deprecation) and the minimum transition times between deprecation and deletion.

Updating a data product
A data product may be updated during its lifetime. Schema evolution for accommodating consumer needs remains one of the most common changes to an event-driven data product. Other updates include changes to the metadata, such as a lowering of the SLA or changing the owner of the data product in case of a staff departure. New tags may be added, existing tags may be removed, and new infosec regulations based on legal requirements may come into effect, changing the permission access model to the data product. Updates may affect both current and prospective consumers, so it's a good idea to have a notification and messaging system set up to enable communication.

The breaking changes process
Communicating an upcoming breaking change such as a major restructuring of the data product requires established rules of engagement. A data product owner needs to provide consumers with sufficient forewarning to give them time to understand the impact, plan, and react. We'll cover the breaking change process extensively in "Negotiating a Breaking Schema Change" on page 140.

Messaging
Self-service platform users should be able to subscribe to granular notifications about data products. The person or team that owns a service account registered as a data product consumer should receive notifications when the data product is updated. Ideally, the data product owner should send out notification of an upcoming change to all consumers so they can investigate if it requires action on their end. Other users may want to receive notifications when new data products

are published, deprecated, or deleted or when ownership of an existing data product changes to a new person or team. You will most likely need your messaging API to integrate with the corporate instant messaging service (like Slack or Microsoft Teams) or your corporate email server. Don't create your own messaging system.

Search and discovery

Users must be able to search through the available data products, people, teams, and services to see what's going on in the data mesh. Search functionality can usually be provided by the data catalog itself, though you'll need to pass sufficient information to the API users to ensure they know how to compose their queries. Discovery is largely a function of a simplified search—simply return all of the data products, people, teams, or services that meet my criteria.

The decisions you make regarding your API should be based on the needs of your users but will initially be driven entirely from the requirements of the UI ("The Data Product Management Service and UI" on page 106). You are likely to find that you can reuse the same API for both the UI and other automation use cases, but may need to evolve some of the functionality and standardize the interface. Again, evolve it based on the needs of your users, and don't invest more into it than your immediate needs.

Monitoring and Alerting

Monitoring data products and alerting on abnormal behavior is part and parcel for building a reliable data mesh. In "Metadata Standards and Requirements" on page 77 we assigned an SLA of a data product using a tiered system: Tier 1 means "Get out of bed and fix it," while Tier 4 means "It can wait until we have some free time." Similarly, we assigned tiered *quality* ratings, ranging from bronze to gold. The exact definitions of the ratings aren't as important as ensuring that we can *measure* the quality and the SLAs to make sure they are met.

There are two main components to meeting the SLAs: update frequency and the time since the last event was written to the data product. The more frequent the writes, the more likely there is a problem if updates suddenly stop. It's important to have a good understanding of the update frequency of the data product, since a data product may be updated rapidly and then remain unchanged for many hours or days. Smart alert services can train against historical patterns to come up with a custom alert, that takes into account cyclical update patterns.

Meeting data quality requirements starts with well-defined schemas, as will be covered in Chapter 6. Schemas provide strong typing and clear requirements for the data product's data model and prevent malformed data from getting into the event stream. Data quality measurements can go beyond simple type checking, however, and can include operations such as validating field contents (e.g., verifying that numeric values fall within a certain range, strings are properly formed, or data is falling within the expected distributions). Some data products, such as those pertaining to financial transactions, will likely require perfect data quality—any abnormality is a problem and must raise an alert. Others, such as analytical aggregations, may be able to tolerate unexpected values within a certain margin. Data quality metrics can be measured by creating a purpose-built data product consumer that reads the stream, compares each event to expected values, and reports any abnormal values to the monitoring system.

Monitor your data products like any other application. You should make sure that the application code that composes the data product is healthy and has sufficient resources, that the event stream contains the expected data, and guard against quality issues through both rigorous testing and direct data analysis.

Multiregion and Multicloud Data Products

A data mesh may be composed of multiple cloud services across multiple regions. For example, you may have multiple Kafka clusters, multiple Kubernetes deployments, and multiple cloud storage buckets. Scalability requirements typically play a significant role in adopting multiple infrastructure deployments, though data locality and regional regulations are also important considerations. Data regarding business activities that may be illegal in other countries (e.g., marijuana and alcohol sales) should remain in the country of origin. Similarly, GDPR and data privacy laws tend to require that data about citizens also remain in the country of origin.

Applying governance controls at the self-service platform level gives you a primary point of control for what is and isn't allowed. There are several factors to consider when building out your own multicloud deployments:

Regional permission requirements
    Federated governance plays an important role in determining the boundaries for where data products can be accessed and copied to. For example, an application running in the United States may be unable to access a data product because of legal restrictions. Similarly, you may be unable to copy a data product from one region to another based on data domiciling restrictions.

Streamlined data product replication
    Setting up cross-cloud or cross-region data product replication can be challenging. Not only will you need to replicate the data itself, but you'll also need to update the metadata to reflect the new dependencies, the new cloud information, and also the ownership permissions (e.g., who owns the replication process itself). For Kafka-backed event streams, you may choose to use the open source MirrorMaker 2.0 (*https://oreil.ly/gH6cZ*). If you want precise byte-for-byte replication, including offsets, consumer groups, permissions, and schemas, you'll

want to look into something more powerful, like Confluent Replicator (*https:// oreil.ly/3gJoF*).

Augmented data product metadata

You could augment your metadata to include regional and cloud service provider restrictions and permissions. For instance, you could restrict copying a data product with encrypted PII outside of the eurozone to ensure you keep compliance with GDPR. Data product processing would similarly need to remain within deployments from the curated list of permitted cloud environments (e.g.,can use Azure or GCP, but can't use AWS).

> Cloud service providers can make it easy for you to spin up a whole dedicated environment that mirrors your production environment. You could then replicate production-level data products to your new environment and perform development, QA, or testing on real production data products. Once complete, you simply delete the environments.

Figure 5-8 illustrates a visual topology of the data product source, dedicated replicator applications, and the destination clusters.

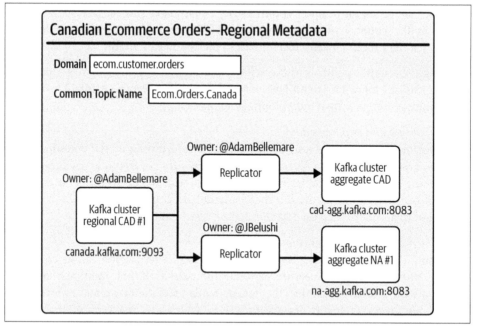

Figure 5-8. Metadata showcasing the topology of multiregion data product replication

Exactly what and how you choose to replicate will vary depending on your organization's needs. However, one key aspect that remains the same is the need to track *what* is being replicated, *who* owns the replication, and *where* it is going. Track this information and these dependencies as part of your self-service platform's metadata entries.

Level 3 Wrap-Up: How Does It Work?

The main themes of the Level 3 platform consist of unified identity management and streamlined data product operations. There is a lot of work to put in to reach this point, and the investment should be driven only by need—not simply for the challenge. Governance requirements pertaining to infosec and limiting access to sensitive information remain the biggest driving force toward unified identity management, authentication, and authorization. Widespread adoption of data products and event-driven applications drive the streamlining of all of the overhead related to simply creating data products and putting them to use.

Summary

The precise evolution of your self-service data platform will be unique to your organization but will touch on all of the features listed in this chapter. You may find that you implement a feature from Level 3 before you implement another from Level 2—and that's completely fine. The levels presented in this chapter are simply a coarse guideline for how your platform may evolve over time.

The guiding light you should follow in creating a self-service platform is to focus on the use cases of your platform users: the data product owners and the data product consumers, be they data analysts, data scientists, application developers, or any other job title. You want to focus on making it possible for your colleagues to serve their own needs, without letting them do things that they shouldn't (like delete someone else's data product).

As we covered in Level 1, the minimum self-service platform is actually quite small and lean, without much in the way of guardrails for what you can or cannot do. However, it's an excellent starting point to kick-start the real discussions about how your platform should change, separating what it *must* have from that which is nice to have, and focusing the discussion on useful iterative improvements. You will make mistakes as you build your platform. Errors will happen. But it is part of the development process to figure out how your unique composition of legacy systems, technology choices, business needs, and teammates' skill sets relate to your business use cases.

Focus on using off-the-shelf components whenever possible, and don't reinvent the wheel. Leverage cloud services whenever possible and avoid writing custom in-house tools unless absolutely necessary. For example, use Kubernetes instead of writing your own cloud-scale container management system. Use Apache Kafka instead of writing your own event broker. Use OAuth2 instead of writing your own identity management service. Use Terraform to streamline the coordination of infrastructure and service resources among your various platform components. The whole point of the self-service platform is to make it *easy* to access and use important business data, and this must remain your guiding principle for focusing your efforts.

The last few chapters have focused heavily on the whys and hows of data mesh and the critical role that event streams play. In the next chapter, we'll focus on event schemas and how they're essential for defining a common data contract between the data product producer and the each of its consumers.

CHAPTER 6

Event Schemas

A well-defined schema is essential for any data product. For events, the schema consists of an explicit declaration of the field names, types, defaults, and boundaries, providing clarity into the contents of the data for both human and machine alike. Schemas provide a clear and common understanding of the data for both the data product producer and consumer. Schemas eliminate ambiguity, support both discovery and self-service, and reduce the risk of misunderstanding the data by those who use it.

Schemas simplify data discovery and self-service. You can embed documentation within the schema itself, keeping the data definition and the documentation tightly coupled. Code generators, in conjunction with the schema, can generate classes and objects suitable to the consumer's programming language of choice. Similarly, event generators can use the schema to generate events that match the definitions, providing a mechanism to generate a wide range of test data for boundary conditions.

Schemas provide a framework for evolving data through time, though your options for schema evolution depend on your technology selection. The main goal of using schema evolution is to update and change data as new business requirements are added and as domains shift and expand, without unduly affecting consumers of the data product.

This chapter is a *prescriptive and opinionated* look at schemas for your event-driven data mesh. There are many different schema technologies and many different ways to communicate data between systems through events. However, some methods and technologies are better than others—they're more common, they're more flexible, and they also reflect the ways most businesses use and communicate events.

Before we get too far into schemas, let's step back and get a better picture of how they relate to making important business data available through data products. For this, we're going to need to take a look at how an event is created, serialized, and sent across a network for storage in an event stream. We'll also take a look at the reverse of this process, where an event is consumed from an event stream, deserialized, and processed by the consumer.

A Brief Introduction to Serialization and Deserialization

Serialization is the action of taking an event object with a well-defined schema and converting it into a sequence of bytes. The representation in the producer's memory is serialized (converted) into a sequence of bytes such that it can be easily sent across the network and written to the event stream. The schema provides the constraints for ensuring that the data can be converted into a sequence of bytes. For example, a schema that specifies that the field named length must be an Integer will throw an exception when attempting to serialize with length set to a String value of "six feet".

Figure 6-1 shows the producer workflow of converting a producer-language object into a sequence of bytes that is then written to the event stream. Note that the schema is attached to the serialized event, such that the consumer is provided with a copy for deserialization. There are some tricks we can use to remove the need for sending a schema with every event, which we'll look at later in this chapter.

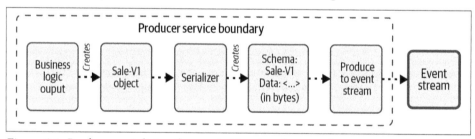

Figure 6-1. Producer serializing the event object into bytes and writing it to the event stream

On the other end of the event stream, a consumer reverses this process and deserializes the byte sequence into an object. Figure 6-2 illustrates the process of consuming, deserializing, and converting the data into a representation of the event that can be processed by the consumer's business logic code.

Schema technologies are an essential part of an event-driven data mesh, because they underpin the contract of the data product with its consumers.

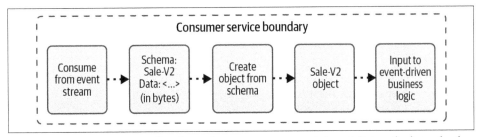

Figure 6-2. A consumer reading from the event stream and deserializing the bytes back into an event representation

What Is a Schema?

An event schema is synonymous with the definition of a database table: at a minimum, it specifies names, types, restrictions, and default values. Schemas ensure that both the event data producer and all of its consumers have a shared common understanding of the data. The schema, in conjunction with the event-stream API, forms part of the API of the event stream. You can think of this as equivalent to a REST API that serves JSON-encoded data—both have a communications protocol and both return a well-formed payload of information:

```
Event stream API + event schema == REST API + json schema
```

The data product owner is responsible for creating and managing the event schema definition, including conformance with any federated governance standards, such as standard time formats and PII requirements. Prospective consumers and stakeholders provide feedback to schema proposals, often in the form of code review in this era of remote work.

We'll start this section with a simple Protobuf-powered example (*https://oreil.ly/TctNo*) to illustrate some of the more compelling reasons for using schemas. Let's start with Example 6-1, which showcases a schema for `Person`.

Example 6-1. `Person` schema with Protobuf

```
message Person {
  //The person's unique ID
  int32 id = 1;
  //The person's full legal name
  string name = 2;
  //Measured in centimeters, rounded to the nearest centimeter
  int32 height = 3;

  enum CountryCode {
    ABW = 0;
    AFG = 1;
    ...
```

```
    ZWE = 248;
  }
  //ISO3166-1-alpha-3 standard. AAA=OTHER
  CountryCode country = 4;
}
```

The event schema details the id, name, and height of a person, along with their ISO 3166 (*https://oreil.ly/yw581*) three-letter Latin-script country code. This schema forms part of the *data contract* between the producer and the consumer of the data. It is the common understanding of how one party writes the data and the other party reads the data.

Figure 6-3 shows two clients: a Java producer that writes to the event stream and a C++ consumer that reads the events out of the stream and into its own memory space. The producer can use the Protobuf code generator for Java (*https://oreil.ly/lrssD*) to automatically create classes and client code for the Person schema. The consumer can similarly generate its own structs and client code using the C++ code generator (*https://oreil.ly/7_OTW*).

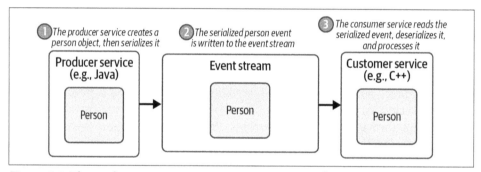

Figure 6-3. The producer to event stream to consumer workflow of an event serialized with a schema

 Both Avro and Protobuf have many code generators that support a wide variety of languages. You can find support and code generators for C++, C#, Dart, Go, Java, Kotlin, and Python, to name a few.

Example 6-2 shows a producer Java client with which we create a Person named "Mackenzie Bellemare" and the associated properties. Next, we serialize the object and write it to a file named *ProtoPerson.data* (We're using a file as a placeholder for the event broker client, simply to avoid bogging this example down with the proper event-broker client produce, retry, and error-handling code).

Example 6-2. Using Java to populate a `Person` object, generated from the Protobuf schema

```
Person mack = Person.newBuilder()
    .setId(4291)
    .setName("Mackenzie Bellemare")
    .setHeight(45)
    .setCountryCode("CAD")
    .build();
output = new FileOutputStream("ProtoPerson.data");
mack.writeTo(output);
```

The consumer reads the `Person` data from the file (i.e., the event), deserializes it using the schema, and finally converts it into an object or structure native to the consumer's language. Example 6-3 shows a C++ consumer using the `ParseFromIstream` function to convert the serialized bytes into a well-structured `Person` class object.

Example 6-3. Using C++ to parse the serialized Protobuf `Person` object

```
Person mack;
fstream input(argv[1],
    ios::in | ios::binary);
mack.ParseFromIstream(&input);

//mack is now populated with the id, name, and height received in the event
id = mack.id();
name = mack.name();
height = mack.height();
cc = mack.countryCode();
```

So what are the main benefits of this approach?

Standardized data contract

The schema forms the basis of understanding between the producer of the data and all of its consumers, both now and in the future. The producer responsible for producing data according to the schema and will be prevented from serializing the object if the data is not in compliance. The consumers in turn can rely on the schema to provide strongly defined types, names, documentation, and additional information about the data. Maintaining a high standard of quality from the moment the data is created is essential for a healthy data mesh.

Provides a foundation for discussion

Schemas give us the basis for tangible arguments over the content and form of the data. Explicit schemas, in conjunction with pull request reviews, enable productive discussions over what should and should not be in an event, and if the data product will solve the problems it's meant to solve.

Code generation

Code generation lets the application operate on the events as objects in its native language, handling the parsing, conversion, and object creation for you. It greatly simplifies business logic by letting you write code against well-defined classes in your programming language instead of against a map of generic object types.

Schema evolution

Your data contract will change over time. The best schema options provide a safe path for schema evolution, including rules, restrictions, and safeguards that prevent you from inadvertently violating your data contract with your consumers. Schema evolution is covered in more detail later in this chapter.

Test event generators

Event generators let you create data that matches your schemas, including specific parameter constraints such as foreign-key and primary-key relationships. You can use these events to test your event-driven service code and use it to produce sample events for consumers to try in their services. Kafka Connect Datagen (*https://oreil.ly/2J1kI*) is an example of such a generator, where you can specify constraints and ranges on the data being generated. Example 6-4 shows a snippet of a schema that contains a userid, where the range of valid data output will vary from User_1 to User_9.

Example 6-4. Kafka Connect Datagen specification

```
{"name": "userid",
 "type": {
    "type": "string",
    "arg.properties": {
        "regex": "User_[1-9]{0,1}"
    }
}},
```

As we can see, there are some significant benefits to schemas, so the next question is: what schema technology should you use?

What Are Our Schema Technology Options?

There are many schema technologies available for building event-driven data products. However, there are a few that stand above the rest of the field in terms of features, commonality, community development, ease of use, and supportive tooling. Google's Protobuf (*https://oreil.ly/JgAYo*) and Apache Avro (*https://oreil.ly/ZpfTm*) both fit this bill. JSON Schema (*https://oreil.ly/r90bk*) is somewhat popular for those who favor JSON, but please do not confuse it with the tangled mess that is schemaless JSON (more on this in a bit).

Martin Kleppman has written an excellent breakdown and analysis of JSON, XML, Protobuf, Thrift, and Avro in *Chapter 4 of _Designing Data-Intensive Applications* (O'Reilly). Consider giving it a read if you would like to learn more about how these schema technologies work under the hood.

We won't be touching on other serialization technologies (including Thrift), because they're not commonly used for event-driven data meshes. This isn't to say they aren't ever used, or that they cannot be used, but rather they're simply not in the top choices. The three most common choices include Protobuf, Avro, and JSON Schema. Let's take a look at each.

Google's Protocol Buffers, aka Protobuf

Protobuf became open source in 2008 and has long been popular for its gRPC format. More recently, it has proven to be a strong competitor to Avro for top schema format. Here are a few notable points about Protobuf's data types and schema management:

- There is support for scalar (*https://oreil.ly/ie-Gj*) (e.g., string, integer, boolean, etc.) and complex data types (*https://oreil.ly/sozYk*).

- The schema is not stored as part of the event but is maintained in a separate file. Protobuf files are commonly shared via a *schema registry*, as covered later in this chapter in "The Role of the Schema Registry" on page 143.

- You can compose complex schemas by referring to schema declarations stored in other files.

- There is no support for dynamic types. However, this is not a significant shortcoming given that data products require strongly typed and well-defined schemas.

The following shows the `Person` object again as defined using the Proto3 version of Protobuf:

```
message Person {
  //The person's unique ID
  int32 id = 1;
  //The person's full legal name
  string name = 2;
  //Measured in centimeters, rounded to the nearest centimeter
  int32 height = 3;

  enum CountryCode {
    ABW = 0;
    AFG = 1;
    ...
    ZWE = 248;
  }
```

```
    //ISO3166-1-alpha-3 standard. AAA=OTHER
    CountryCode country = 4;
}
```

Protobuf has two main versions with differing functionality regarding default values and handling missing data. Protobuf v2 allows marking fields as either `required` or `optional`, the ability to set custom default values, and the ability to determine if a field is included in the message or if it is missing. These are all features that make schema evolution much easier to manage as they provide both stricter boundaries for producers and stronger guarantees for consumers.

Protobuf v3 brought support for JSON encoding, among a number of other features, but this came at the expense of removing `required/optional` and custom default values. As with any open source community, this decision has supporters and detractors in both camps. Numerous organizations have chosen to remain on the Protobuf v2 standard, while others have since moved on to Protobuf v3.

Apache Avro

Apache Avro is another extremely common schema and serialization format, created under the Apache Software Foundation. Initially released in 2009, Avro has been commonly associated with Apache Kafka over the years, as well as a row-based, big data storage format. Here are a few notable points about Avro's data types and schema management:

- There is support for primitive (*https://oreil.ly/hmJmt*) (e.g., string, integer, boolean, etc.) and complex data types (*https://oreil.ly/7w_k0*).
- By default, the schema is stored as part of the data. The schema can also be decoupled from the data and stored independently.
- By including the schema with the event, Avro offers dynamic deserialization. A consumer can deserialize the event into a `GenericRecord` object built and populated dynamically from the schema and data. This feature is typically used when a consumer client does not have a code generator.
- You can compose complex schemas by referring to schema declarations stored in other files.
- While schema evolution is possible, *it is not explicitly defined* as part of the standard.

The following shows an Avro schema of the same `Person` object from the previous code snippet:

```
{
  "type": "record",
  "name": "Person",
  "namespace": "com.event.driven.datamesh",
  "doc": "Example of a Person record",
  "fields": [
    {
      "name": "id",
      "type": "integer",
      "doc": "The person's unique ID"
    },{
      "name": "name",
      "type": "string",
      "doc": "The person's full legal name"
    },{
      "name": "height",
      "type": "integer",
      "doc": "Measured in centimeters, rounded to the nearest centimeter"
    },{
      "name": "countryCode",
      "type": "enum",
      "symbols": ["AAA", "ABW", ... "ZWE"],
      "doc": "ISO3166-1-alpha-3 standard. AAA=OTHER"
    }
  ]
}
```

You may have noticed that the Avro schema is a bit more verbose than Protobuf. In Avro, all of the properties, such as type and doc, are contained entirely within the field definition. In contrast, comments in Protobuf are simply added with C/C++ style syntax. Semantically, they are quite similar.

The next and final schema technology that we'll look at in this chapter is JSON Schema.

JSON Schema

JSON Schema format (*https://oreil.ly/r90bk*) allows you to annotate and validate JSON documents. Unlike Avro and Protobuf, you can use JSON documents *without* a schema. A schemaless JSON means that there is really no definition of what *should* and *should not* be in the schema nor of any typing or defaults. Schemaless JSON is not suitable for use in data products as it leaves too much room for errors, misinterpretations, and missing data.

Here are a few notable points about JSON Schema's data types and schema management:

- There is support for six primitive types (*https://oreil.ly/DF7-F*) (null, boolean, object, array, number, string) as well as some more complex typing.

- You can compose complex schemas by using references to schemas stored in other files or locations.

- Data validation is similar to that of Protobuf and Avro. Producers validate their data against their schema prior to writing it to the event stream.

- There is support for adding validation keywords for data quality enforcement to numbers, strings, arrays, and objects.

The following shows a JSON Schema representation of the same `Person` object from the previous code snippet:

```
{
  "$id": "https://example.com/person.schema.json",
  "$schema": "https://json-schema.org/draft/2020-12/schema",
  "title": "Person",
  "type": "object",
  "properties": {
    "id": {
      "type": "number",
      "description": "The person's unique ID"
    },
    "name": {
      "type": "string",
      "description": "The person's full legal name"
    },
    "height": {
      "type": "number",
      "description": "Measured in centimeters, rounded to the nearest centimeter",
      "minimum": 1,
      "maximum": 300
    },
    "countryCode": {
      "type": "string",
      "enum": ["AAA", "ABW", ... "ZWE"],
      "description": "ISO3166-1-alpha-3 standard. AAA=OTHER"
    }
  }
}
```

JSON Schema is the only technology discussed so far that contains both a *language* for specifying schemas and *validation parameters* that restrict the ranges of certain properties. As exemplified in the `height` property, the height of a person is restricted to between 1 and `300` cm, with the `description` including further information about rounding to the nearest number. These constraints will prevent a system from accidentally inputting the height as millimeters, but would unfortunately still fail to prevent it from writing it as inches.

Schema Evolution: Changing Your Schemas Through Time

Even if you create the perfect data model in your first attempt, it will inevitably need to change over time. New business responsibilities can cause a domain to expand, in turn creating new demands for the data products. While new systems may need access to the latest data format, existing systems that have no need for the new data require a guarantee that their data contract won't change. *Schema evolution* allows us to change our schemas such that we can meet the use cases of new consumers without breaking compatibility for existing consumers.

There are a few properties of schema evolution that are common between Avro, Protobuf, and JSON Schemas. The first is compatibility modes, where events can be converted forward or backward depending on the changes made between schema versions. Compatibility modes are essential for change management, for guarding against (unintentional) breaking changes, and for alleviating consumers of the need to write custom code for each version of the schema (e.g., if `schema.version==1` do this, if `schema.version==2` do that, etc.).

The main compatibility modes are as follows:

Backward compatibility
> Consumers using the new schema can read data produced with the old schema. This compatibility mode is important for ensuring that consumers using the latest schema can still read and process older data encoded under earlier versions. For example, deleting a field is backward compatible. Say we have the record shown in the following:
>
> ```
> {
>   "type": "record",
>   "name": "Example",
>   "doc": "This is Version 1",
>   "fields": [
>     { "name": "id", "type": "integer" },
>     { "name": "foobar", "type": "string" }
>   ]
> }
> ```
>
> We could remove the `foobar` field for Version 2, as shown in the following:
>
> ```
> {
>   "type": "record",
>   "name": "Example",
>   "doc": "This is Version 2",
>   "fields": [
> ```

```
      { "name": "id", "type": "integer" }
    ]
  }
```

Note that the schema converter (as part of the Schema framework) can take Version 1 data and convert it to Version 2 simply by dropping the `foobar` field. Thus, Version 2 is backward compatible with events written using Version 1.

Forward compatibility

Consumers using an old schema (Version 1) can still read new events written with a newer schema (Version 2). They will only be able to access data that matches their Version. This compatibility mode is important for when an existing consumer coded against a current schema version rewinds its consumer offset to read historical data in the event stream.

From the previous example, you'll note that we can't convert Version 2 to Version 1, so it is *not* forward compatible. Why? Version 1 lacks a *default value* for the field `foobar`, which is needed by the consumer to fill in the missing value during conversion.

We would need to modify our Version 1 schema to add a default value *before* we published it (good thing we always create compatibility test cases as part of our pull request, right?). In Avro, specifying a default is as simple as the following:

```
{
  "type": "record",
  "name": "Example",
  "doc": "This is Version 1, but with a default value for foobar",
  "fields":
[
{
  "name": "id",
  "type": "integer"
},{
  "name": "foobar",
  "type": "string",
  "default": "DEFAULT_VALUE_STRING"
}
]
}
```

The term "default value" can be a bit misleading. Unlike a relational database table, where the default value is populated at *write time*, these default values are used at *read time*. Furthermore, the default value is only applied if the record itself does not contain the field. To further our previous example: if you try to convert a record written with schema Version 2 to schema Version 1, the converter will notice that the field `foobar` does not exist in the original event. Thus, it will set `foobar="DEFAULT_VALUE_STRING"` upon creating the converted Version 1 record instead of throwing an exception.

> Avro, JSON Schema, and Protobuf v2 each enable custom default values. This can be a powerful option for ensuring that records remain compatible through multiple changes. Developers often use default values to flag the fact that data is missing due to a compatibility conversion (e.g., `DEFAULT_VALUE_STRING`) and not because the payload was actually received with `foobar=null`.
>
> Google's Protobuf v3 removed custom default values as a deliberate design decision, so you may find Protobuf v3 a bit more difficult to use for evolutionary purposes.

As with all things schema-related, ensure that you check out the specifics of your schema selection for more details. Each of these four standards has much more content than can comfortably fit into this single chapter.

Full compatibility

When an event can be converted both immediately forward and immediately backward.

Full-transitive compatibility

When an event can be converted both forwards and backward to *any other version in the event stream*. This is the strongest guarantee, and it means that every single schema evolution is fully compatible with previous schemas. A Version 3 schema would be able to be converted to Version 2 and Version 1, and vice versa.

> Event-driven data products should adhere to full-transitive compatibility whenever possible. It provides the strongest guarantees for consumers and ensures that they need to update their code only when business use cases change and not because the schema was broken. While you can loosen the compatibility level of your data product as you choose, you will need to ensure that it does not adversely affect your consumers.

While schema evolution is extremely helpful, there will inevitably come a time when your domain shifts significantly enough that it is insufficient. A breaking change will need to occur, and it must be navigated carefully.

Negotiating a Breaking Schema Change

Breaking changes most commonly occur due to shifting boundaries of a source domain model, often due to the expansion of the business model. Adding new product lines or services may necessitate rethinking and redefining data ownership, leading to new boundaries that don't map 1:1 to the existing data products. As a simple example, a `User` data model may have previously modeled `address` with a simple `string`, as shown in the following:

Example 6-5.

```
{
  "type": "record",
  "name": "User",
  "namespace": "user.namespace",
  "fields": [
    { "name": "first_name", "type": "string" },
    { "name": "last_name", "type": "string" },
    { "name": "address", "type": "string" }
  ]
}
```

But new locality features require the creation of an `Address` object containing `home_address`, `work_address`, and `phone_number`.The following is an Avro schema of the new standardized `User_v2` object. Note that both `home_address` and `work_address` are `Address` objects, and that the `Address` object allows for optional inclusion of `phone_number`:

Example 6-6.

```
{
  "type": "record",
  "name": "User_v2",
  "namespace": "user.namespace",
  "fields": [
    { "name": "first_name", "type": "string" },
    { "name": "last_name", "type": "string" },
    { "name": "home_address",
      "type": {
          "type" : "record",
          "name" : "Address",
          "namespace": "user.namespace.inner",
          "fields" : [
              {"name": "phone_number", "type": ["null", "string"]},
              {"name": "address", "type": "string"},
              {"name": "city", "type": "string"},
              {"name": "country", "type": "string"}
          ]
```

```
      }
    }, {
      "name": "work_address",
      "type": "user.namespace.inner.Address"
    }
  ]
}
```

The old, singular `string address` field will no longer be available to downstream consumers. But do all of them know about this change? What happens to systems that still rely on the `string address` field?

Coordinating a change that concerns multiple teams can be challenging, and the same is true for renegotiating the boundaries of an already published data product. However, we don't have to reinvent the wheel; we can draw on existing precedents for navigating this process.

It is common policy for a well-maintained API, be it a library, framework, or REST API, to maintain a degree of backward compatibility with legacy clients. New clients can use the latest calls to power their business logic, while older clients can continue to use older API calls. Eventually, the API calls are deprecated and subsequently removed, giving maintainers of the application time to migrate to the newer APIs. We can adopt this same process for addressing breaking changes in data product schemas, as outlined in a series of steps.

Step 1: Design the New Data Model

The data product owner, in conjunction with their team, must come up with a new candidate model for the data product. In cases where the entire source domain requires substantial change, such as a single domain splitting into two or two domains becoming three, the biggest challenge can be redefining the boundaries of the new domains and the new constraints to the existing data products. The existing data products need to be reviewed against the changes made to the source domains, such that the new candidate data products can be presented to the existing consumers for review.

Step 2: Iterate with Your Existing Consumers and the Federated Governance Team

Once your candidate data product is ready, it's time to book a meeting with your existing customers (or a subset of the most important ones, at least for the earliest feedback). Discuss the changes to the domain models, the proposed changes to existing data products, and any new data products that you plan to create to account for the shifting model. Similarly, some existing data products may have no direct equivalent in the new models and will subsequently be removed.

These discussions usually yield rich feedback for the data product owners to bring back to their teams and apply to their data products. This is an iterative process of review and revision but provides the best overall result as it maintains the consumer-driven nature of the data mesh while reducing the amount of wasted effort.

It's a good idea to involve the federated governance team in the first couple of breaking schema changes your organization undergoes, because it provides valuable experience and feedback for refining the process. For example, the data product owners may have trouble identifying all of the stakeholders and consumers (due to poor data discovery and self-service tooling) or lack the ability to mark older data products as deprecated. Just like we're not likely to get our data product schemas right the first time, we're also likely to have some issues with our first breaking schema change. Identifying and resolving common issues is critical to improving the self-service nature of data mesh.

Step 3. Create a Release Schedule, a Data Migration Plan, and a Deprecation Plan

Once the new schemas and data products are cleared to move forward, the next steps involve creating a release guide and deprecation plan. Identifying the affected consumers in combination with the impact of the required changes provides us with an idea of how much time and effort they'll need to do the necessary migrations. Accordingly, it will also provide an indication of how much support the data product owners will need to provide during this migration. The release schedule should reflect the estimated time it will take to migrate all of the consumers, along with some extra padding for safety's sake.

Data migration is a significant factor for a breaking data product change. Maintaining a full history in the event stream will require either migrating the previous event data model to the new one, or recreating the events from the source data. The former can work when the breaking change is simply a remodeling of existing fields, but tends to fall short when new data is created. In our example, we redefined Address, adding both a work_address and a home_address. We lack information about whether the current address is a work or home address, and even if we can find that out, we still have only one address and need to collect information to populate the other field.

The data product owner could backfill the User_v2 event stream by creating new records to match the new schema. However, these new records would only represent the User at the current point in time. Historical events in the original User stream would not be migrated without additional work.

Finally, the data product owner must support both User and User_v2 data products for a period of time (such as 8 to 12 weeks) so that consumers can migrate from the old one to the new one. The data product owner's team will assist them with their migration needs, including clarifying details about the new domain, any changes to semantics, and assisting in rebuilding internal state stores.

Step 4. Execute the Release

The new data products are released alongside the existing ones, such that consumers have time to migrate over. Mark the original User data product as *deprecated* to block new consumers from registering as readers, and instead redirect them to use the latest version, User_v2. The User data product with the old string address value will co-exist with the new User_v2 data product for a predetermined period of time.

While most consumers will work in a timely manner to migrate their applications to the new data product, there will be those who lag behind due to lack of resources and competing priorities. While you can certainly send them ever-more-frequent reminder messages, at some point the integrity of the data mesh will become at risk: it is unreasonable for the producer service to maintain two versions of the data product indefinitely, especially since the business domain model has permanently shifted. Noncompliance is not abnormal in a data mesh, and at this point it would be best to consult your federated governance team on how to proceed: migrate the code of non-complying consumers, escalate up the business chain, or simply proceed with the deprecation plan and halt production of new events to that event stream. Usually the threat of a production outage is sufficient to finish the migrations.

Navigating a breaking schema change is a fairly involved process that requires explicit communication between the data product owner and all of its consumers. The precise steps in your process will depend on your own implementation details, but should look similar to what we just covered.

Managing schemas well requires keeping track of previous versions and ensuring compatibility rules are followed. Consumers additionally need the ability to discover which schemas belong to which event streams as part of self-service tooling require-ments. A *schema registry* provides a solution for these needs, among others, and is an essential part of an event-driven data mesh, as we shall see in the next section.

The Role of the Schema Registry

A schema registry is a service that allows us to register schemas in association with their event streams. One of the main roles of the schema registry is to reduce the number of bytes sent over the network. Back in "A Brief Introduction to Serialization and Deserialization" on page 128, we saw that the basic serialization process appends a full copy of the schema to each event record, which results in a significant amount of duplicated data sent over the network. Figure 6-4 shows a producer writing events with a full copy of each schema, reducing throughput, increasing data replication costs, and increasing the load on consumers.

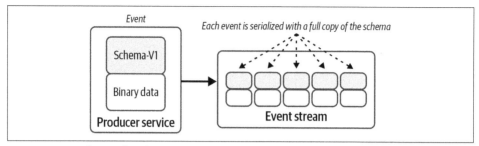

Figure 6-4. Each serialized event published to the event stream with the entire schema, resulting in excessive network utilization and storage overhead

A schema registry can absolve us of the need to write the schema with each event. Instead, we can store the schema *external* to the event and just use a unique ID in its place to track the associated schema. Thus, whenever a consumer reads an event, it can simply reference the schema registry to obtain the schema associated with that ID.

Figure 6-5 shows the entire end-to-end process. Instead of serializing the schema along with the event, the producer service queries the schema registry (1), registers the schema (2), then replaces the schema with a short unique ID (3 and 4). This event is then produced to the event stream (5). The process is performed in reverse on the consumer side: the event is read from the stream (6), the schema registry is queried using the unique ID (7 and 8). Once the schema is obtained (9), the record can then be deserialized (10 and 11) for processing by the consumer's business logic.

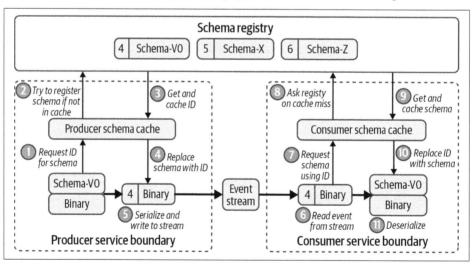

Figure 6-5. Leveraging a schema registry in an event-driven producer/consumer workflow

Precisely *how* the schema is replaced by the unique ID depends on both the producer's serialization logic and any limitations in the format of events in the schema registry. For example, Confluent's Kafka Schema Registry (*https://oreil.ly/TTkv-*) replaces the schema with a 5-byte prefix (*https://oreil.ly/kBGRz*).

Using a schema registry requires serializers and deserializers to adhere to the proprietary format. And while Confluent's schema registry is fairly widely used with Kafka, it's not the only schema registry, and not all schema registries will use the same format. As part of building self-service tools, your governance team will need to negotiate which schema to support for building your data mesh.

A schema registry provides other benefits in addition to network and disk I/O savings. Here are a few other significant benefits provided by a schema registry:

Data discovery
> The schema registry provides a mapping of event streams to its registered schemas. Prospective consumers can examine the schemas to see if the stream contains the data they're interested in. Self-service tooling can provide search functionality on top of the schema registry API to search for specific fields, documentation, or metadata tags.

Schema evolution validation
> Registering a schema with the schema registry is a mandatory part of the write path of an event to a stream. This action provides a hook for validating the producer's current schema against that stored in the registry. Did the user evolve the schema in a way that is unauthorized by the schema registry (e.g., the new schema does not support backward compatibility)? Throw an exception. Is the schema completely invalid compared to what was registered under that ID before? Throw an exception. Is the event malformed? Throw an exception. The schema registry provides a safeguard against unintentional and unauthorized changes, protecting the data integrity so that the data product can meet its quality and reliability SLAs.

Automatically updated documentation
> The schema registry provides a minimal form of automatically updated documentation for each event stream. Users can view all the registered schemas, including the names, types, and doc fields. Embedded schema docs are very useful for highlighting any idiosyncrasies or corner cases in the data. They are also far more likely to be up to date because they are embedded, as opposed to documentation maintained independently by an outside party.

Downloadable schemas to generate code
> A consumer can download schemas to generate class definitions and test events for their unit tests.

You can write a custom registration script to evaluate the schema during the registration process. A simple and common check is to verify that every value in a schema has a "doc" string of nonzero length to ensure that there is *some* documentation for each field. Another option is to scan for PII patterns and request an additional verification step if something suspicious is found. Similarly, you can automatically generate class definitions and run validation tests prior to deployment.

Schema registries provide many benefits for a low overhead and are an essential component of an event-driven data mesh. The savings on network and storage costs alone make them a valuable choice, with the remaining functionality providing the icing on the cake.

So now that we've covered schemas, schema registries, and the benefits of using both, we have one last schema-related question before winding up the chapter. How do we manage schemas in relation to our data product producer and consumer applications?

Best Practices for Managing Schemas in Your Codebase

There are several schools of thought for storing event schemas in your codebase. One is to centralize all of your data product schemas in one big repository, using references to tie them to the codebase that actually owns the schema. Another is to decentralize and store schemas in the code repository of the producers and rely on the self-service data platform to tie them all together.

However, the best practice is a combination of the two: a centralized code repository for shared-use schemas with data product owners retaining their own schemas internal to their projects. Let's take a deeper look at how this works in practice by first examining *schema composition* and its role in a data mesh.

Apache Avro, Protobuf, and JSON Schema each provide the ability to import schemas from other files just as you would import a class or a library into your code. This is a powerful feature that enables us to compose a schema from simple common building blocks.

First, you'll need to consult with your federated governance team to come up with standardizations of common cross-domain entities. In this case, previous meetings, discussions, and arguments have led to the standardization of two simple (but useful!) entities within the organization—base_user, representing the unique ID of a user:

```
package myorg.common;

message base_user {
  String uuid = 1;
}
```

and `base_item`, containing a unique ID of a specific ecommerce product:

```
package myorg.common;

message base_item {
  int64 id = 1;
}
```

The data product owner can import both of these base definitions into the `user_clicked_on_item` schema definition, along with a common timestamp field, to compose their event definition:

```
import "common_schemas/base_user.proto"
import "common_schemas/base_item.proto"
import "google/protobuf/timestamp.proto";

message user_clicked_on_item {
  myorg.common.base_user user = 1;
  myorg.common.base_item item = 2;
  google.protobuf.Timestamp timestamp = 3;
  String websiteURI = 4;
}
```

Composing schemas using standardized forms makes it much easier to combine data products from across the organization. For example, this event can be aggregated with other events by `base_user`, `base_item`, or `Timestamp`, or even a combination of these three. Furthermore, adhering to common definitions means that you can also leverage common unit tests and validation plug-ins to significantly reduce the chance of making mistakes, keeping data quality and reliability high.

Common schema components should remain fairly minimal and only include fields that are mandatory for the data product owner to populate. Keep in mind that you can always create additional components that have more extensive field listings. For example, you may choose to create a common `item_details` component containing all of the standard information to extend `base_item`, and include it as an additional component in your data product's schema.

Store the common schema components in a centralized repository and pull them into your local system at compile time. Store your application's schemas alongside the code in its own repository. You can then choose to publish your event schema to the data product discovery platform upon promoting it to a data product.

Keeping your data product's schemas alongside the code that creates the events streamlines the entire review process. Yoou can simply create a code review, determine the existing consumers, and add them as reviewers. A strict approach requires each consumer to approve the changes, ensuring that everyone is aware of changes that could impact their applications.

In the next and final section of this chapter, we'll take a look at how you go about choosing which schema technology to use.

Choosing a Schema Technology

There are several major factors for choosing which schema format to adopt. The first is precedence: are you already using a given schema format? If you are, this would be the best candidate to look at first. Your federated governance team would be responsible for investigating its suitability in your organization and discovering if there are any significant impediments or pain points that need to be addressed that prevent further adoption. Managing just a single schema format is much easier than managing multiple.

The second major factor is the availability of supportive tooling and how it integrates into your self-service environment. Code generators, event generators for testing purposes, schema registry support, and data discovery support are all significant subfactors. While both Avro and Protobuf tend to have a lot of support, other schema frameworks may not have nearly as much support, adoption, and available tooling, especially in the context of event streaming. The entire goal of using a schema technology is to improve self-service capabilities, ensure high-quality data products, and remove the margins for error. Use something that is reliable, widespread, and well-supported.

The third major factor pertains to schema specific traits and if they'll be suitable for your use cases. For example, you may require nonnull and nonzero defaults, as provided by JSON Schema, Protobuf v2, and Avro. You may also prefer to have JSON Schema's built-in data quality checks (e.g., minimum, maximum) or instead prefer the faster serialization and deserialization of Avro and Protobuf.

For a real-world example, we can look to Paul Makkar from Saxo Bank. In his talk "Kafka and the Data Mesh" (*https://oreil.ly/yNjdI*), he outlines the decisions he and his team made in selecting Protobuf over Avro. I have summarized the evaluation in the following sidebar.

Why Saxo Bank Chose Protobuf over Avro

Saxo Bank's engineering organization is primarily a .NET shop, and it initially attempted to use Apache Avro as the main schema technology for generating code, validating schemas, and integrating with its workflows. However, the organization found that this didn't work as well as was hoped. Avro integration with .NET was simply too difficult. The C# and Python clients for Avro lagged behind the Java implementation, required more manual steps, and introduced a number of friction points. You can read more about the specific issues and evaluation on Confluent's blog (*https://oreil.ly/S-q1J*).

Saxo Bank then trialed Protobuf as the schema of choice and encountered fewer issues. The code generators worked precisely as needed for the data format specifications, there were no issues with (de)serialization, and the company was more satisfied overall with the experience for both the developer and the data product owner.

Based on the principle of building out self-service tooling, Saxo Bank also chose to invest in using Buf, an opinionated tool for managing and using Protobuf schemas that provided them with linting tools, style guides, naming conventions, and enum usage tooling.

Protobuf annotation functionality allowed Saxo Bank's engineers to directly embed metadata, such as tagging of PII and specifications about encrypted data, into their schemas. These annotations can be ignored by consumers that do not care about the field, such as encrypted PII, but enabled by those consumers that do need access to more information about how to unlock that data (such as a reference to the authentication and decryption components).

The decision to move to Protobuf was based on identifying the pain points of using Avro, investigation of alternatives, and assessment of common use cases. Further testing of Protobuf showed that it was far more suitable for the needs of Saxo Bank, so the federated governance team chose to align on and support a single standard for all to use.

For Saxo Bank, in-use technology (.NET) and important integrations with supportive tooling (such as Buf) played significant roles in the adoption of Protobuf.

Summary

Schemas form an essential part of event-driven data products. They provide structure and clarity for both the producers and consumers of the event stream and form a reliable and explicit definition of the contents of the data product.

Code generators bridge the gap between the schema itself and the business logic and provide a benefit to both the producer and the consumer. The former benefits from the strict type definitions and distinction between optional and mandatory fields, ensuring that no data is accidentally malformed or excluded. Subsequently, the latter benefits from the same well-defined type-system, absolving it of the need to interpret and standardize the data. Schemas provide the means to impose quality controls as close to the source as possible.

Schema evolution provides the ability to evolve and change schemas over time, with explicit up-front rules as to which changes are allowed given compatibility requirements. While breaking changes can still occur, schemas provide the common framework for determining what the new data products may look like. And since they're commonly integrated as part of the codebase, schema changes can follow the same review processes as standard business application code changes.

While there are many options available for you to choose from, Apache Avro and Google's Protobuf remain your best options, with JSON Schemas as a reasonable third choice. Your investment into one of these will vary depending on your preexisting technology choices, but remains best discussed and decided centrally by your federated governance team.

In the next chapter, we'll take a look at leveraging what we've learned with schemas and apply it to the problem of event design. There are many different ways to model and design events. We'll explore the best ways to do it and the pitfalls and gotchas that are best avoided.

CHAPTER 7

Designing Events

There are many ways to design events for event-driven architectures. However, some are more suitable than others for use in an event-driven data mesh. This chapter covers the best strategies for designing events for your event-driven data products, including how to avoid the numerous pitfalls that you will encounter along the way.

Introduction to Event Types

There are two main types of events that underpin all of event design: the *state* event, as we first introduced in "State Events and Event-Carried State Transfer" on page 55, and the *delta* event, which we'll cover in more detail in this chapter.

Figure 7-1 shows a simple square wave in steady state, periodically altering from one state to another based on a delta. Similar to this square wave, we model our events to either capture the state itself or the edge that transitions from one state to another.

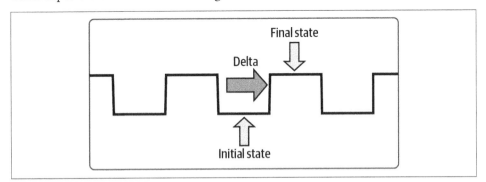

Figure 7-1. State and delta during a change

There are three stages to any occurrence in a system:

1. The initial state
2. The delta that alters the initial state to produce the final state
3. The final state (which is also the initial state for the next change cycle)

The majority of events we encounter can be fully categorized as either state or delta. Looking at events in this way helps separate concerns and focus design efforts:

State events

State events fully describe the state of an entity at a given point in time and are the best choice for communicating data products between domains. State events are typically the most flexibile and useful event types for use in an event-driven data mesh.

Delta events

These describe the transition between states and typically only contain information about what has changed. Delta events have the distinction of being the first type of event that many event-driven application developers encounter. However, these events are generally not well-suited for an event-driven data mesh, as we'll discuss shortly.

While there can be *hybrid* events that have characteristics of each, these tend to be less common because they can cause undesirable strong coupling. We'll talk more about those later in this chapter.

Let's take a look at state events first.

Expanding on State Events and Event-Carried State Transfer

"State Events and Event-Carried State Transfer" on page 55 introduced both state events and ECST. As a refresher, a state event showcases the current state of an entity at a precise moment in time, much like a row in a relational database. ECST allows for any consumer of the event stream to materialize, aggregate, and store whatever selection of data it needs in its own domain boundary, to use as it sees fit. In this section, we'll look at some useful options for extending state events.

State events can contain just the "now" state or they may contain the "before/after" state (a pattern we'll cover with "Change-Data Capture" on page 179 in the next chapter). Both options have their own advantages and disadvantages, which we'll examine in turn. For starters, let's take a look at how each of these options affects *compaction* of event streams.

There are two main design strategies for defining the structure and contents of ECST events:

Current state
Contains the full public state at the moment the event was created.

Before/after state
Contains both the full public state *before* the event occurred and the full public state *after* the event occurred.

Let's look into each of these in detail to get a better understanding of their trade-offs.

Current State Events

The event contains only the current state of the entity and requires comparison with a previous state event to determine what has changed. For example, an `inventory` event for a given `item_id` will contain only the latest value for the `quantity` in stock at that point in time. This design strategy has several main benefits:

Lean
The state events consume a minimal amount of space in the event stream. Network traffic is also minimized.

Simple
The event broker stores any previous state events for that entity, such that if you need historical state, you simply rewind and replay your consumer offsets. You can set independent compaction policies for each event stream depending on your consumer's needs for historical data.

Compactable
You can keep the number of events in the stream proportional to the key space of the domain.

It also has a few nuances that are not quite drawbacks, but rather things to consider:

Agnostic to why the state changed
The downstream consumer is not provided with the reason *why* the data has changed, only the new public state. The reason for this is simple: it removes the ability of consumers to couple on the *internal state transitions* of the source domain. Think about data in a relational database table—we typically do not communicate *why* that data has changed in the data itself, and the same holds true for state events (Note: We'll look at bending this rule a bit with hybrid events a bit later).

Consumers must maintain state to detect transitions

A consumer must maintain its own state to detect specific changes to certain fields, regardless of how simple or complex its business logic is. For example, a customer changing their address to another country may require you to send them new legal documents, which can differ depending on the country they left and the country they moved to. By making it the consumer's responsibility to materialize state for tracking transitions, the onus of computing these edges is placed entirely within the domain of the consumer.

Data products built using *current state events* are flexible and fairly easy to use and should form the basis of most of your data products. If you want to package up state transitions into your event as well, look no further than before/after state.

Before/After State Events

This strategy relies on providing the state before a transition occurs and the state after it has occurred. Change-data capture (CDC) systems, as covered in "Change-Data Capture" on page 179, regularly make use of the before/after strategy. The following showcases two before/after user events with a simple two-field schema:

```
Key: 26
Value: {
  before: { name: "Adam", country: "Atlantis" },
  after: { name: "Adam", country: "Canada" }
}
```

A follow-up before/after state event that shows the deletion of Key = 26. Note that old data still remains in the before field:

```
Key: 26
Value: {
  before: { name: "Adam", country: "Canada" },
  after: null
}
```

There are some benefits to this design:

Simple state transitions in a single event

The before/after event showcases every field that has changed within a single transaction, in addition to all of the fields that have not changed. The reason for the change, however, is not included.

Consumers can detect simple changes without maintaining state

Some consumers can forgo maintaining state if they are only interested in detecting a simple state transition. For example, if we want to send documents to a user who moves from Madagascar to Canada, then our consumer can simple check to see if the before and after fields of the event match their criteria. However, this doesn't work if Adam moves from Madagascar to Ethiopia, and then soon there-after moves to Canada, causing two events to occur. The consumer business logic would not be able to trigger on this sequence of events since it doesn't maintain any state. In practice, the theoretical stateless consumer is seldomly realized, since the vast majority of services of any reasonable complexity need to maintain state.

There are also a few drawbacks to this design:

Compaction is difficult

Deleting an event using the before/after logic results in the `after` field being set to null—but the entire value itself is not null. By default, event brokers like Apache Kafka will not recognize this as a tombstone and thus will not delete it. While it may be technically possible to rewrite the compaction logic, it usually isn't feasible, especially if you are relying heavily on SaaS solutions.

There are, however, some options, depending on which tooling you use. Debezium has worked around this limitation by allowing you to produce a tomb-stone after the before/after event, generating two events instead of just one. According to Debezium's documentation (*https://oreil.ly/_Jq8*):

> A database `DELETE` operation causes Debezium to generate two Kafka records:
>
> - A record that contains `"op": "d"`, the `before` row data, and some other fields.
> - A tombstone record that has the same key as the deleted row and a value of `null`. This record is a marker for Apache Kafka. It indicates that log compaction can remove all records that have this key.

Risk of leftover information

As we saw earlier, previous data may be accidentally maintained indefinitely in the `before` field unless you issue a series of deletions.

Doubled data storage and network usage

Before/after events double (on average) the amount of data going over the wire and stored on disk. Consumers, producers, and the event broker each bear part of this load. In some cases this may be trivial. Seldom-updated events or those with low volume are probably nothing to worry about, but extremely high volume event streams can quickly add up the costs. This can be particularly expensive depending on the cross-regional data transfer fees associated with high-availability producer, consumer, and event broker deployments.

I recommend using current state events over before/after when designing event-stream data products. The consumers will need to maintain state for the records they care about for their business processes, but disk space is relatively cheap and they need to select only a subset of the domain that they need. This also simplifies operations for the event broker when compared to before/after, with lower cross-region traffic costs, less broker disk usage, and less broker network usage replication overhead. Further, the risk of leaking data from improper compaction deletion is eliminated.

In the next section, we'll take a look at delta events, where an event is modeled after the change and not the state itself.

Delta Events

The delta event represents a change that has occurred within a specific domain, represented as the edge of a transition in Figure 7-1. Delta events contain *only* the information about the state change, not the past or current state. Delta events are usually phrased as verbs in the past tense, indicating that something has occurred. For example:

- `itemAddedToCart`
- `itemRemovedFromCart`
- `orderPaid`
- `orderShipped`
- `orderReturned`
- `userMoved`
- `userDeleted`

You may find that you're more familiar with these types of events than you are with the state types used for ECST. Delta events have historically been fairly common, particularly in the context of the Lambda architecture (see "The Lambda Architecture and Why It Doesn't Work for Data Mesh" on page 62). Delta events are also commonly used *inside* a domain for *event sourcing*, a subject we'll now take a look at before going back to data products.

Event Sourcing with Delta Events

Event sourcing is an architectural pattern based on recording *what happened* within a domain as a sequence of immutable append-only events. These events are *aggregated* to build up the current state by applying them in the order that they occurred, using domain specific logic, one after another.

This architecture is often promoted as an alternative to the traditional create, read, update, delete (CRUD) model commonly found in relational-database type frameworks. In the CRUD model, the fully mutable state of the entity is directly modified such that only the final state is retained. Though the databases underpinning CRUD can generate an audit log of the changes that occurred, this log is used primarily for auditing purposes and not for driving business logic.

There are some limitations to the CRUD model that may make event sourcing an attractive alternative. For one, operations must be processed directly against the data store as they are invoked. Under heavy use, this can significantly slow down operations and result in timeouts and failures. Second, high concurrency operations on the same entities can result in data conflicts and failed transactions, further increasing load on the system.

But the CRUD model also contains several distinct advantages. Though it depends largely on the database, most CRUD implementations offer strong read-after-write consistency. It's also fairly intuitive and simple to use, with lots of tools and frameworks supporting it. For many software developers, this is the first model of maintaining state that they encounter. Figure 7-2 shows a series of CRUD events (one create, two updates) applying changes to the refrigerator state. The state is completely mutable, and only the updated state is retained after a create or update command is applied.

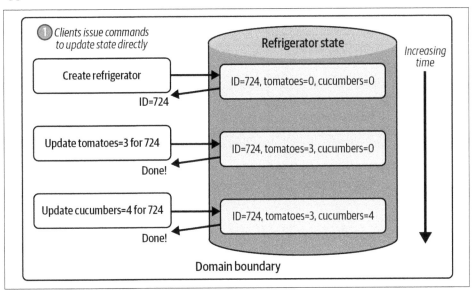

Figure 7-2. Using CRUD commands to update the contents of the refrigerator, reflected in the database

Under the event sourcing architecture, these create, update, and destroy operations are instead modeled as events that are written to a durable append-only log that retains them indefinitely. It is not uncommon to use a single database table to act as the append-only log. It is also possible to use an event broker like Apache Kafka to host the append-only log, although this does introduce additional latency. In either case, the current state is generated by consuming events in the order they are written in the log and applying them one at a time to create the final state.

Figure 7-3 shows the same refrigerator example, with the CRUD operations instead modeled as domain events. And although these sample events are CRUD-like, the domain owner has free reign over designing the deltas to suit their own business use cases. For instance, they could extend the set of events they're creating to also incorporate deltas such as:

- turn_lights_on/turn_lights_off
- turn_cooling_on/turn_cooling_off
- open_door/close_door

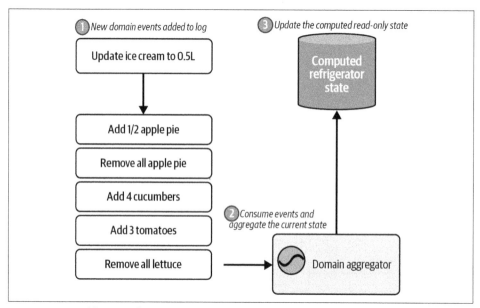

Figure 7-3. Building up the contents of a refrigerator using event sourcing

The domain aggregator (2) is separate from the process that writes the new domain events into the log (1), and allows the write and aggregation processes to be scaled independently. A domain can also contain multiple domain aggregators and may aggregate the same log to two different internal state stores depending on the domain needs.

One of the main drawbacks of event sourcing is that it is eventually consistent, which can be a significant obstacle for some use cases. There will always be some delay between writing the event to the log and seeing the materialized result in the state. And because multiple concurrent clients can each write events about the same entity, it becomes difficult to attribute any specific modification in final state to the delta your client just appended. This can make it unsuitable in applications that require strong consistency.

Event sourcing is a reasonable alternative to the CRUD model for building up internal state. The problem with event sourcing comes when it is *misused as a means for interdomain communication*, exposing the internal domain deltas to the outside world for others to couple on (and misinterpret). These domain-specific events and their relationship to the aggregate and to each other can change over time, so the events defined within a domain for event sourcing *are not suitable for interdomain communication as a data product!* Just as we do not allow services outside of our domain to couple directly on our data model, we also must not allow services to couple on our private domain events data model.

This isn't to say you cannot expose any events outside of the domain's boundaries. But *any* event that you expose outside of your domain boundary becomes part of the public data contract and requires your domain data product owner to support it as such. This means ensuring that its semantic meaning doesn't drift over time, that the data doesn't evolve, and that others don't try to use it to reconstruct your private internal domain on the outside using a copy of your logic. A failure to maintain the boundaries of "events in here" and "events out there" can lead to very tangled coupling, excessive difficulty in refactoring, and subtle errors due to misinterpretation of events by outside consumers.

Why Delta Events Don't Work for Event-Driven Data Products

The next few sections illustrate the problems with using delta events for event-driven data products. There are several issues with using delta events as the means of communicating data between domains. Let's take a look at each issue in turn.

There is an infinite set of possible event types

First and foremost, there is an infinite number of delta events that can occur in any nontrivial domain. This alone should stop most folks from trying to create event-stream data products with the delta model, but unfortunately it does not. But surely, can it really be the case that there is an *infinite* number of delta events?

In reality, the actual set of delta events necessary for your domain is undoubtedly finite. The real problem is that every consumer of a delta event needs to know precisely how to correctly integrate it into the aggregate—without this ability, you cannot effectively communicate state through your data product.

Let's take a look at an example. Figure 7-4 shows a simple set of ecommerce events for constructing the contents of a shopping cart.

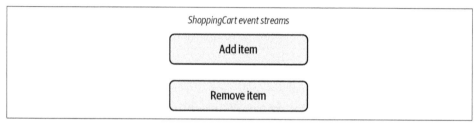

Figure 7-4. Shopping cart delta events, used to construct the current state of the shopping cart

Add and remove are fairly simple: items can be added, or they can be removed. The consumer will need to interpret and apply each of these events, in the correct order, to build up its aggregate. Suppose, though, that a new feature in the domain allows users to update the quantity of items they have in their cart: where previously the domain owner may have issued a remove event first, then an add event with the new quantity, now they may instead simply issue an update.

Figure 7-5 shows this new Update Item Quantity event stream published to the world. Now if a consumer needs a model of the shopping cart, they must also account for these updated events in their aggregation code. As the scope of the domain changes, so do the meaning of the events and their relationship to the aggregate.

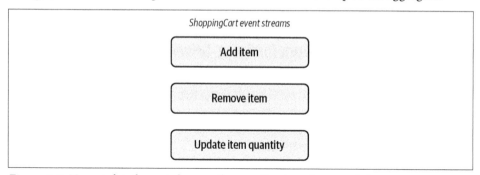

Figure 7-5. New updated event changes the way the shopping cart delta events are interpreted

One of the common reasons that people (wrongly) choose to use delta events for cross-domain communication is that they don't believe that other consumers should be required to maintain state to trigger on specific changes. However, the range of possible deltas makes this untenable. The simple expansion of the shopping cart domain to incorporate features such as coupons, shipping estimates, and subscriptions increases the amount of information that a consumer must account for, as shown in Figure 7-6.

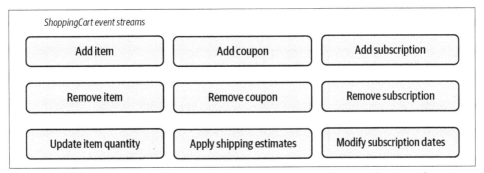

Figure 7-6. The delta events defining the shopping cart sprawl as new business functionality is added

Exposing this expanded shopping cart domain to consumers requires that the consumers can identify, use, and build a correct aggregate out of these events. This leads us to the next major problem of using delta events cross-domain.

The logic to interpret the events must be replicated to each consumer

How can a consumer know they're correctly interpreting the delta events? And how does the consumer stay up to date when new domain events are introduced? The key is to make it possible for a consumer to correctly operate without having to continually update their logic to account for new and varied delta events.

In the state model, a consumer only needs to materialize the state events to know they're getting the complete public domain. They may not know *why* the transition occurred (we'll touch on this a bit more later in the chapter), but they can be assured that the entire public domain is there, and that as a consumer, they don't need to worry about correctly building an aggregation.

Figure 7-7 shows two consumers, each of which has replicated the logic from the producer for building up the aggregate state. Consumers are responsible for identifying, understanding, and correctly applying the add, remove, and update domain events to generate the appropriate final state of the aggregate. The complexity of the domain is paramount; very simple domains may be able to account for this, but any domain of meaningful complexity will find this solution untenable.

Intermittent issues can cause further complexities—an event stream hosted on a lagging broker may experience delays in providing some events, resulting in the consumer receiving them out of order from events in other streams. Deltas applied in the wrong order often yield incorrect state transitions and may trigger incorrect business actions.

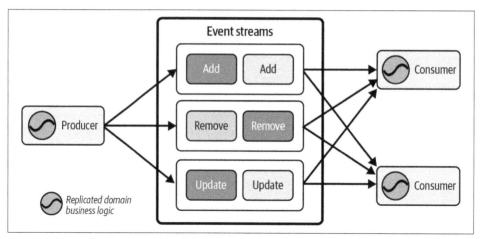

Figure 7-7. The logic to interpret delta events to build state is copied into multiple locations

Additionally, each consumer may implement its own aggregation logic slightly differently—often because a consumer fails to update the aggregation logic as the domain evolves. One consumer may wait up to 30 seconds for late-arriving events, while another consumer may not wait at all and simply discard any late arrivals, resulting in similar yet different aggregates.

Any changes to how the producer aggregates its internal domain, including new events or changed delta semantics, must be propagated to the consumer logic—if you have worked on distributed services (or microservices) before, you may be shuddering at this idea. Using delta events to communicate between domains tightly couples the producer, the event definitions, and the consumers together, and trying to manage this is an exercise in futility.

These events map poorly to event streams

In the problems discussed so far, we've operated under the assumption that any new delta events will be immediately identifiable and understandable to consumers, though they may not yet understand how to apply those events to the domain. The reality is far messier. Delta event consumers will need to be notified when new deltas are created so that they can update their code to integrate the event into their data model. Coordination can be quite difficult, particularly when there are many different consumers. Herein lies the main problem of this subsection: how do consumers know about the new domain events that they must consider in their model?

One common suggestion that unfortunately misses the point is to simply "put it all in the same event stream so that the consumers have access to it and can choose if they need to use it." Although existing consumers will end up receiving these new event types, this proposal does nothing to solve the code changes and integrations for consumers to use that data.

Additionally, it is far more likely to cause the consumer to throw an exception, get thrown away as "bad data," or, worse yet, cause silent processing errors in the consumer's business logic. This also violates the convention of using a single evolvable schema per event stream, which is a de facto standard for many of the frameworks and technologies that process event streams.

The critical issue here is that new event definitions require working with those that aggregate the events into a model. If you put the new delta events into new individual streams, you make discovery easier and follow the one-schema-per-stream convention, but your consumers will still need to be manually notified that this new stream exists! In either case, a code update is required to make any sense of this data, while a failure to incorporate it runs the risk of an incorrect aggregate.

I like to contrast this with the state model, where the state domain can change as needed and the composition of the data product is encapsulated entirely within the producer service. Any modifications made to the business domain occur in one place and are reflected in the updated data model published to the event stream.

Inversion of ownership: Consumers put their business logic into the producer

The fourth problem with deltas revolves around the ownership and location of business logic. For example, a consumer may need to know when a package has been shipped so that it can send out an email to the intended recipient notifying them that it's on its way. The business logic for determining that the package has shipped must necessarily live in the producer, as in Figure 7-8.

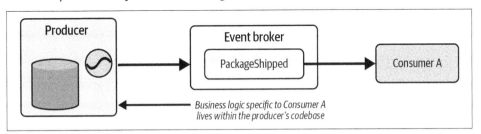

Figure 7-8. Consumer business requirements are pushed into the business logic of the producer; in this case, Consumer A only wants to know when a package is shipped, but not when the package has any other status

However, this quickly becomes untenable with the growing scope of business use cases. Each new business requirement that relies on state transition will similarly need to place its business logic within the producer service (see Figure 7-9) to generate events whenever that "edge" happens. This is prohibitively difficult to scale and manage, let alone track ownership and dependencies.

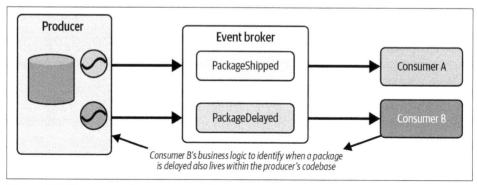

Figure 7-9. The scope of consumer requirements can grow quite large, as there are many possible deltas for most domains of any complexity

The entire purpose of delta events is to avoid maintaining state in the consumer service, but they require that the producer be fully able and willing to fulfill business logic solely for the consumer. For example, consider these reasonably plausible use cases:

- I want to track returns where a user had previously called in to complain: a `user ReturnedItemAfterTelephoneComplaint` event.
- I want to know if the user has seen at least three ads for the item and then subsequently purchased it: a `userSawAtLeastThreeAdsThenPurchasedIt` event.

These sample events may seem a bit over the top, but the reality is that these are the sorts of conditions that businesses *do* care about. In each case, the consumer should maintain its own state and build up its own computations of these occurrences but instead avoids it by pushing the responsibility of detecting the edge back to the producer. The resultant highly specific events are *not* data products but a tightly coupled system of untenable complexity.

A final factor is that a single system is seldom able to provide all of the information necessary for these highly specialized events. Consider the example of Figure 7-10. In this example, the consumer needs to act when state from the `advertising` service and the `payments` service (both within their own domains) meet a certain criterion: the user must have been shown an advertisement three times and then eventually have purchased that item.

Even if we convinced the advertising team to produce `userSawAdvertisementThree Times` and `userRe turnedItemAfterTelephoneComplaint` events, the consumer would still need to store it in its own state store and await the matching purchase from the `payments` service. Even the most complex and convoluted event definition cannot account for handling data that resides entirely in another domain. The consumer must still be able to maintain state, despite our best efforts to avoid it.

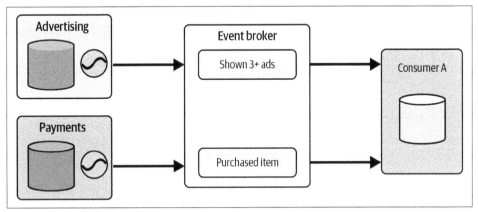

Figure 7-10. Consumer-specific delta event triggering logic is pushed upstream to both the advertising and payments service

And what if our consumer wants to change its business logic from three ads to four? A whole new event definition needs to be negotiated and put in the producer's boundary, which should give you an idea of how poorly this idea fares in practice. It is far more reasonable that the producer output a set of *general purpose state* and let the consumer figure out what it wants to do with those data sets.

Inability to maintain historical data without excessive complications

The fifth and final point against delta events for event-driven data products is based on the difficulty of maintaining *usable historical data*. Old state events can simply be compacted, but delta events cannot. It becomes substantially more difficult to manage the ever-increasing log of events as a source of historical information.

Each delta event is essential for aggregating the final state. And there may not only be a single event stream to deal with, but multiple delta streams relating to different deltas within the domain. Figure 7-11 shows an example of three simple shopping cart delta events that have grown very large over the past 10 years—so large that a new consumer might take, say, three weeks of nonstop processing to make it through the volume of data, just to catch up to the current state.

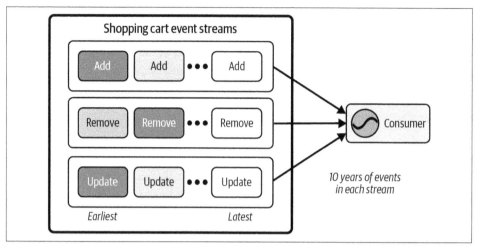

Figure 7-11. There are simply too many delta events in this stream for a new consumer to reasonably consume

While purging old data is certainly one solution, another solution that I have seen attempted is to offload older events into a large side state store, which can be sideloaded into a new consumer. The idea here is that the consumer can load all of these events in parallel, booting up far more quickly. The problem is that the order in which these events are applied can matter, and just moving the events to a non-streaming system only to stream them back into new consumers is a bit nonsensical. So the next solution is to build a *snapshot* of the state at that point in time based on all of the delta events. This is shown in Figure 7-12.

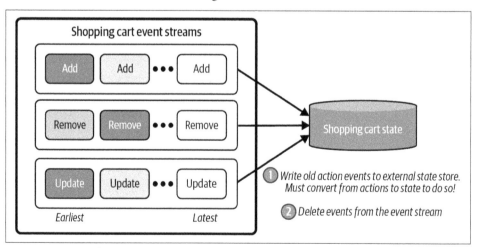

Figure 7-12. Loading the old events into a bootstrapping side store requires aggregating into a state model

There is a bit of irony here. In the attempt to avoid creating a publicly usable definition of state, we find ourselves doing exactly this to store the data in a side store. New consumers can certainly boot up far more quickly using it, but now they have to both read from the snapshot state store and then switch over perfectly to the event stream.

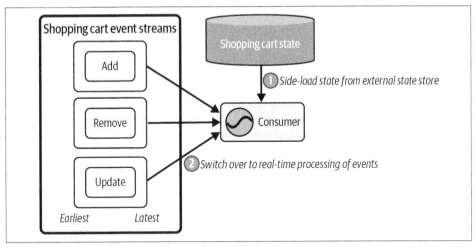

Figure 7-13. This brings us back around to the Lambda architecture involving both delta events, aggregated state, and the need to handle both batch and streaming

Figure 7-13 shows that we have now come full circle, back to the very Lambda architectures that we have been trying to avoid this whole time, along with all its operational complexity and inherent problems.

The following are unfortunately common yet insufficient arguments for using delta events for interdomain communication:

> Maintaining duplicate state is wasteful, it's going to take up too much disk.
>
> The consumers will know what the event means. How could they possibly misinterpret it?
>
> C'mon, I really only care about this one transition, it's not a big deal if I couple on it. Just publish a custom event for me.
>
> —That person who doesn't want to use state events

Delta events are fine within the internal boundary of a private domain, where the tight coupling of the event definitions and the logic required to interpret and apply them can be applied consistently. However, using the same delta events across domain boundaries is perilous, and using them as the means to build up state in other applications is really out of the question. Focus on using state events for your data products and leave delta events communicating within a closed system.

That said, there are times when it may be reasonable and useful to look at event design through a different lens. Let's take a look at measurement events and what makes them useful.

Measurement Events

Measurement events are commonly found in many domains and consist of a complete record of an *occurrence* at a point in time. There are common examples of this in our everyday world: website analytics, perhaps most familiarly embodied by Google Analytics (*https://oreil.ly/jdlm2*), is one. The user behavior tracking that occurs on every single website, social media experience, and mobile application is another. Every time you click a button, view an ad, or linger on an Instagram post, it is recorded as a measurement event.

What does a measurement event look like? Here's an example of a user behavior event recording the event of a user seeing an advertisement on a webpage:

```
Key: "USERID-8271949472726174"
Value: {
  utc_timestamp: "2022-01-22T15:39:19Z"
  ad_id: 1739487875123
  page_id: 364198769786
  url: https://www.somewebsite.com/welcome.html
}
```

A measurement is a snapshot of state at a specific point in time. However, measurements have a few characteristics that differentiate them from the state events we discussed earlier.

Measurement Events Often Form Aggregate-Aligned Data Products

Measurements are often used to create an *aggregate-aligned* data product. For example, the userViewedAd measurement could be used to compute a multitude of data sets, answering questions like "What is the most popular page_id?", "When do users see the most ads?", and "How many ads does each user see, on average, in a session?" In contrast, basic state events are usually used as *source-aligned* data products.

Measurement Event Sources May Be Lossy

It is not uncommon to lose measurements somewhere between their creation and ingestion into the event stream. For example, ad-blockers are very good at blocking web analytical events, such that your reports and dashboards are unlikely to be completely accurate. They are, however, often *good enough* for many analytical purposes, especially for building aggregations.

Measurement Events May Power Time-Sensitive Applications

Consider a factory that measures temperature, humidity, and other air quality metrics on its assembly line. One *analytical* use case for these measurements may be to track and identify long-term trends of the factory environment. But an *operational* use case may be to react quickly in the case of divergent sensor values, altering the assembly line throughput or shutting it down altogether if the environmental conditions fail to meet specifications.

In the case of network connectivity issues, it may be the case that the sensors are waiting to publish data that is now 30 to 60 seconds old, while new data piles up behind it. Depending on the *purpose* of the measurement stream and its pre-negotiated service-level objectives (SLOs), it may choose to discard the old events and simply publish the latest. It really depends heavily on whether this data is being used for real-time purposes or whether it's being used to build a comprehensive historical picture that is tolerant of outages and delays, as is the case in web analytics.

Collecting and Using Measurements in Practice

Early in my career, I worked at RIM, now BlackBerry, collecting measurement data from internal developer BlackBerry devices. Basically, whenever a "bad thing" happened on a device, we would generate a dump of measurements, package it up, and send it to our backend servers for further processing. "Bad things" included dropped calls, dropped text messages, BlackBerry Messenger failing to send messages, cellular modem chip resets, along with custom triggers generated by key business applications. The purpose was to collect all of these measurements for both automated generation of problem reports and to aid developers in debugging.

There are a couple of key things about collecting measurements that I learned then and have carried with me ever since. For one, it was extremely important to have a well-defined schema for the payloads under your control, as it made automated post-processing so much easier (null pointers anyone?) and reduced time spent adding special logic to handle malformed data. Secondly, measurement completeness was more important than real-time performance. It wasn't uncommon for us to receive measurement events that were hours, days, or even weeks old—this could be due to test devices that may have been temporarily disconnected, such as an executive flying from North America to Asia, or even just one of our developers getting stuck in a tunnel on their commute to work. But the SLOs that we had issued to our dependent consumers reflected this, and we only started getting hounded for data if we missed our daily report.

Hybrid Events—State with a Bit of Delta

Hybrid events are a mixture of state and delta. It's best to think of these as state events that may contain a bit of information about *why* or *how* something happened. Let's look at an example for clarity.

Consider the following scenario. A company provides an online service that requires a user to sign up before using it. There are several that a user can sign up:

- Via the main sign up button on the home page
- Via an email advertising link
- Using a third-party account (a Google account, for example)
- The account was manually created for them by an administrator

The hybrid data product consumer wants to know *how* the user signed up. For operational use cases, we want to know which onboarding workflow to serve them when they next log in. For analytical purposes, we want to know which of our methods of sign-up are the most common so we can allocate our development resources.

One way to model this sign-up is with a user state event, with a single enumeration indicating the sign-up mechanism (after all, you can only sign up once!). An example of the record would look like this:

```
Key: "USERID-9283716596927463"
Value: {
  name: "Randolf T. Bandit"
  signup_time: "2022-02-22T22:22:22Z"
  birthday: "2000-01-01T00:00:00Z"
  //An enum of (MAIN, VIA_AD_EMAIL, THIRD_PARTY, or ADMIN)
  method_of_signup: "VIA_AD_EMAIL"
}
```

To create the hybrid event, we incorporated what would otherwise be delta events into a single state event. Instead of `signed_up_via_email`, `signed_up_via_homepage`, `signed_up_via_third_party`, and `signed_up_via_admin` events, we flattened them down into a single enum and appended them to the user entity. The domain of values in the user state event needs to account for each of the possible enum settings: for example, we may also want to include information about which third-party sign-in provider was used or which email campaign got the user to sign up.

And herein lies the main issue with hybrid events. The precise mechanism of *how* something came to be in a domain is by and large a private detail, but by exposing this information we also expose the internal business logic process for coupling on by downstream consumers.

The main risk to the consumer of this information is that *how* a user signs up will change over time. This can be both a semantic change in meaning (what exactly is the "main" way to sign up now versus 5 years ago and 5 years in the future?), as well as the expansion or contraction of values in the enum. These semantics are usually only the concern of the source domain, but by exposing these delta-centric seams, they become a concern of the consumer.

There is also the chance (or likelihood) that the producer must update the hybrid event to account for a new means of sign-up: via the company's newly released mobile application (add `VIA_MOBILE_APP` to the `method_of_signup` enum). Consumers of this event must be kept informed of impending changes to this event and must confirm that they can handle processing of this new `method_of_signup` before the event definition is updated. If not, the consumers run the risk of encountering fatal errors during processing, because their business logic won't account for the new type. This is just another aspect of the same issue we saw in "The logic to interpret the events must be replicated to each consumer" on page 161.

However, in this example, the risk to the consumer is low, but not zero, for the following reasons:

- How a consumer signed up is immutable. The real risk lies in the meaning of `method_of_signup` drifting over time. The owner of the event can prevent this by providing very clear documentation of the enumeration's meaning (e.g., in the event schema itself) and adhering closely to its own definitions.

- The logic that populates `method_of_signup` is fairly simple overall, and so is much less likely to drift over time. Registering via an email link is a binary delta—you either registered via the email link or you didn't. In contrast, an enum based on the `userReturnedItemAfterTelephoneComplaint` delta event from earlier in the chapter has many more sequential dependencies and ways of misinterpreting it, and is far more likely to drift in meaning over time.

A hybrid event is a trade-off. The risk you incur in using a hybrid event is proportional to the complexity of the delta you are trying to track and the likelihood that it will change over time (intentionally or not). I advise that you try to further decouple your producer and consumer systems to avoid communicating the details of *why* or *how* data has changed. If you choose to include a delta-type field in your event, be aware that it becomes part of your data contract, and carefully consider the coupling it introduces with the source system.

Notification Events

There's one last event type to discuss before we wrap up the chapter. A notification contains a minimal set of information that *something has happened* and a link or URI to the resource containing more information. Mobile phones are probably the most familiar source of notifications—you have a new message, someone liked your post, or you have enough hearts to resume your free-to-play game—click here to go to it.

An example of a simple behind-the-scenes notification you may receive on your cell phone could look something like the following. Your instant message application sends out a "NEW_MESSAGE" notification, including a status (for icon display), the name of the application, and a click-through URI to the application itself:

```
Value: {
  status: "NEW_MESSAGE"
  source: "messaging_app"
  application_uri: "/user/chat/192873163812392"
}
```

Notification events are often misused as a means of trying to communicate state without sending state itself. Instead, a pointer to the state is sent in the notification, with the expectation that the recipient will log into the source server and obtain the data. The following shows just such an example, where the notification includes that the status has changed, and there is an access URI to find the complete current state:

```
Key: 12309131238218
Value: {
  status: "PARTIAL_RETURN"
  utc_timestamp: "2021-21-13T13:11:42Z"
  access_uri: "serverURI:8080/orders/values/12309131238218"
}
```

At first glance, this seems to be a neat and trim solution: it allows the consumer to simply query for the full public state upon receiving the event without copying or exposing that data elsewhere. One of the major issues is that the event doesn't actually provide a record of the state *at that point in time*—unless the data contained at access_uri is completely immutable (it usually isn't). Since this anti-pattern is usually built on top of a mutable state store, by the time you receive the PARTIAL_RETURN notification, the associated state at access_uri may have already been updated again to a new state.

This race condition makes notifications an unreliable mechanism for communicating state. For example, a sale with status updates of SOLD -> PARTIAL_RETURN -> FULL_RETURN will emit three distinct events, one for each state. A consumer lagging behind on its processing may not be able to access the PARTIAL_RETURN state before it finalizes to FULL_RETURN and thus completely miss that full state transition. To make matters worse, a new consumer processing the backlog will not see any of the previous state—only whatever is stored in the `access_uri` at the current wall-clock time.

A final blow to this design (further cementing it as unsuitable for use in a data product) is that it adds far more complexity. Not only must the domain owner of the notification publish events, but it must also serve synchronous requests pertaining to that state. This includes managing access control, authorization, and performance scaling for both the event-stream producer and the synchronous query API.

Instead, it is far better just to produce the necessary state of the event as an immutable record of that point in time. It takes very little effort and greatly simplifies data communication between domains.

Summary

We covered a lot of ground in this chapter, so let's take a moment to recap before moving on.

Events can primarily be defined as state or delta. State events enable event-carried state transfer and are your best option for communicating data between domains. State events rely on event broker features, such as indefinite retention, durable state, and compaction to help us manage the volume of events. The state design allows us to leverage the event broker as the primary source for our data product, enabling the use of the Kappa architecture while deftly avoiding the pitfalls associated with its predecessor, the Lambda architecture.

Delta events are a common way of thinking about event-driven architectures, but they are insufficient for cross-domain communication. Deltas belong firmly in the camp of the event sourcing and can be invaluable for communication within a singular bounded context. Misuse of delta events occurs when coupling by external parties is allowed. This results in the exposure of internal business logic, processes, and events that should remain private. Simply put, do not use delta events for cross-domain coupling.

Measurement events record occurrences, such as those from human users, distributed systems, and Internet of Things (IoT) devices. Measurement events have their roots in the data analytics domain and consist of a snapshot of the localized state at a precise moment in time. These events are frequently used to compose detailed aggregates or to react to rapid measurement changes.

Both hybrid and notification events should be used with caution, if at all. Hybrid events are primarily a state event but can expose information pertaining to *why* something happened, akin to a delta event. This forms a seam that introduces tight coupling, particularly when the *why* changes with time. Notifications are fairly inconsequential for the domain of data products unless they're misused as a means to communicate pointers to external mutable data. Avoid this at all costs.

In the next chapter, we'll take a look at integrating what we've covered here with existing data systems and how to go about making useful data products for our consumers.

CHAPTER 8

Bootstrapping Data Products

There are two main scenarios for creating event-driven data products. The first involves the creation of data products from existing data sources that are not already in the form of events. As we have alluded throughout the book, these include conventional databases (relational, document, key-value, etc.), cloud filesystems, and even FTP file dumps. In this chapter, we'll be looking at *bootstrapping* these existing data sources into the event-driven data mesh.

The second scenario involves data sources that are in event streams, such as data produced by native event-driven services. Since the data source is already event-driven, creating data products tends to be more a function of formalizing what data is emitted and what data should remain concealed within.

Don't worry too much about getting your first data products exactly right. In fact, it's best to get some experience under your belt, find what works and what doesn't work so well, and iterate from there. You can draw a parallel between building data products and building your self-service platform. "Level 1: The Minimal Viable Platform" on page 99 is a basic but useful platform for getting started with a data mesh that you'll increment and improve as necessary. Think about your first data products in this very same manner—MVP data products that will start you off on your road to real-time, event-driven processing and get the data available for others to use as they see fit.

In this chapter, we'll look at several techniques, including CDC and the transactional outbox, that help you *bootstrap* your data from wherever it is now into useful data products. We'll look at some of the pitfalls and issues that can crop up and some possibilities for solving them. Let's get into it.

Getting Started: Bootstrapping with Connectors

Connectors enable you to easily bootstrap existing data into event streams without having to totally refactor your source applications. The reality is that most systems that create data, such as business entities and operational facts, are also the only sources for it. Similarly, these systems also have thousands (or millions?) of developer hours poured into them—we're not going to be substantially overhauling the system just to get data out of it. Instead, we need to meet the systems where they currently are. as we discussed in "Connectors" on page 101, this is where connectors come in.

Bootstrapping data starts the conversation of who owns the data, the connector, and the transformations between the internal and external data model. Modifications to the internal data domain may break the connector, which breaks the downstream data product's SLAs. Outages and failures tend to drive the need for remediation, resulting in clearer delegation of responsibility.

 When bootstrapping data, be sure it's clear who owns what parts of the process and that each party knows its responsibilities. Renegotiating social contracts underpinning data mesh is as important as technical considerations.

Bootstrapping existing data isn't *just* about sourcing it from the ol' reliable monolith—data can be held in a database of any type, including relational, document, key-value, time-series, streaming, and large files in cloud storage. And though each mode of storage is different, obtaining data typically falls into two main camps: periodically querying the database or tailing a change log. Ultimately, we want to extract the important business data, model it into a form that is useful to the intended consumers, and emit it as a well-formed data product. But before we get into querying and change logs, let's take a look at a common anti-pattern.

Dual Writes

The dual write, as shown in Figure 8-1, is one of the most common things that people do when starting out with event-driven systems. In brief, the application's owner tries to write an update to a database record *and* to an event stream at the same time. However, there is no atomic write guarantee between the two since the application's database and the event stream are completely independent data storage engines.

The tricky part to dual writes is that they work most of the time. As long as you don't have any intermittent failures, you're not going to encounter an issue. But every now and then you're going to encounter an issue—the network may timeout, there may be a bug in your application code, the event broker or database may be intermittently unavailable, etc. If you do not test and monitor for these specific failure modes, you'll often find that a few weeks or months down the line some critical data is missing from your data products. And tracking it back to the source will likely reveal that a short intermittent outage resulted in dropped events.

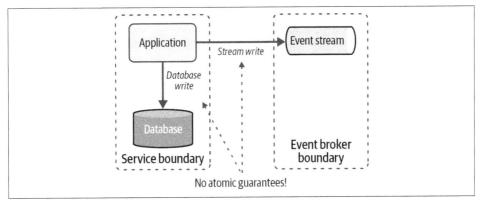

Figure 8-1. Dual write between a database and an event stream

While it's possible to create a coordinating system and introduce a two-phase commit to orchestrate atomic write-guarantees across heterogeneous systems (*https://oreil.ly/WXfMV*), it tends to be complex and can generally be avoided. We'll look at some other options in the remainder of this chapter that can help you find better ways to get your data into event streams.

Dual writes are fine if you don't mind some data loss—for example, if you're writing measurements or other forms of loss-tolerant data to the data product. But for all other instances where you need a complete representation of data in your event stream, you're going to want to use query-based polling, CDC, or the transactional outbox table. Let's take a look at each of these now.

Polling the Database to Create Data Products

Databases are built to be queried, and we can simply periodically query the database, convert the results into events, and publish them to an event stream. Tools like Kafka Connect (*https://oreil.ly/IlT-E*) are purpose-built to provide you with a framework to do just that, with both a suite of off-the-shelf connectors and the means to code and deploy your own.

Query-based polling tends to work best when you can easily identify which records have changed since the last poll. For example, an `updated_at` or `modified_at` timestamp is a common choice, as illustrated by the Kafka Connect JDBC connector (*https://oreil.ly/zJBpQ*). Each time your polling loop kicks off, it uses the highest `updated_at` timestamp that it saw from the last loop and inputs it as the minimum timestamp for the current loop. The returned rows are converted into events and the connector updates its stored `updated_at` timestamp for the next loop.

Event schemas are automatically inferred from the format of the query results. If the upstream database definition is changed, the schema of the events may also change if included as part of the query results.

> Ensure that the ownership and responsibilities of the connector platform, the connector execution, the connector code, and the resultant events' owners are clear. You and your peers should be able to easily identify who to talk to when an issue arises.

There are several major pros for using query-based polling:

Query flexibility
> Databases are purpose-built to serve queries in an efficient manner, so querying the database is an easy and low-effort way to get started moving data from rest into an event-driven data product.

Period flexibility
> You can query as frequently as necessary to ensure your SLAs are met.

Data model isolation
> You gain isolation between the internal data model and the data product model published to the event stream. You can create views and materialized views to denormalize the data model, selecting only the data that needs to be emitted externally.

There are also several major cons for using query-based polling:

Database resource usage
> A database query may be quite extensive in terms of complexity and performance usage. You may find that you cannot get sufficient performance to meet your SLAs due to query complexity, volume of results, or regular operational load. While you may be able to mitigate this issue to some extent with read-only replicas, it does introduce additional costs and complexity, and not all database systems may have this option.

Will miss hard deletes
> Records that have been hard-deleted from a database will not be returned in a query (they're deleted, after all). You may need to convert your database to using *soft-deletes* to track deletions. You will then have to convert the soft delete events to tombstones or else your consumers will need to account for soft deletes on their own. This complexity is overcome by using CDC.

Will miss intermittent changes

Since we're polling at a specific interval, multiple changes that occur between one poll and another will show up as only a single result in the query. If you're trying to capture all changes, you're going to need to look at CDC, as covered in the next section.

One more thing—when you bootstrap data from a database into an event stream, you'll likely need to ingest the entire set of existing data through a process known as *snapshotting*. Taking a snapshot can be a resource-intensive activity because you'll need to load the entire data set from the data under capture into the event stream before moving on to iterative polling loops. While snapshotting a few thousand records will be quick, snapshotting a few billion will necessarily take much longer.

Snapshotting a database is further complicated by its operational requirements. A database is often serving live traffic and cannot be interrupted or put into a state of degraded performance. However, snapshotting most often requires that the table (or data set) in question be *locked* to prevent any new writes while the snapshot process is occurring. Depending on your database implementation and the size of the data, the table may need to be locked for only a moment, or it may need to be locked through the entire snapshotting process. Even if the lock is brief, the database in question may have such a high rate of traffic that any locking is completely unacceptable.

Read-only replicas are a common solution for avoiding operational impediments while snapshotting a database. The snapshot is performed against the replica, whose tables are locked to writes (and replications) until the snapshot is complete. Next, the replica table is unlocked and the queued updates are applied to the database tables. The snapshotting connector then switches over to iterative update mode based on updated_at time. Once caught up to the current time (or as close as is satisfactory), the connector can be switched over to point at the main database, and the read-only replica can be torn down.

Query-based polling and locking of tables is a dated process for bootstrapping data out of a database. While it's still perfectly *valid*, it's becoming more common to use CDC techniques for bootstrapping. Additionally, some recent innovations have made it possible to get eventually consistent snapshots without the need to lock the data source—but this relies on having access to the database's change log. Let's take a look at using CDC and how this solution can provide a better solution to bootstrapping.

Change-Data Capture

CDC is the process of capturing changes from the database's underlying log and converting them to events. What is a log, you may ask? PostgreSQL has a write-ahead log (WAL) (*https://oreil.ly/6kksP*) as part of the process of preserving data integrity—changes made to the database are first written into the durable WAL before being applied to the underlying data model. In the event of a database failure, the WAL, in conjunction with the data preserved to disk, ensures that no information is lost.

Many databases provide programmatic read-only access to these logs—for example, MySQL provides a binary log (*https://oreil.ly/HsHwN*), while others, like MongoDB, provide CDC events in a more direct manner (*https://oreil.ly/wck0V*) instead of tailing the log. CDC provides with many options for constructing your data products.

First and foremost, CDC gives you *everything* about changes made in the database. Your event stream will receive every update to a given row or document, such that you will not miss any transitions. Second, CDC gives you options for what fields to include in your event as well as specific metadata, such as information about the connector or database-specific information. Additionally, you can choose to include both before and after fields detailing the full state of the row or document before the change and the full state after the change. We touched on this previously in "Before/After State Events" on page 154.

For more information on what you can and can't do, you'll need to check out your CDC or database's documentation. Debezium's PostgreSQL documentation (*https://oreil.ly/XFTOp*), for example, includes a full description of all of the data available to you and how to configure your connector to select just what you need.

Some CDC frameworks also provide a way to snapshot certain databases much more efficiently and without locking the table. Normal operational reads and writes can continue uninterrupted with the resultant snapshot being eventually consistent with the current table's state. A Debezium blog post (*https://oreil.ly/HzC57*), explains this innovation. It was based on a paper from Netflix (*https://oreil.ly/0RaUL*) that states:

> DBLog utilizes a watermark based approach that allows us to interleave transaction log events with rows that we directly select from tables to capture the full state. Our solution allows log events to continue progress without stalling while processing selects. Selects can be triggered at any time on all tables, a specific table, or for specific primary keys of a table. DBLog executes selects in chunks and tracks progress, allowing them to pause and resume. The watermark approach does not use locks and has minimum impact on the source.
>
> —Andreas Andreakis and Ioannis Papapanagiotou, Netflix

Live table snapshots that don't block operational use cases are a huge boon for bootstrapping event-driven data products. The snapshot mechanism can be configured to minimize resource usage, leaving plenty of headroom for surges in activity, though it may result in the snapshot taking longer to complete. Meanwhile, behind the scenes, the CDC system interleaves the results from the incremental snapshot queries and the log events together, converting them to events and writing them to the stream.

Once the snapshot is complete, the CDC process continues tailing the database's event log and converting the changes into events.

CDC has become increasingly popular in recent years. Many databases now provide native integration with popular CDC tools, while some cloud service providers have their own fully managed connectors that hook directly from your database to an event stream with little to no work on your part.

CDC offers several pros:

Nonblocking snapshots
CDC can create snapshots without interfering with the normal operations of the source database.

Minimal performance penalty
Capturing events from the database logs won't affect normal operational performance. The CDC service runs on its own dedicated resources and needs only a tiny bit of performance from the host machine in the form of tailing the output logs.

Very low latency
Creating events via CDC is very fast. Changes made to the database tables are typically reflected in the associated event stream within just a second or two.

Compatible with hard deletes
Hard deletes show up in the database log and can subsequently be converted into deletion events. Deletions can also be modeled as tombstone events, such that entities that are no longer relevant can be completely removed from both the event stream and the downstream consumers' materialized views (Figure 3-12).

There are also several cons to using CDC:

Exposure of the internal data model
The internal data model is directly reflected in the database log and thus in the extracted events. Isolation of the underlying data model must be carefully and selectively managed, unlike query-based updating, where views can be used to provide isolation. Perfectly valid schema changes to the internal database model will be reflected downstream in the event schema and may cause breakages for your consumers.

Highly normalized event streams
Internal model coupling results in event streams that mirror the source relationships. Normalized database tables result in normalized event streams and often require consumers to denormalize data before use. While joining events across streams of data is possible, it remains more complex and less efficient than resolving the joins inside a relational database built for this purpose. We'll discuss this in more detail in "Denormalization and Eventification" on page 186.

CDC connectors are a significant improvement over query-only connectors. They reduce the barrier to bootstrapping data products and make it easier to get started with event streams. However, there still remains room for improvement, particularly as regards further isolating the internal data model from that which is published to the external world. Let's take a look at the transactional outbox pattern next.

Change-Data Capture Using a Transactional Outbox

A *transactional outbox* is a dedicated database table that acts as a temporary output buffer for events to be written to the event stream. When you update your *internal domain model*, you select only the data that you want to expose to the outside world and write it to the outbox. Then, a separate asynchronous process, such as a dedicated CDC connector, consumes the data from the outbox and writes it to the event stream. Figure 8-2 shows the end-to-end process.

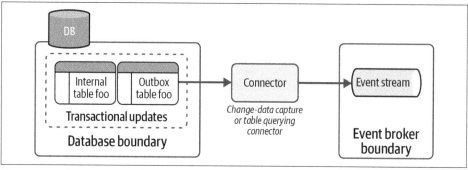

Figure 8-2. Getting events from a database using a transactional outbox and a dedicated connector

The transactional outbox pattern is a more invasive alternative to simply capturing existing internal model tables because it requires altering both the database and the existing code. First, we'll need to create an outbox for the data we want to turn into events. The most common option is to create one table per domain entity and enforce data types based on the table's schema.

Secondly, we'll need to modify the application code by wrapping relevant internal entity updates in a *transaction*. Your database must support transactions for this pattern to work. Within the transaction, you will need to select the data you want to expose and write it to the outbox. Finally, you can close and commit the transaction. Updates to the internal domain model either happen atomically or not at all.

The Python code of Example 8-1 illustrates an atomic update of an EcomItem in a MySQL database. The internal model update is executed prior to the transactional outbox update, though both are wrapped within a single transaction for consistency.

Example 8-1. Atomic update of the internal model and the transactional outbox

```
try:
    conn = mysql.connector.connect(host='localhost',
                                    database='python_db',
                                    user='abellemare',
                                    password='definitelynotpassword')
    conn.autocommit = False
    cursor = conn.cursor()

    # Perform the internal domain model update
    internal_model_update = """
        Update EcomItem
        set price = 1299.99
        where id = 4291"""
    cursor.execute(internal_model_update)

    # Select the subdomain of the internal model we want to write to
    # the transactional outbox
    internal_sub_model_query = """
        Select name, price
        from EcomItem
        where id = 4291"""
    cursor.execute(internal_sub_model_query)
    name_and_price = cursor.fetchone()

    if (name_and_price == None):
      raise Exception("Unexpected missing record. Can't get name_and_price")

    # Insert the selected data into the outbox
    outbox_insert = """INSERT INTO EcomItem_Outbox (id, name, price)
                    VALUES (4291, %s, %s)"""

  # Pass the name and price in to replace the query wildcards
  cursor.execute(outbox_insert, name_and_price)

  # Commit the internal and outbox updates atomically
  conn.commit()

except mysql.connector.Error as error:
    # reverting changes because of exception
    conn.rollback()

finally:
    # Close the database connection
    if conn.is_connected():
        cursor.close()
        conn.close()
```

In this example, we first update the EcomItem price to $1299.99. Next, we select the name and price from the table we just updated—we are forced to query name at the very least since we want to produce a state-based event that contains all of the current state for the item we just updated. Finally, we compose the event and write it into the EcomItem_Outbox format, as shown in Table 8-1, just as we would any other relational database table.

Table 8-1. EcomItem_Outbox table definition

id	name	price	Datetime
4291	"Fancy Laptop"	1299.99	2022-06-22 11:33:12

There are two things to note about our SQL table definition. One, we are using NOT NULL for each of the mandatory fields that we expect in our event. Inserting a new event into the outbox will fail unless all constraints are met. Two, we're populating the Datetime field by default using CURRENT_TIMESTAMP if it is not provided by the application's code. You may use this timestamp as part of the schema for your event, or you may use it to populate the event's metadata to indicate when the event was created.

Ensure that the internal model, the transactional outbox table model, and the event schema are compatible. Use pre-deployment to ensure that internal model updates correctly transcribe to the outbox table model and event schema to avoid easily preventable runtime errors.

Obtaining data from the outbox can be accomplished using exactly the same techniques we've talked about earlier in this chapter: either by directly querying the outbox via a polling connector or by using a CDC connector.

You'll also need to *clean up* the outbox table from time to time. If you're using a query-based polling mechanism, cleanup is as simple as deleting each of the rows from the outbox as they are written to the event stream.

Debezium offers a full-featured outbox to Kafka topic mechanism known as the outbox event router (*https://oreil.ly/rl_he*). It prevents propagation of DELETE events from outbox tables but can still send out tombstones by setting route.tombstone .on.empty.payload to true. Additionally, it will automatically clean up the outbox table to prevent it from growing unbounded.

You should use off-the-shelf, freely available products such as Debezium whenever possible to simplify your data mesh journey. A great many developer hours and testing hours have gone into hardening it, and it'll provide you with a far more robust solution than most home-grown solutions. You'd be better off spending your efforts on building your data products and establishing a self-service platform than on trying to reinvent CDC solutions.

Some database storage engines allow you to create a table that doesn't save the data to the database but instead writes it to the database's log. MySQL's BLACKHOLE storage engine simply discards all writes but preserves all INSERT, UPDATE, and DELETE operations to the log. The BLACKHOLE storage engine requires minimal disk IO and it absolves you of having to clean up the table since nothing is ever written to it.

There are a number of pros to using a transactional outbox:

Internal data model isolation
The outbox provides isolation of the internal data model from the external data model, allowing both to evolve independently.

Exactly-once outbox semantics
Transactions ensure that both the internal model and the outbox data are created together or not at all. A failure to update the internal model will prevent an event from being written to the outbox, but so will the reverse. Test your code and exercise each code path.

Early schema enforcement
The outbox table schema determines the event schema. All events written to the outbox will comply with the event stream schema requirements, significantly reducing the chance for errors.

Denormalized data
You can choose to denormalize data during the transaction, such that downstream consumers do not have to join the data themselves. We'll go into this more in "Denormalization and Eventification" on page 186.

Producing events via a transactional outbox also has several cons:

Database must support transactions
It bears repeating that your database must support transactions. If it does not, you'll have to choose a different data access pattern.

Application code updates
The application code must be updated to enable this pattern, which requires development and testing resources.

Outbox write may fail the transaction
A transaction failure due to a write issue to the outbox will also cause the write to the internal model to fail. This may be unacceptable for your use case, but is easily prevented by comprehensively testing your code and validating your transactional updates prior to deploying your code.

Database performance impact

> The performance impact to the data store may be significant, especially when large quantities of records are written, read, and deleted from the outbox. This could have a negative impact on response times and customer experience.

The outbox provides an abstraction layer between the internal domain model and the external event model. We can use this layer to further denormalize and restructure our data to suit the needs of our data product consumers. Let's take a closer look at this aspect.

Denormalization and Eventification

One of the main goals of normalizing data is to minimize redundancy. However, normalization tends to work best when the stored data is attached to a processing engine that can easily resolve and denormalize it as needed.

Some consumers will want only a really simple event-driven data product with a minimal amount of information. Others may want one that has a lot of extra information about the entities and request extensive denormalization to get the flattened result. It is more challenging to deal with denormalization in a set of event streams than it is a set of tables, so it's a very good idea for us to carefully consider what *should* and what *should not* go into a denormalized event stream.

For example, consider the following relational ecommerce, merchant, and inventory data model. The EcomItem shown in Table 8-2 has a foreign-key relationship (merchant_id) to the Merchant table in Table 8-3. EcomItem also has a primary-key relationship (inventory_id) to the Inventory table in Table 8-4, which contains the quantity of items currently in stock.

Table 8-2. EcomItem table definition

id	name	price	merchant_id	inventory_id	updated_at
4291	"Mirage Block Set"	1299.99	4	44291	2021-03-22 13:05:00

Table 8-3. Merchant table definition

id	name	premium_partner	updated_at
4	"Devin's Trading Cards"	true	2019-08-12 19:00:37

Table 8-4. Inventory table definition

id	quantity_in_stock	updated_at
44291	3	2021-01-09 07:33:13

Though this model is simplified, you'll commonly find similar models in many online ecommerce marketplace platforms—think of businesses like Amazon, eBay, Alibaba, Etsy, and Shopify, to name a few.

`Merchant.premium_parter` specifies if the merchant has signed on and paid for the premium business experience: better advertising deals, preferred advertisement placement, and preferred search result placement. Additional operational features include the ability to upload videos and additional pictures per `EcomItem`, create item bundles, and offer AI-generated custom deals to find satisfactory price points for cost-savvy customers. Most of these services require the `EcomItem` information to serve to the end customer—but they each also require the merchant information for branding and display purposes as well as determining if the merchant requires `premium_partner` treatment.

Due to the highly relational nature of these streams, each consumer service will need to do the same foreign-key joins of `EcomItem` to `Merchant` to get the data into a proper format for its business use cases. Figure 8-3 shows a small subset of consumers that each need to consume and join each event stream.

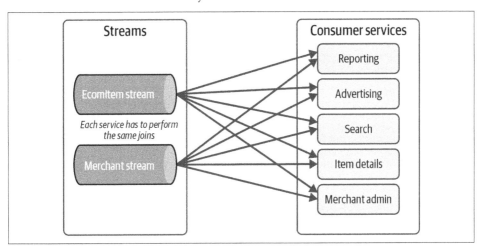

Figure 8-3. Each consumer has to join the same data to determine premium partner status

There are some significant downsides to this arrangement:

Repeated processing

Each consumer needs to execute these joins on its own. Each client will have duplicate code and use a similar amount of resources for the joins. For small data sets, it may be inconsequential, but for processing data at scale, including dealing with partitioned event streams, it can become quite expensive in terms of processing resources.

Significant client code constraints

Each consumer client needs to be able to resolve the joins on its own. The majority of scalable streaming join solutions, such as Apache Kafka Streams, Flink, and Spark, are Java virtual machine (JVM)-based, but some also support Python and SQL. However, there is no first-class support for other popular programming languages such as Go, JavaScript, Ruby, Rust, and so on. You may also resolve joins by using a dedicated relational database, but your client may require a document, key-value, geo, or time-series database instead.

Eventification is a implementation pattern for converting, denormalizing, and remodeling highly relational streams into a format that is more suitable for event-driven consumers. In DDD terminology, we're creating an aggregate root (*https://oreil.ly/sCYr7*) as an event. Our earlier evaluation of using `EcomItem` identified that we'd also need to include the information about the `Merchant`, particularly its `premium_partner` status. In the same vein, we can consider `Inventory` information to be outside the scope of the aggregate root, as it's seldom used by our consumers outside of one or two specific use cases.

There are several factors to consider when performing eventification:

Consumer requirements and use cases

Increasing ease of use is the chief goal of eventification and requires knowledge of your consumers' needs. The aggregate root provides the essential core information in an easy-to-access and readily available format so that your consumers do not have to individually and repetitively do the work themselves.

Degree of denormalization

How much you denormalize the data depends on the consumer use cases as well as the size of the data and the frequency of change. We'll cover this in more detail in "What Should Go In the Event? And What Should Stay Out?" on page 192.

Keys for joining on related streams

As we discussed back in "Event Stream Keying and Partitioning" on page 82, the event keys you select during eventification should enable easy joining on other event streams. Ensure your event is keyed in a way that makes it compatible for joining to related streams that are not required by most consumers. `Inventory` would be an example of such a stream.

Structuring the external data model

Eventification provides you with the opportunity to convert and standardize data as well as conceal portions of the internal data model from downstream coupling. The resultant denormalized and remodeled schema becomes a part of the the data product's API.

There are two main areas where you can implement the eventification pattern: when writing to the outbox table and when using a dedicated service to join normalized streams. Let's look at each of these in turn.

Eventification at the Transactional Outbox

One option is to select internal model data and denormalize it prior to writing it to the outbox. If we take the sample code from "Change-Data Capture Using a Transactional Outbox" on page 182, we can tweak it to add a query to select and join the EcomItem and Merchant data, then remodel it into the outbox table's external model. Example 8-2 shows a code sample for remodeling the relational data into a more suitable denormalized event format.

Example 8-2. Eventification prior to writing to the outbox

```
...
    # Assume that we have just updated the internal model
    # Next, we select fields from the internal model and denormalize it
    # by joining against the Merchant table.
    internal_model_query = """
     select e.name, e.price, m.name as merchant_name, m.premium_partner
     from EcomItem as e, Merchant as m,
     join on e.merchant_id = Merchant.id
     where e.id = 4291"""

    cursor.execute(internal_sub_model_query)
    result = cursor.fetchone()

    # Create the insert statement for the outbox table
    outbox_insert = """
      INSERT INTO
        Enriched_EcomItem_Outbox (id, name, price, merchant_name, premium_partner)
      VALUES (4291, %s, %s, %s, %s)"""

    cursor.execute(outbox_insert, result)
    # Commit the internal and outbox updates atomically
    conn.commit()
...
```

In this code snippet, we create an entry for Enriched_EcomItem_Outbox in response to the application creating or updating the data for EcomItem.id=4291. The internal relational model remains encapsulated within the database, while the outbox provides a data model more suitable for event-driven consumers. But what about when the Merchant data changes? Consider a single merchant that decides to pay for premium partner status.

Any previously created `Enriched_EcomItem` events must *also* be updated to reflect the current premium status. A failure to do so means that the event stream is permanently inaccurate and no longer reflects reality, which will likely cause problems in how downstream consumers react to and process that merchant's data. Simply put, if you're going to denormalize data, you're going to need to update the event whenever *any* field changes. This remains true regardless of *how* you go about denormalizing data, be it from the inside with an outbox table or with a dedicated eventification service, as we shall see in the next section.

A transactional outbox table works really well as a low-overhead way of isolating the internal and external data models. If your source data resides inside a relational database, it's very easy to rely on the database engine to quickly and efficiently denormalize data into an event-friendly format instead of leaving it up to each consumer to handle. By making event streams easy to use, you improve the data product user experience for your consumers, helping them get on with the business of using the data instead of just struggling with it.

However, it's not always possible to build an outbox table into a database, let alone denormalize your data within the transaction. Aside from databases that simply do not support transactions, legacy systems with no active development as well as those with strict performance requirements may not be suitable candidates. Whenever a transactional outbox isn't feasible, it's best to look at eventification in a dedicated service residing outside of the source domain. Let's take a look at that now.

Eventification in a Dedicated Service

Eventification *outside* of the source database requires a purpose-built microservice or stream SQL application. For example, Figure 8-4 shows a high-level overview of a dedicated eventification service joining `EcomItem` and `Merchant` data together to form a single enriched stream for downstream use. Event-driven processing technologies like Apache Kafka Streams and Flink provide simple high-level frameworks for joining data together.

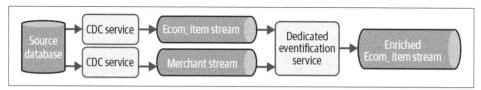

Figure 8-4. Eventification within a dedicated service using CDC event streams

Take Kafka Streams for instance—if we take the same `Merchant` and `EcomItem` models from the previous section, we could create a simple Java application to join two into a single state-based event. The code would look something like Example 8-3, though you may also prefer to look at a full-featured example (*https://oreil.ly/m7Qb_*):

Example 8-3. A Kafka Streams microservice joining and enriching `EcomItem` with Merchant data

```
public Topology buildTopology(Properties envProps) {
    //Configuration code not shown for brevity
    //Create the Serdes
    MerchantSerde merchantSerde = new MerchantSerde(...);
    EcomItemSerde ecomItemSerde = new EcomItemSerde(...);
    EnrichedEcomItemSerde enrichedEcomItemSerde = new EnrichedEcomItemSerde(...);

    //Create the application builder and create two tables.
    KStreamBuilder builder = new KStreamBuilder();

    //A KTable is the materialization of a state-modeled event stream
    KTable<Long, Merchant> merchantTable =
        builder.table(Serdes.Long(), merchantSerde, merchantTopic);
    KTable<Long, EcomItem> ecomItemTable =
        builder.table(Serdes.Long(), ecomItemSerde, ecomItemTopic);

  ecomItemTable
    .join( merchantTable,
         EcomItem::getMerchantId,
         new EcomToMerchantJoiner() )
    .toStream()
    .to(enrichedEcomItemTopic, Produced.with(Serdes.Long(), enrichedEcomItemSerde));

    return builder.build();
}
```

The `EcomToMerchantJoiner` class is shown in Example 8-4. It specifies how to join the two entities together by extending the ValueJoiner class (*https://oreil.ly/L775t*).

Example 8-4. The EcomToMerchantJoiner definition used by the joiner service to populate the EnrichedEcomItem

```
public class EcomToMerchantJoiner implements
    ValueJoiner<EcomItem, Merchant, EnrichedEcomItem> {
    public EnrichedEcomItem apply(EcomItem e, Merchant m) {
        return EnrichedEcomItem.newBuilder()
                .setId(e.getId())
                .setName(e.getName())
                .setPrice(e.getPrice())
                .setMerchantName(m.getMerchantName())
                .setPremiumPartner(m.getPremiumPartner())
                .build();
    }
}
```

Or if you want to simplify it even further, you can rely on something like Flink SQL to do the same thing using a pretty simple SQL-like query. Example 8-5 shows a much simpler way of joining the same entities together using Flink SQL (*https:// oreil.ly/FD_r1*).

Example 8-5. A Flink SQL version of the eventification service

```
SELECT *
FROM EcomItem
INNER JOIN Merchant
ON EcomItem.merchantId = Merchant.id
```

The SQL layer makes it even easier to resolve streaming joins and denormalize entities, and it opens up the self-service platform capabilities to non-JVM developers. A simple SQL layer is ideal for the purposes of eventification since we're *not* executing any complex business logic, simply resolving joins and emitting enriched entities.

There are some significant advantages to using an external eventification microservice, including:

- Reduced demand on the database's resources
- Simplification of the source domain's application logic

However, there are also some challenges to handle:

- Synchronizing changes to the database tables, the connectors, and the eventification microservice
- Finding a robust stream joiner framework; there are only a few options, and they're all JVM-based
- Arguing over ownership of the microservice (hint: the domain owner is responsible for building useful data products)

Regardless of whether you choose to denormalize your business entities inside the source database, outside the database using a purpose-built microservice, or at the consumer itself, it's important to consider the impact on your consumers. Focus on making your domain data as easy to use as possible for them and work together to come up with an agreeable solution.

What Should Go In the Event? And What Should Stay Out?

There is a fine balancing act for determining what data to include and what data to exclude in an event. There are several factors that influence this decision. Consumer needs, the update frequency, the data size, and the resultant total load are all considerations.

Let's consider an extension of our ecommerce example. `EcomItem.inventory_id` specifies a relationship with the `Inventory` data (Table 8-4), indicating how many of the item are in stock.

Every time the inventory changes, say due to a sale, a return, or a received shipment, the inventory domain can emit a new state event with the updated inventory. For products that change extremely frequently (think a Black Friday "door crasher" sale), you could end up with a veritable barrage of inventory events. While it remains a valid option to publish only a sample of the events, you lose accuracy about exactly what happened while increasing the latency for an event occurring and a consumer's ability to react to it.

If we join the `EcomItem` with `Inventory` (`EcomItem.inventory_id = Inventory.id`), then every single `Inventory` update will trigger a corresponding join on the materialized `EcomItem` table. This can be quite a lot of events, and consumers that don't care about the inventory quantity will be spammed with inconsequential updates.

Similarly, consider a `Reviews` aggregate data product that contains the top 100 reviews for a given `EcomItem`. While this data may not change frequently, joining it with `EcomItem` means that every single time we update either `Reviews` or `EcomItem`, we also re-emit the entire payload containing the top 100 reviews. Just like with frequent updates, many consumers may not care at all about the contents but still need to contend with the very large data size coming through the stream.

Finally, you may discover that you have both data with a very high rate of change from one stream and data with a very large payload size from another stream. Joining the two means that you'll now have *a lot* of data with a high rate of change. This can cause a compounding high load on your event broker, your eventification process, and your consumers.

You'll need to find your own appropriate balance for your data products by talking to your consumers and working with your federated governance team to come up with some guidelines for helping your peers make similar decisions.

As a general rule, avoid joining in data that changes frequently or is a very large size. You may be better off leaving those components out of the enriched event and letting your consumers choose to integrate it into their own service. Of course, you can always create a new data product that includes `Inventory` as part of `EcomItem`.

Slowly Changing Dimensions

Let's continue with our ecommerce example. We saw that there are many `EcomItems` for a given `Merchant`, and if we want to denormalize the `EcomItem.merchantId` data, we'll have to join against `Merchant`. However, `Merchant` data may not change for a very long time, though it certainly *could* be changed at any moment.

This type of data is known as a slowly changing dimension (SCD) (*https://oreil.ly/4liIP*), which is usually static but can change unpredictably. SCDs have long been the provenance of data warehouse and data lake models, deliberately modeled for handling large analytical queries that span wide time ranges. But how do we model them? And what impact will they have on our data products?

Although there are numerous SCD subtype classifications, the two most relevant for data products are the `Type 1` and `Type 2` data model approaches. Let's take a closer look at each of these to see how they affect the way we build our data products.

Type 1: Overwrite with the new value

With `Type 1` modeling, only the most recent value is retained. Say we have a merchant *without* premium status, as per the account shown in Table 8-5. If this merchant decides to pay for premium status, we'd need to produce a new entity event to overwrite the previous one.

Table 8-5. Type 1: The first state event of Devin's Trading Cards

id	name	premium_partner	updated_at
4	"Devin's Trading Cards"	false	2010-04-22 23:15:01

Table 8-6 shows the results of the updated merchant entity event with `premium_partner=true`.

Table 8-6. Type 1: Updated premium status for Devin's Trading Cards

id	name	premium_partner	updated_at
4	"Devin's Trading Cards"	true	2019-08-12 19:00:37

The previous record is no longer required, and the event broker can compact away the old event at a later date. While you may choose to retain the data for a longer period of time, `Type 1` dimensional modeling doesn't account for a history of changes—this is where `Type 2` comes in. Let's take a look.

Type 2: Append the new value

With `Type 2` dimension modeling, the changed value of `Merchant.premium_partner` is appended to and integrated with a single new state event. The event consumer has access to the previous versions of that field and can use it for determining what the entity looked like at a specific point in time. For example, building an analysis of engagements over time, based on the merchant's `premium_partner` status. Similarly, the same event provides the latest `premium_partner` value for operational purposes, ensuring that the merchant receives the proper premium treatment by the endpoints serving its content.

Table 8-7. Type 2: Updated Merchant data is appended to the event, complete with version IDs for previous updates

id	name	premium_partner	updated_at	version
4	"Devin's Trading Cards"	false	2010-04-22 23:15:01	0
4	"Devin's Trading Cards"	true	2019-08-12 19:00:37	1

Both the Type 1 and Type 2 SCD modeling strategies can power both operational and analytical use cases. Operational cases typically only care about the most recent value—when a change occurs, the operational system can react to the new state event and act accordingly. Analytical systems tend to need a history of data, including *when* the fields changed, so that they can build accurate aggregates based on those properties.

The default selection for a state event is usually Type 1 modeling—your application publishes only the latest data, leaving it up to the event stream to provide the history of previous values. Your consumer model needs to *opt in* to maintaining the previous values within its own domain data store.

Type 2 models *force* the consumer to consider the impact of SCDs as the state event data model contains the full history of previous values. If the consumer wants only the latest value, it still needs to explicitly select out of the history. Thus, while Type 2 models are more verbose and require a bit more overhead for consumers to use, they reduce the chance of a consumer overlooking the history of changes.

Before we wrap up this chapter, let's take a look at one more necessity: getting data out of files stored in cloud storage (HDFS, S3, etc.) and into an event stream.

Bootstrapping Cloud Storage Files to an Event Stream

Connectors let us acquire data from an event stream, recompose it into files, and write it to cloud storage so that it can connect up with existing batch-based pipelines. But what if we want to do the reverse and take data stored in cloud storage and load it into an event stream? Migrating to an event-driven data mesh doesn't happen overnight, and bootstrapping existing data at rest into event streams is an important option.

Batch-computed data has long been a staple of many data analytics platforms. Data is usually structured as a set of large files in a columnar format such as Parquet. This data is periodically computed by a *scheduled job*, which reads an input data batch, processes it, and writes a resultant data batch back out to cloud storage. Batch-computed data is also typically partitioned based on time, often aligned on natural periods such as hourly, daily, weekly, and yearly.

There are a few main ways that we can get data at rest into event-driven data products. These options include:

Refactoring the job to produce events

This option requires that you have an event-producer client available in the language of your job. You simply include the event-broker producer code within your job, such that it writes to both the cloud storage *and* the event broker. This approach does introduce a dual write risk, as covered earlier in "Dual Writes" on page 176.

Writing to broker after job completes

Since you're already using a scheduled batch job, you can simply add a step to read the new data, convert it into events, and write it to the event broker. One of the big benefits of this approach is that you can use any technology or language you want. Your initial job could be an old Apache Pig (*https://oreil.ly/KsVC9*) workflow that you don't want to touch with a 10-foot pole, while your event-broker job could be a very simple and lean application in another language. The downside is that you'll have to read the data back into memory again, which increases both cost and latency.

Using a connector

You can also use a connector to simply listen for the creation of new files and folders. For instance, this Kafka Connector (*https://oreil.ly/KRaL9*) can read files formatted with Avro, Parquet, CSV, text, JSON, or binary/byte information from an S3 bucket and write the data into a Kafka topic. This option allows you to rely on your existing batch jobs to create the data and on the self-service connectors to bring that data into your event streams. From here, you can start remodeling the data into well-formed data products.

Bootstrapping your data into event streams is a big step toward an event-driven data mesh. These bootstrapped streams are usually too slow for operational use cases, but they usually suffice for transitioning batch-based analytical jobs over to streaming applications. Your consumers will be able to use a single streaming protocol for all of their data sources instead of having to mix and match various cloud and stream protocols.

Once you have bootstrapped your batch data into an event-driven data product, start sourcing feedback from your consumers. Once they get used to using streams, they may ask that you bring the data product up to real-time speed. By following data as a product principle, you can plan out the work, prioritize it, and build a roadmap of data pipelines to port over to real-time streams.

Summary

A data mesh is built upon the foundations of your existing systems and data stores. Bootstrapping data from existing sources into preliminary data products is an essential step in building a successful data mesh. Many existing systems and data sources are simply going to remain as they are, with no real chance of extensive refactoring and re-creating into something new. It's critical that we can meet these systems where they are and get the data out, with minimal trouble.

Connectors play a pivotal role in the self-service bootstrap process. They fulfill the basic goal of extracting data into a stream form, where you can start negotiating the finer points of the data product: latency, event size, denormalization, and update frequency. Precisely what you put in and what you leave out varies depending on the consumers' needs. Talk to them, work with them, and iterate on your products.

But what if you don't want to provide all of your data products via event streams? What if you can't, due to third-party APIs and the sheer gravity of existing batch-processed data? The next chapter takes a look at these questions and discusses how you can integrate nonevent-driven data products into your data mesh.

CHAPTER 9

Integrating Event-Driven Data into Data at Rest

Event-driven data products provide exceptional flexibility for consumers but they may not be suitable for every use case. Existing systems and dependencies play a big role in any architecture, and shifting to a data mesh depends on supporting existing use cases while simultaneously promoting incremental change. Many systems, processing jobs, and computations rely heavily on data at rest, particularly those in the analytics domain.

In this chapter, we'll focus on integrating event-driven data into data at rest. We'll look at the Medallion architecture and the role it plays in modern data analytics workflows. We'll explore strategies and trade-offs for determining when to convert data from a flow of events into a batch of files at rest. Finally, we'll take a look at a real-world example to tie theory into practice. Let's get into it.

Analytics and the Medallion Architecture

Change works best by first meeting your users where they are. Batch-based data analytics pipelines and workflows are extremely common in most industries, and many organizations have invested heavily in batch-based data engineering, data science, data analytics, and reporting workflows. "Data Products Are Multimodal" on page 31 introduced the idea of multimodal data products, but until now we've been working primarily in event streams. While they're often the best choice for driving both operational and real-time analytical use cases, we still need to integrate with our batch-driven workflows.

Figure 9-1 shows the typical end-to-end distribution of a data analytics pipeline using the *Medallion terminology* introduced in "Data quality classifications" on page 79.

Generally speaking, data engineers extract (E) data from a source, load (L) it into a staging ground, and perform any necessary initial transformations (T)—an ELT process. This *bronze data* then feeds the next step of the pipeline, further cleaning up and standardizing the data, and composing it into a higher-quality *silver data* format.

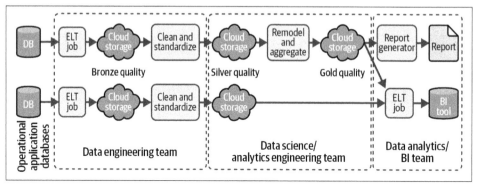

Figure 9-1. A typical batch data processing workflow spanning multiple teams

Silver data may then undergo further processing and aggregation into a *gold* data set, representing the highest level of quality, most often built to serve a singular business function. It may also be used as is to build business-specific aggregations that are not part of the Medallion-graded data sets available for others to use.

Data analysts rely on the well-modeled silver and gold data (along with SLAs and support), ingesting it into business intelligence (BI) and analytical tools. Here they perform analyses, compose reports, and influence data-driven decisions.

Integrating event-driven data products into existing batch-data workflows is an acid test to see if your data mesh is actually the foundation of a new means of data communication or simply another ad hoc mechanism serving only a limited subset. Figure 9-2 illustrates how to integrate event streams as the source of the batch-data workflow instead of using the existing purpose-built code.

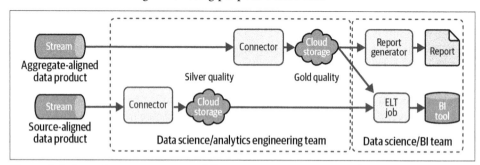

Figure 9-2. Powering an existing workflow using event streams and connectors

You may first notice that the data engineering team is no longer to be seen—they're now off building the data mesh's self-service platform and supporting its adoption. Additionally, the work of ensuring data quality and standardization has been pushed upstream to the data product owner. A data scientist or analytics engineer may yet still be involved in building the data products, though their participation is not mandatory.

The remaining duties of the data product users in Figure 9-2 involve creating and configuring the connectors that sink the event-driven data into cloud storage. The self-service platform should provide them with everything they need to serve their own connector use cases, as discussed back in "Connectors" on page 101.

Event-driven data products let us remove custom-built, point-to-point data pipeline jobs that often connect one system to another. But it requires that we provide the data in a format and cadence that the consumers are already expecting, based on the existing jobs. Let's take a look at this in the next section.

Connecting Event Streams Into Existing Batch-Data Flows

Data flows are rarely simple and clean—they're often layers upon layers of unsatisfactory compromises, "temporary" solutions that become permanent, and hacky workarounds that end up supporting critical business use cases. The codebase is littered with "TODO—Temporary hack! Fix this!" and ancient backlogged work tickets detail essential changes that need to be implemented, written by people who often no longer work at the organization. In short, data flows look a lot like any other application's code—but they're also spread across multiple jobs incorporating diverse frameworks, languages, and databases.

Just as building up a data mesh's self-service platform is an incremental process, so is connecting data products to existing batch-based data flows. First and foremost, you're not going to refactor and replace years of extensively crafted business logic any time in the near future. And in many cases you shouldn't even try. It's not worth trying to change things that work *good enough* just for the sake of change. Instead, you should focus your efforts on the critical business use cases that are either sensitive to bad data or that require results much more quickly than existing data flows can support.

Integrating event-stream data products requires consuming the events, converting them into a suitable format (e.g., Parquet), and sinking them to the cloud filesystem. Our integration strategy is to replace the batch-created data sets with those new ones derived from our purpose-built data products. But that's not the only thing we'll need to do. In fact, it's probably best if we just take a look at an example to see how this strategy can work in practice.

Consider an ecommerce and advertising platform company that offers its business partners pay-to-promote advertisements. Business partners create advertising campaigns, allocate budgets, and bid against one another for the right to display their advertisement to the end user. The advertising platform company must provide both billing results and insight reports for their business partners. After all, they want to know how effective their advertisements are, who is clicking on them, and how much they owe.

However, there is a problem. Business partners routinely receive bills from the finance team that do not match the engagements that the analytics team is reporting. For example, a partner may be billed for 1,200 unique engagements, yet their analytics report shows only 1,154 unique engagements. What gives? Let's take a look at the data flow that has built up over the years to get a sense of the complexity and where errors can creep in.

Figure 9-3 shows the end-to-end process, beginning with ingesting and parsing raw data from the analytics server logs (1). The data is extracted (2) from the server logs every 15 minutes, transformed into a rough unstructured batch file, and loaded into the cloud filesystem (3) as basic HTTP log events. Next, a periodic job that kicks off every 15 minutes processes the *previous* 15 minutes' worth of data, cleans it up, standardizes the fields, and emits it into distinct data sets (4) depending on the user actions (e.g., click, view, scroll).

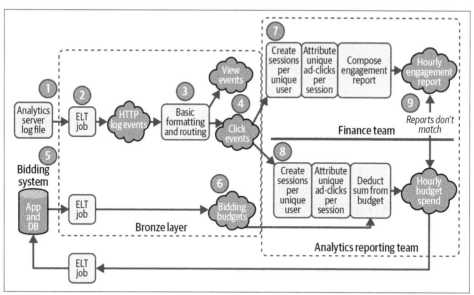

Figure 9-3. Divergent batch-computed engagement and budget reports

Thus, we want to take batches of server log events that look like the following:

```
42.241.222.101 - - [22/Jan/2021:23:27:13 +0000]
"GET /ad/131241232?a=click&b=29&uid=A675E09&device=iPhone12
 HTTP/2.0" 200 5316 "https://sample.domain.com/"
"Mozilla/5.0 (Windows NT 6.1) AppleWebKit/537.36
 (KHTML, like Gecko) Chrome/72.0.3626.119 Safari/537.36" "2.75"
```

And convert them into batches of well-structured data with a schema that looks like the following table:

long	string	datetime	int	string	enum
adId	userId	datetime	bidInCents	url	device
131241232	A675E09	22/Jan/2021:23:27:13 +0000	29	sample.domain.com/	iPhone12

Next, we source data from the advertisements and budgets database (5) and ELT it into a data set available on the cloud filesystem (6). This job kicks off every 60 minutes and creates a full snapshot of budget data, including any rows that haven't changed since it last ran.

Both the finance team (7) and the analytics reporting team (8) begin their work from the same set of click events—a good practice and one we'll return to later in this chapter. But each team acts independently of the other, and this is where differences in reporting (9) can creep in, causing confusion as to which report, if either, is correct.

First up: user-session definitions. Each team computes user-sessions in its own way. While both teams know that the advertisements are only unique within a session, the precise business logic that each team uses to compute the sessions varies. One common definition relies on a 30-minute timeout—the session will remain open so long as the user performs some sort of activity within that 30 minute period. *But* it's also common practice to cut off a session at the midnight mark, closing the session at midnight and opening another immediately after.

The financial team respects the midnight cutoff—after all, it's a good way to get another billable event in and it's also a pretty standard (though dated) practice. Meanwhile, the analytical reporting team simply uses a 30-minute timeout. That's discrepancy number one.

Second up: unique-user attribution. The analytics team started a long time ago and has been struggling to identify unique users through a period of many years. Account IDs, phone numbers, device IDs, and, more recently, iOS and Android advertising IDs have complicated the legality and logic of identifying and tagging unique users. In contrast, billing for pay-for-promotion advertising is fairly new—but they believe that unique identification is simply a matter of using the device-advertising ID. After all, "everyone knows" that's what you're supposed to do.

The end result is that both teams have well-defined business logic that passes their unit tests, identifies unique users according to their test cases, and outputs a reasonably accurate result. Sure, they may not match, but they're off by only a few percentage points. That's discrepancy number two.

It's no wonder that there are some problems, and while there are many other and more nuanced areas where issues can creep in, these two will suffice for our analysis. And while I have no doubt that you're probably already envisioning a solution, let's back up and take a look at where things went wrong through the lens of data mesh.

Through the Lens of Data Mesh: What's Going On?

First, these original data sets are not data products. They are not purpose-built, they are not created with a well-defined structure, and there is no requirement to meet the specific requirements of downstream consumers. Logs are simply extracted and parsed into a batch of data with best-effort. Structure is added after the fact, by people that neither own the data nor own the application that emits it.

Second, there is no domain ownership. How does a user go about asking questions about what the data means? While you may be able to talk to the team that owns the advertisements and budgets database and get an answer out of them, you're going to be hard-pressed to get a clear explanation of bootstrapped nginx logs from the application developers that wrote the frontend service. There's no data product owner. There's no official point of contact. Communication to downstream users is based almost entirely on tribal knowledge and manual investigation of currently registered data pipelines. Changes to upstream data are detected by downstream consumers when their jobs break.

Third, the lack of domain owners and data product owners has cultivated a protective and siloed culture. Why rely on upstream data sets when they're prone to sudden and unexpected breaking changes? It's best to get your data from as close to the source as possible so that others can't break it on you. Rely only on your own team's work and minimize dependencies on others. While your company's colleagues are certainly well-meaning, you *know* your direct teammates and work together tightly to ensure that *your* data flows work.

The end result is a reactive, protective, and isolationist culture, not caused by maliciousness or negligence, but rather the complete absence of codified duties and roles.

Through the Lens of Data Mesh: How Do We Solve It?

Let's look back at Figure 9-3. I suspect that one of the first things you thought of was that we should push the duplicate logic in (7) and (8) back upstream to do session-building and unique user identification in one common location. If so, your instincts are correct. Let's take a look at Figure 9-4 to see what this same workflow may look like when powered by an event-driven data mesh.

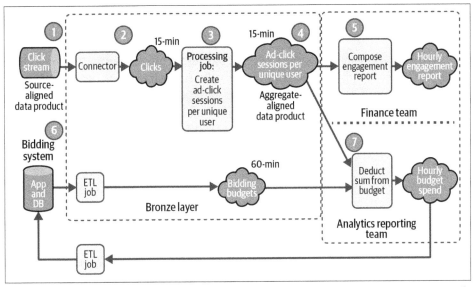

Figure 9-4. Integrate with event-driven data products and push common computational logic upstream

The first thing to note is that click events (1) have been promoted to a source-aligned data product and made available through an event stream. This was a fairly easy conversion since all it took was to natively produce the click events from the analytics server whenever they occurred. No need to parse nginx logs when the data was already fully available. The domain owner accepted the mantle of data product owner and committed to creating a click-event data product. Data that starts in motion simply stays in motion, and we can just slow it down to a 15-minute batch format file when we connect it (2) to cloud storage.

The schema for the *source-aligned click-stream data product* is specified as follows:

```
Key: String, //user_account
Value: {
  user_account: String,
  utc_timestamp: Datetime,
  ad_id: long,
  page_id: String,
  bid_in_cents: int
}
```

Next, we got representatives from the finance and the analytics reporting teams together to work out the common unique-user and session-creation logic. We extracted the existing business logic from their domains, unified it, and came up with a common definition for both. As their use cases require both sessions and uniqueness, both steps occur within a single process (3) and the data is emitted in batch every 15 minutes (4). Note that if we decide to treat the data in (4) as an aggregate-aligned data product, we will need to assign a data product owner and ensure we follow all common data product management and metadata requirements.

The hourly engagement report (5) has been updated to draw from the common data in (4). While the hourly engagement report still remodels the data according to its own requirements, it does not make decisions about unique user or session classifications. The bidding system (6) remains untouched for now. It continues to receive hourly budget spend inputs from the analytics reporting team.

The budget report (7) continues to draw on hourly snapshots of data batch-created by the ETL job attached to the advertisements and budgets database. Why not upgrade to an event-driven data product? Because in the constraints of our example, there is simply no business need to make the change—the batch-based budget file creation works well enough and isn't causing any problems.

Implementing a data mesh is incremental, and it's important to identify the problem areas that benefit most from data as a product. While in an ideal world we would want to have every source a well-formed data product with no duplicate business logic anywhere, the reality is that we need to pick and choose where to invest our time and efforts.

Balancing File Sizes, SLAs, and Latency

There are a few technical issues to address when integrating event-driven data products from streams into batches, particularly when writing to a cloud filesystem. Here are some of the main factors you're going to need to consider:

Performing data format conversions
Event schemas are generally unsuitable for modern big data processing, so you're going to need to convert your events into blocks of files with a suitable schema format. While Avro and Protobuf remain common choices for event streams, columnar formats such as Parquet tend to be the most common for cloud filesystems because they offer significantly higher performance processing for batch workloads than do the event-centric formats of Avro and Protobuf.

Handling schema evolution
Schema evolution adds some complexity to the picture. Typically, each event evolution requires its own file because the columnar format schema is determined on a per-file basis. Thus, version 1 events go to the version 1 file, while version 2 events go to the version 2 file. The more schemas you have in an event stream, the more files you're going to end up with in the cloud filesystem.

Balancing file size versus latency

Your downstream consumers can't use the data until the files are written to the cloud filesystem. If you want to minimize the delay between an event occurring and it showing up in the cloud filesystem, you'll to end up with a large number of small files written frequently. Your latency will be quite low, but applications that want to load and process this data will be slow and inefficient. One major issue with cloud filesystems is that they need to reconcile schemas for all the data that they're loading—and by having a vast amount of small files, you end up with a lot of overhead for processing. Alternatively, you may choose to write files only when they've reached a certain size (e.g., 100 MB) or a certain time boundary (e.g., hourly), with the trade-off being a longer delay until the data is available.

Implementing post-connect file amalgamation

A common technique is to frequently write many small files (e.g., every minute) to ensure a very low latency for specific batch consumers. Then, at the end of a time boundary (e.g., every hour), you kick off a new batch job to recombine the many small files into just a few large ones. As a final step, you update the cloud filesystem's metadata entry (such as Apache Hive) to redirect future batch jobs to the amalgamated files, substantially increasing their performance.

Integrating events from streams into data at rest requires careful consideration of your data product's use cases. If your organization has existing batch-computed data, you can usually repurpose the existing conventions and SLAs for your own. If people are used to having their data updated every 30 minutes, it's fine to start with a 30-minute update cadence as your SLA. Data format conversions and schema evolution are similarly not new to event streams, and you may find you can draw inspiration for handling these issues from your existing data pipelines and workflows.

Budget Blues: A Tale of Overspending

Migrating to a common `Ad-Click Sessions per Unique User` data product has worked well—the discrepancies have disappeared and there have been no more business partner complaints. However, there's still an issue that we've simply chosen to ignore until now.

Currently, ads are served to an end user via a bidding process. Business partners are presented with information about the end user, such as age, location, and interests, and can submit a bid for the right to serve the end user an advertisement based on relevance. The winning bidder's advertisement is then pushed to the end user's UI. However, the business partners are charged only in the event that the end user *clicks* on the event. Viewing it is simply not enough.

Ads are served on a wide variety of properties and across many systems, and we don't know that an ad has been clicked on until after we've already served out the ad and loaded the page. At that point, we can only wait to see if the end user clicks on it.

Currently, the budget spend report is computed in hourly batches. Every hour we export the data from the Bidding System to get the new and updated bidding budget facts. The consequence of an hourly cadence is that the absolute earliest that we can compute budget fulfillment is one hour—in practice, it's going to take longer than this, as we'll also need to account for the processing time and the time to ETL it back into the Bidding System. Our goal is to shorten the time between aggregating clicks, computing the remaining budget, and informing the Bidding System about which budgets should and shouldn't be allowed to bid anymore.

As it currently stands, we often have business partners whose budgets have technically already been filled, but the Bidding System has not yet received the hourly report with the updates. In the meantime, the algorithms continue to use the business partner's budget entry to aggressively bid on advertisement placement, out-bidding other business partners who *do* have budget left, but have bid a lower amount.

The end result is lost income because we cannot bill a business partner for additional ad-clicks beyond their explicitly stated budget limit. Instead, we need a much tighter loop to reduce the time between a budget fill and the Bidding System deactivating the associated bids.

Figure 9-5 illustrates the evolution of our architecture to one that will help us meet these goals.

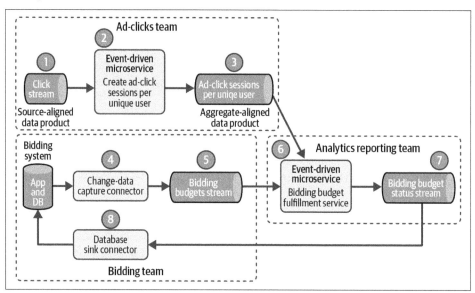

Figure 9-5. Further evolution of the budget fulfillment system to use event-driven data products

The source-aligned click events (1) are aggregated into sessions by a purpose-built microservice (2), resulting in an aggregate-aligned data product (3). This stream has been deliberately promoted to data product status by the Ad-Click Team domain owners because it powers not only the workflow in Figure 9-5, but other applications and processes as well (not shown). The aggregate data product has the following schema:

```
Key: String, //user_account
Value: {
  user_account: String,
  session_start: Datetime,
  session_end: Datetime,
  //Map of unique ad_id clicked and the corresponding bid amount
  unique_ad_id_to_bid_price_in_cents: Map[Long, int]
}
```

unique_ad_id_to_bid_price_in_cents is simply a map that contains the unique set of ad_ids mapped to a bid amount. For example, consider the following snippet:

```
unique_ad_id_to_bid_price_in_cents: Map[Long, int] =
  [ [77883344, 29],
    [12937163, 14],
    [01845672, 0]
  ]
}
```

The user in this session clicked on three ads. The winning bid for each ad was 29 cents, 14 cents, and 0 cents, respectively. The last value indicates that no one was willing to pay any money for the right to serve that ad.

Further to Figure 9-5, the Bidding Team has set up a CDC connector (4) to emit a stream of facts detailing the Bidding Budgets (5). This enables the Bidding Budget Fulfillment Service (6) to accommodate new, modified, and canceled budgets as soon as the updates occur.

Note that the Bidding Team *did not* establish the CDC stream of Bidding Budgets as a data product. It remains a private event stream within the team's domain and is only visible and usable by the service (6) owned by the Analytics Reporting Team. If Bidding Budgets becomes more widely needed, the Bidding Team can revisit the decision to promote it to a data product, complete with all the governance and support requirements.

The Bidding Budgets entities have the following schema:

```
Key: long, //budget_id
Value: {
  budget_id: long,
  ad_id: long,
  amount_in_cents: long,
  remaining_amount_in_cents: long,
```

```
    maximum_bid_in_cents: int,
    start: Datetime,
    end: Datetime
}
```

For simplicity in this example, each `budget_id` is attributed 1:1 to a specific `ad_id`. Each budget contains the full budget amount, the remaining amount to spend, and the maximum bid, all expressed in cents. Because most campaigns are run against a date range, there is also a start and end date for further bidding eligibility differentiation.

The `Bidding Budget Fulfillment Service` (6) materializes `Bidding Budgets` into its own state store. It also materializes each `Ad-Click Sessions Per Unique User` session, assigning the unique session clicks to each budget. The service checks every new fact for changes, be it another attributed click, closing out of the session, or a modification to the budget, and updates the allocated budget spend accordingly.

To reduce the potentially extremely high frequency production of `Bidding Budget Status Stream` events (7), only one update per `budget_id` is emitted every 60 seconds, *unless the event indicates a fulfilled budget*. In that case it is emitted immediately to reduce the end-to-end latency between when a budget is filled and when it is removed from paid promotion.

Finally, the `Bidding Budget Status Stream` events (7) are integrated back into the `Bidding System` via a `Database Sink Connector` (8), which converts the events into database UPSERT commands. This completes the budget calculation loop, providing the `Bidding System` with nearly real-time data about the fulfillment of its budgets, drastically cutting the unrecoverable bidding costs in comparison to the legacy-based hour-plus feedback loop.

The `Bidding Budget Fulfillment Service` (6) remains owned by the `Analytics Reporting Team` due to legacy reasons. After all, they computed the batch report before, and therefore they still remain responsible for it now. Social change may come slowly, and perhaps one day the `Bidding System` will be able to compute its own results inside its own domain. Accepting and focusing on incremental change remains a key part to adopting a data mesh.

Technical change may also come slowly. While there are two event-driven microservices in this example, the `Bidding System` remains firmly a nonevent-driven application that simply needs access to a stream of data. "Connectors" on page 101 are a vital tool for bridging the gaps between existing nonstreaming systems and event-driven data products and really make incremental changes both possible and practical.

If you decide to support nonstreaming data products, you'll have to consider how they fit in alongside your event streams. Let's take a look at that now.

Extending the Self-Service Platform for Nonstreaming Data Products

You'll need to choose which nonstreaming data products to incorporate into your platform based on your unique use cases. "Data Products Are Multimodal" on page 31 introduced the multiple modes that a data product may have, including batch-computed files, request-response APIs, and event streams. But what counts as a separate data product and what counts as a *mode* of a single data product? How do you represent it in your self-service platform? Let's take a look at a few factors that influence our options:

Ownership
> The person with the role of data product owner is the sole individual who can own a data product. There cannot be multiple owners. If a single data product is to be made available via multiple modes, there must be a common owner that can guarantee support and consistency for each of the modes.

Technical boundaries
> "Change-Data Capture" on page 179 is very useful for extracting events from databases, particularly when the database owner is not willing or able to provide the business data as a natively produced event stream. In this case, the CDC stream is a separate data product with ownership that is separate from any request-response data product provided by the source database owners. Keep in mind that if the owner of the transaction system is not willing or able to work with the CDC stream owner, you will have at best a Band-Aid solution prone to failed SLAs and broken data models. It's essential to work together to maintain data product continuity and schema compatibility whenever possible.

Alignment and composition logic
> A batch of 60-minute sales aggregates derived from a stream of 1-minute sales aggregates are two separate data products, despite both being aggregations of the same data.

A multimodal data mesh should identify the relationships between data products, presented either as modes of the same product or via their relationships to other products. For example, you may choose to put SQL-queryable and event streaming as two modes of a single data product. The metadata entry, as found through your self-service discovery tooling, would look something like Figure 9-6.

Regardless of how you display your batch-created data products, you'll need to ensure that you have first-class support for discovery, compute, and publishing. There are no shortcuts or easy outs when integrating multiple data product modes, which is why it's always easier to start with as few as possible and expand your selection only as necessary.

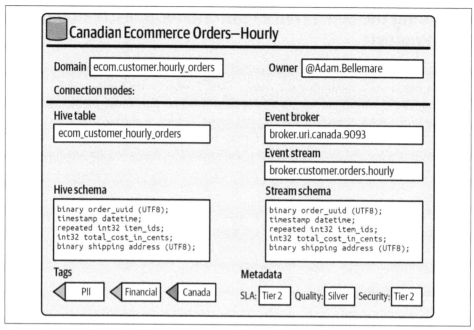

Figure 9-6. A self-service UI showing both a Hive table and Kafka topic mode for a single data product

Summary

A data mesh is inherently multimodal, and data products can be provided via a variety of means. Event streams remain the best option for the majority of data products, as it is far easier to power both operational and analytical use cases through a stream than a batch of files at rest.

Batch-based compute has been the predominant way to build data pipelines and provide analytical results since the inception of big data. Replacing the batch-computed files with an event-stream source is one of the most common first integration steps. A sink connector recomposes the event stream into a batch of files, matching the format and aggregation requirements. The end result is a set of event streams that can power real-time operational and analytical systems while simultaneously powering the sources that power the existing batch-based data pipelines.

How you choose to classify a batch of files created by a sink connector is up to you. You may choose to consider it to be two modes of the same data product, but you must ensure singular ownership and responsibility. You may also choose to consider them different data products. An event stream may be source-aligned, while the data sunk to the cloud storage may be an hourly aggregate-aligned data product. Lineage and dependency tracking remain important for discovery of closely related data products.

Self-service platform support for multimodal data products remains a key requirement. Aside from discovery, you'll need to ensure that your data mesh users can register their services as consumers and manage the publication of their own nonstreaming data products. Metadata requirements will vary from product mode to product mode, as will the means of secure access, information handling, scaling, and evolution. Ensure that representatives from your federated governance team have carefully evaluated and prioritized the features necessary to support your data product modes.

There's one more subject to deal with as we approach the end of the book. Distributed systems must often deal with eventual consistency, and a distributed and asynchronous event-driven architecture is no exception, as we will see in the next chapter.

CHAPTER 10

Eventual Consistency

Eventual consistency is one of the main concerns that people have with distributed systems and event-driven data products. But eventual consistency can mean different things to different people. For example, an application developer may be using a database that doesn't offer consistent read-after-writes, such as in the case of a large distributed database or when using event sourcing to build up state. In an event-driven data mesh, we're more concerned with the effects of multiple consumer systems subscribing to event-driven data products and how to work with individual consumers each reading data at their own rate.

There are people who have been looking at, working on, and thinking about eventual consistency for quite a long time. Pat Helland is just such a person and has written an excellent piece that collates insights and opinions (*https://oreil.ly/gym1j*) from numerous thought leaders on the subject.

> Since Doug [Terry] coined the phrase eventual consistency in the Bayou paper in 1995 (*https://oreil.ly/LmBEu*), I was interested in his perspective. When he defined eventual consistency, it meant that for each object in a collection of objects, all the replicas of each object will eventually have the same value. Then, he said: "Yeah, I should have called it eventual convergence."
>
> —Pat Helland

Helland goes on to discuss a definition by Peter Alvaro, from his 2015 PhD thesis "Data-Centric Programming for Distributed Systems" (*https://oreil.ly/85Yli*):

> A system is convergent or "eventually consistent" if, when all messages have been delivered, all replicas agree on the set of stored values.
>
> —Peter Alvaro

Both Terry and Alvaro converged (ha!) on the same definition of eventual consistency, putting the focus on independent replicas eventually converging on the same set of stored values. We'll keep using the "eventual consistency" terminology, but keep in mind we're really talking about *convergence of data*.

A consumer that is continually materializing an event stream can easily provide you information on what data it *does have* in its data store, but it can't tell you what it *doesn't have*. Because the data store is eventually converging, it may tell you it doesn't have a piece of data when queried, but then immediately receive and process that data in the very next clock cycle. However, a consumer does have the ability to tell you if it is *caught up* to a *given offset*, and we can use this knowledge when resolving questions about convergence.

Many of the questions and concerns regarding eventual consistency in the event-driven world stem from a concern that "bad things" will happen because of it. It's often used as a threatening term, listed in the cons section of a architectural rundown treatise. But it doesn't have to be a con, because there are only a few big things to watch out for. There are two main reasons why two independent consumer services may have not yet converged:

A service is lagging behind
> All of the data in the data products is consistent, but one service is simply lagging behind on its consumption, processing, and storage of the data.

A data product is lagging behind
> The data within the data products is *not* consistent, but each service is fully up to date with the latest data. For an event-driven data product, either the producer has failed to write the data or the event stream may be unavailable. In the worst case scenario, the data product would lag so far behind that it may violate its SLAs.

Note that these two options are not mutually exclusive. It is entirely possible that one or more consumers' services *and* one or more streams are both lacking data. Although convergence will eventually bring consistency, it will only be fleeting until again our services and data products are temporarily lacking data and in need of processing to catch up.

The thing is, eventual consistency isn't really as impactful as you may think, and we'll examine some good ways to handle it later in this chapter. The vast majority of time your event-driven services will be up to date with the latest events and effectively within the same time bubble, much like regular old synchronous services. This is one of the reasons why I think it generates a lot of apprehension—you never know *when* your service is going to start lagging and shifting into its own time bubble, and if it does, how to detect it and what to do about it.

The crux of the matter is that eventual consistency really only starts to become an issue when one independent context asks a synchronous question to another independent context, with no guarantees that their internal data sets are synchronized.

Let's take a deeper look at how contexts, event time, and boundaries relate to convergence.

Converging on Consistency, One Event at a Time

Each event-driven processing instance effectively exists in its own time bubble, with its internal time based solely on the event timestamps that it has consumed and integrated into its state. The vast majority of event streams provide data in an incrementing offset and timestamp order, though certainly the events can also be out of order (more on this later in the chapter). Thus, while the consumer service is free to look at the wall-clock time, its own internal time is based completely on the timestamps of the events that it has consumed.

Take Figure 10-1, which shows two independent consumers reading from a single event stream. Each service is fully independent, chugging along on processing the events, applying business logic, and saving the data in state.

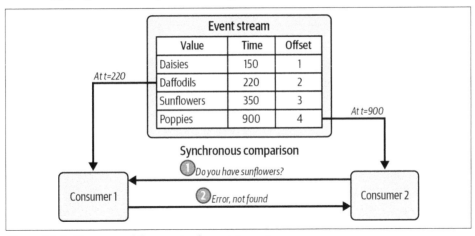

Figure 10-1. The crux of the eventual consistency issue

The results that each service provides to the outside world, be it by request-response API, an output event stream, or other means, are very unlikely to be precisely synced with similarly materialized data in another service. This is where discrepancies and confusing results can creep in. Consumer 2 at time t=900 asks Consumer 1 at t=220 for its copy of Sunflowers data. Having never even heard of Sunflowers, all Consumer 1 can do is reply with Error, not found.

In contrast to event-driven data product consumers, think of two synchronous services that communicate over request-response APIs and that own and store all of their data within their own services. When one of these services issues an API call to another, it's not thinking, "I wonder what time it is over there."

In addition to using offsets or incrementing event IDs, you may choose to use the event time, representing when the event occurred, to account for convergence. In cases where events are created via CDC, event time is typically defined as the time the data was upserted into the source database.

The assumption is that these two services are in the *same time bubble* and have the same wall-clock time or are close enough that we don't care. This assumption is largely true, because a synchronous service doesn't buffer work in a large queue to get to at a later date like an event-driven system does. Rather, it handles or fails the requests immediately and returns the most up-to-date data that it has available, representing the current wall-clock time.

Let's take a look at a simple shipping and delivery company. In this model, a driver is an employee who can drive a truck. We need a driver for each truck we want to send out for deliveries, otherwise that vehicle isn't going anywhere. How would the assignment of a driver to a truck be affected in synchronous and asynchronous systems?

Figure 10-2 shows a set of synchronous services on the left residing in a single time bubble. All data is maintained in a fully consistent state, such that a point-in-time query will return a complete list of both trucks and drivers at that instant.

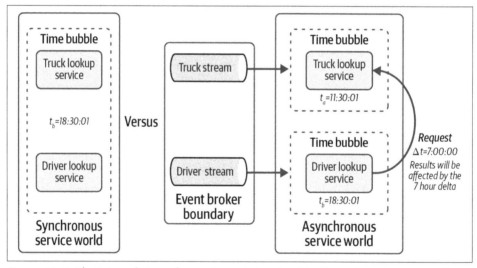

Figure 10-2. The internal time of a service is determined by the union of its input offsets

Meanwhile, the services on the right are sourced from event streams. In this example, notice that there is a time lag of 7 hours for the truck lookup service, as it has fallen behind in materializing its incoming events. If the driver service asks the truck service to provide a new truck for assignment, it may not have any available, despite new trucks having been published to the event stream. The service must *catch up*; otherwise, it'll give nondeterministic results.

Though it may seem tempting to require that all drivers and trucks be registered together in a single atomic event, it unfortunately doesn't work out for our business use cases. There are many professional drivers who do not own their own truck and there are companies that lease trucks but do not provide drivers. Each must be registered independently.

 System times are largely synchronized to within milliseconds, thanks in large part to frequent synchronizations with Network Time Protocol (NTP) servers. If you require perfect time alignment between two events, you should refactor your domain to put the critical time-sensitive data into the same singular event. Otherwise, you'll have to plan to handle eventual consistency.

While a lagging service is one source of convergence issues, a second source is an event stream that is not yet updated despite all consumers being fully caught up. This is especially problematic when the events in one stream are related to the data in the other stream, such as by a foreign or primary key. Let's do away with lag, latency, and processing time and just pretend for a moment that you have a service that can instantly consume and materialize any number of events, from any number of streams. In the case of Figure 10-3, we have a `Flower Pot Builder` service that is consuming and joining data from two streams to determine what's the best soil to put in the pot for each flower type.

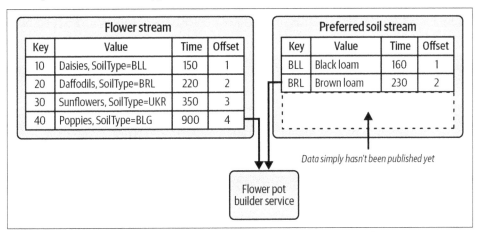

Figure 10-3. The data in the source event streams hasn't yet converged

Although the service is fully up to date with each event stream, there are no matching records in the `Preferred Soil` stream for `Sunflowers` and `Poppies`. The `Flower Pot Builder` service will need to wait until it can obtain the matching `Preferred Soil` events for those flowers. There are many reasons why these two streams may be out of sync: they may be sourced from different domains, they may have different SLAs, the producer for `Preferred Soil` may be down, the network may be partitioned, or the event broker may be unavailable, to name just a few.

While it's possible that the data may simply not exist *at all, anywhere*, in many cases we expect data to exist based on certain business rules and properties. For example, `Preferred Soil` has a foreign key relationship with `Flowers`, so we can expect any `Flower` record with a populated `Soil Type` field to have a corresponding `Preferred Soil` record. The records for both `Sunflowers` and `Poppies` are missing, however. This data may yet show up, but as this example shows, even fully up-to-date consumers of the existing event streams may be inconsistent with upstream systems through no fault of their own.

The eventual consistency issues we face basically boil down to consumers that have not yet converged and event streams that have not yet converged. Next, let's take a look at a few more detailed practical scenarios and some strategies for dealing with eventual consistency.

Strategies for Dealing with Eventual Consistency

You have two main options when dealing with eventual consistency, either between services or within a single service. The first option is to simply wait for the state to become consistent, such as waiting for the event that completes the join, ends the session, or finalizes an aggregation. This option works equally well when querying an external service that gives you an inconsistent answer—you can simply wait and retry the query again at a later time. You may also choose to output an incomplete result that indicates a lack of consistency, but you will need to update it with the final results when you receive the appropriate data to act.

The second option is to give up after a certain period of time. *Giving up is final.* If the missing event you were waiting for shows up a split-second after you give up, it's still too late to do anything with it. If the server you were querying finally has the result you need, it doesn't matter as you won't be notified or sent a follow-up request. Timeouts are indicative of a failure in your data product SLAs that needs to be addressed.

Let's take a look at several strategies for dealing with eventual consistency.

Prevent Failures to Avoid Inconsistency

Data meshes are distributed, and as such, we must contend with all of the problems of distributed systems. Systems will crash. Networks will partition. Event streams will be unavailable. Cloud storage will be inaccessible. Amazon S3 will go down, resulting in a host of bored software developers creating memes. Figure 10-4 showcases the areas of major concern in a basic data product creation and usage workflow.

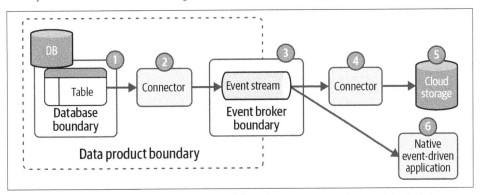

Figure 10-4. Intermittent issues can cause delays in convergence to consistent states

Each of the numbered components can suffer its own range of failures, causing a delay in the events arriving at their final destination. The database (1) can suffer from crashes, network unavailability, and even disk failures. The connectors (2 and 4) can similarly crash, throw exceptions, or fail to connect to the broker (3), a cloud data store (5), or a native event-driven consumer (6).

You can seek to reduce your chance of failure through good DevOps practices, monitoring, resource scaling, and testing. It's also important to ensure your consumer services have sufficient resources to scale up and stay up to date with the latest events and that any outages or failures on your producer side are identified and fixed quickly, in line with your agreed upon SLAs ("Tiered service levels" on page 78).

Use Event-Driven Data Products Instead of Request-Response Server API Calls

Consider the business use case where we need to assign a truck and a driver to a delivery route. Instead of storing the truck data in one service, the driver data in another, and the route in a third, we simply publish the data to streams and leave it up to each consumer to use it as they see fit. We don't make API calls across multiple of systems, but instead ingest it into a single service, with a single temporal bubble, purpose built for composing the driver route assignments.

Adding data sources in the form of event streams is a fairly simple extension for your service. Figure 10-5 shows the addition of a `package` stream that helps improve the selection of trucks and drivers to assign to a route, emitting a waybill to indicate the distribution of packages.

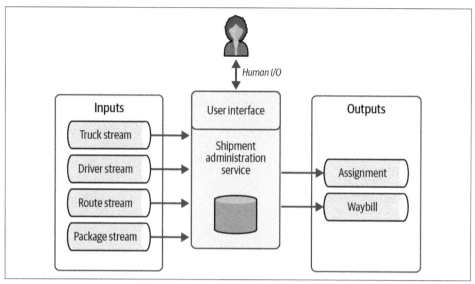

Figure 10-5. Sourcing data only from event streams provides eventually consistent data for making business decisions

The consumer service has full visibility into the timestamps of each event, along with the ability to ask the broker if it's caught up to date on any given input stream. Thus, the consumer service *can figure out for itself* if it's in a converged state or not and act accordingly.

The human user in Figure 10-5 can act as part of the business logic that assigns trucks and drivers to routes. The shipment administration system can propose assignments, and the human user can either accept or reject those assignments, or override them as she sees fit.

You must ensure that your consumer service logic can correctly handle data arriving in any temporal order *between streams and partitions*. For example, consider a driver that owns their own truck, is the sole driver for it, and won't drive any other truck. It is possible that your consumer service may receive the truck registration event before the driver registration event or vice versa. Your business logic must account for the data arriving in any order, as both are perfectly valid use cases and could be equally likely to happen.

Stream-processing frameworks like Kafka Streams, Flink, and Spark accommodate asynchronicity by default, which makes them ideal candidates for processing event-driven data products for more complicated purposes. Simple event-stream consumer clients seldom have the capabilities to account for asynchronous temporal arrival and thus offload the complexity of managing it onto the consumer. Ensure you have a good understanding of what your consumer clients do and do not offer you.

Expose Eventual Consistency in the Server Response

You've probably seen this strategy employed before. Ever book a flight, a hotel, or rent a car online, and see the little spinning icon saying "Please wait to confirm, do not hit refresh"? Exposing the eventually consistent nature of a system is common practice in the world of UIs, and we can adopt this strategy for use in server-to-server communication.

There are a few options for this strategy:

Halt serving when lag exceeds threshold
> The queried service monitors its own consumer lag of its input event stream offsets, and only serves data if the lag is lower than the threshold. Instead of returning the data, your service returns a message indicating that it is not ready, such as an HTTP 503 (Service Unavailable). You may also choose to return a Retry-After response (*https://oreil.ly/qqMro*) indicating when the service should be ready based on typical throughput processing. If the consumer lag is less than the threshold, the service will serve the queries and provide a response as normal.

Provide stale data to requester
> Your service can provide a response to the requester regardless of how stale the data is. You can include a response in the payload indicating that the data is stale and make it clear that it's up to the requesting client to choose how to proceed. In some cases a client doesn't much care about stale data—in other cases it's critical, and the client may choose to hold off further processing until it can have its request served with up-to-date data.

Provide a callback API
> Clients can register to have their request handled when your service is no longer lagging and receive a callback with the requested data. This strategy is more complicated to implement because either the client will have to block and wait for the callback or it'll need to implement context switching logic to work on other tasks until the callback occurs. Additionally, your service will need to buffer and handle the callbacks, plus provide SLAs for its users.

But what about event time? Can you use time since your last new event to detect if you're lagging? For some cases you can, but in many others you cannot. Let's consider an example.

A source-aligned data product of user `click` events provides hundreds or thousands of events per second. Based on historical trends, if more than a few minutes go by without a new `click` event, your service can fairly safely infer that it is lagging behind, or that the source data product has violated its SLA.

However, consider a source-aligned compacted data product of user entity state, where each event represents the user's current state. New events are published only when a user updates a field, when a new user is registered, or when an existing user is deleted. While there could be many hours (or days) between events, the data in the stream remains valid and any service that has consumed the stream remains converged and up to date. It just simply hasn't received any new events (because there are none!), and so cannot tell you any more information than the event time of the last event.

It is easy to falsely infer lag by using the event time of the last-processed event alone. And while you *can* use event time to infer lag in cases of high-frequency updates, it remains unsuitable for many other use cases. You would do well to rely on offsets to detect and expose lag whenever possible.

Plan for New Services and Reprocessing of Data

When you bring up a new consumer service, you're going to need to decide if it's going to process historical data or if it's just going to start from the current wall-clock time. Processing historical data is pretty straightforward for a new service: you simply point the consumer offsets to the start of the input streams and let it go! The service will consume and process the events as rapidly as possible, materializing state, computing results, and writing resultant output events as necessary. The nice thing about new services is that no existing services are querying them or dependent on their output yet, so you don't need to worry about inadvertently breaking anything.

Reprocessing historical data for existing services, however, can be more nuanced. Look to your business use case to figure out how much of the historical data you'll need. For some streams and application use cases, you can restart your consumers to read from an offset based on time (e.g., the last 30 days worth of data). Other streams and use cases, such as creating the fully materialized state of all users from the previous section, require consuming the entire history of the compacted `User` event stream.

One common reason for reprocessing historical data is because you had a bug in your consumer system and it did some bad things. Exactly what these bad things are can vary from service to service but fall into two main buckets: either you served bad data to others via synchronous request-response, or you wrote bad records to an output event stream. With the former you're out of luck—there's nothing you can do to go back and unserve the data. With event stream outputs, you do have a few options, but it all depends on how the output affects your consumers.

 Fixing issues due to bad data is *not* solely the provenance of event-driven data products. Bad data can also be communicated via request-response APIs, batch-computed files in cloud storage and direct database queries. The science of fixing the user impacts of bad data lies heavily in proper workflow design, identification of failure modes, and implementing recovery options ahead of time.

Options to remedying bad event data include:

Publish corrected data to the data product

Produce new events with the corrected data and publish it to the existing output event streams. You may need to rewind your input offsets as part of this process if your service is itself driven by event streams. Your consumers will obtain the corrected events, and it's up to them how to handle reconciliation. This option is suitable when the repaired event streams aren't driving consumer use cases that can't be reversed. For example, a suitable use case involves publishing the corrected translations of product reviews shown on an ecommerce website.

 A bug in a data product may require a formal declaration of an incident. Depending on the severity of the bug, the data product contents, and the importance of the data, you may need to notify all of your consumers and start an incident resolution process. This remains true regardless of whether the data was served via direct requests or via an event stream.

Purge and re-create the data product

In some cases you'll need a much more involved solution to handle the previous bad data. Not all workflows are easily reversible, and you may instead need to create an entirely new stream, deprecate the old one, and move all of your consumers over to the corrected data. This is a heavyweight option that requires stop-the-world coordination, but may be the only choice when further dissemination of bad data is unacceptable.

Finally, if you find you need to reprocess event streams from the start of time (it was a *really* bad bug!), consider the impact to downstream consumers. They'll have to consume every single event that your service writes to the output topic. If you find yourself in a spot where you're going to be doing this, be sure to warn them and coordinate accordingly. You may need to throttle your output, and they may need to horizontally scale their consumers to account for it.

Synchronize Data Products on Time Boundaries

Event-stream data products serve a wide range of consumer use cases, including, of course, sinking the data via a connector to cloud storage. Big data analytical processing by the likes of Apache Spark, Flink, Presto, or BigQuery relies on well-formed, batch-created data, often in the form of a Parquet, ORC, Avro, or other big data format. Many organizations have developed extensive data engineering, science, and analytics pipelines relying heavily on batch data. A well-built data mesh should meet the needs of these people where they are and not force them to move onto event streams.

An event stream is a continuous flow of data, whereas you can consider cloud storage data as data at rest. This means that we really need to be cognizant about how we write the data to disk and should adhere to any partitioning standards already in place by the big data folks. It's quite common to partition data based on timestamps, be it in 1-minute, 5-minute, 30-minute, or 1-hour partitions. Partitioning allows the aforementioned big data processing engines to load *only* the range of data they care about and nothing else. You may, of course, partition data on many other attributes, such as event type, location, infosec regulations, and PII details, but these are policies that you'll need to discuss with your governance team and ideally the people who know and use the data.

Temporal boundaries are important for batch processing in the big data space for several reasons. One, it's much more efficient and affordable to only load and process the required data for computing the pipeline results instead of reading a massive data set from cloud storage into memory just to discard most of it. Second, batch processing jobs require that all of the data be present in a time slot before it can start processing. If data is collected in 30-minute chunks, it means we can kick off a processing job every 30 minutes to compute the next batch of results. Many big data analytics computations deal with temporal analysis, and having a precise time range is essential for accuracy.

Third, but not least, big data jobs often need to join on other data sets. By partitioning all cloud storage data sets in the same manner, on the same date and time boundaries, we enable the users of that data to select and choose the time ranges suitable for their use cases. If they only need the last half-hour, no problem. If they need the last 30 days, it's available.

The simplest way to get started is to check out what sink options you have for your event broker. For example, Confluent offers an AWS S3 sink (*https://oreil.ly/9K2Br*) for free usage with Kafka Connect. It has an easily configurable format option (Avro, Parquet, JSON, Raw Bytes), along with a wide range of data partitioner options (*https://oreil.ly/ECNvm*), including custom time-based, daily, and hourly options. The flexibility of sink solution options makes it easy for you to get your event-streaming data into the format necessary to power your existing batch data pipelines.

There's one more important subject to take a look at before we close out the chapter. Despite all of our best efforts, events may be published out of order to an event stream and require resolution by our downstream consumers. Let's take a look at what options we have for handling these events.

Out-of-Order Events

While it's not too difficult to imagine a world where each event in a stream partition is in perfect incrementing timestamp order, the reality of accomplishing it is much more challenging. Consider the pair of producers in Figure 10-6 that take user-behavior click events on a website and convert them into events.

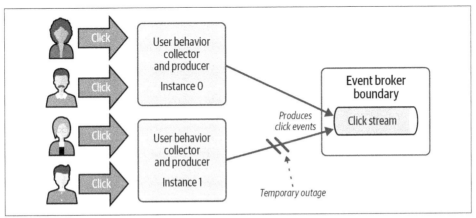

Figure 10-6. Intermittent failures can cause events to be written out of temporal order

Instance 1 is temporarily unable to connect to the event broker but buffers the click events internally until the connection is restored. When connectivity resumes, Instance 1 can write its backlog of events to the event stream with no loss of data. However, the events in stream, time-stamped with the time that the Instance 1 received them, are now temporally out of order with the events from Instance 0.

A temporary outage is not the only scenario where you'll encounter this issue. In fact, the most common source of out-of-order data is due to the inability to perfectly synchronize distributed clocks. Though NTP servers and atomic clocks can bring us *pretty close* to perfect event-time synchronization, the fact of the matter is that we'll always have a bit of skew—a few milliseconds here, a few hundred milliseconds there. Misconfiguration, bugs, and human error also inevitably add their own sources of skew and drift.

You may choose to stamp events with the wall-clock time of the receiving event broker when it receives the event for publishing to the stream. Using the broker-received event time only papers over the clock skew issue as the *true* event time is when the event actually occurred, not when it was recorded to the broker. It's up to you if you choose to use it, but you'd be better off maintaining the original event timestamps and instead commit to handling out-of-order data at the consumer side.

Out-of-order events are important to consider because they affect the state that a consumer converges to. Two independent consumers that treat out-of-order events differently can arrive at permanently different states and never converge at all. In some situations it may not matter, but in others it may be of critical importance.

 I cover the major techniques that stream-processing frameworks use to process events, progress through time, and identify out-of-order data in *Building Event-Driven Microservices*, Chapter 6. Please refer to this chapter if you are interested in the under-the-hood details.

Since events can be written out of order and aren't guaranteed to have monotonically increasing timestamps—how do we handle them? Let's take a look.

Resolving Late-Arriving Events

Events can only be considered late from the perspective of a consumer, and each consumer is free to maintain its own definition of what is late and what is not. Take for instance a consumer maintaining a time-bound window of aggregated data, say *advertisement clicks per hour*, derived from the source-aligned Ad Clicks stream. Windowing operations are excellent forcing functions for handling late arriving data, as they *require* that you answer just one simple question: "Is this specific event part of your time window, or not?"

Figure 10-7 shows the advertisements that the users clicked on, the incrementing offsets, and the *event time* of when the user clicked on it.

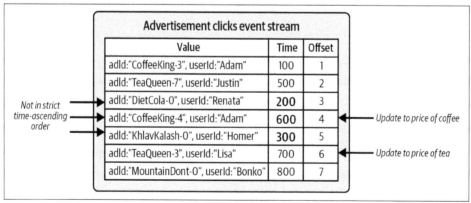

Figure 10-7. Out-of-order events representing advertisment clicks, based on event time

There isn't always a well-defined line between one window of time and another. Note that from offset 2 to 5, the event time oscillates back and forth, indicating a very close race condition, possibly between two producer instances that are *almost* in sync. Overlapping oscillating event times like these are relatively common in event streams created by more than one producer instance, and you'll need to plan accordingly for dealing with them.

Full-featured, event-processing frameworks, like Kafka Streams, Apache Spark, and Apache Flink, have functionality to select and process events in a predictable and deterministic order. Each processing thread selects the event with the lowest (earliest) timestamp and lowest (earliest) offset from among the next possible events, then dispatches it through its business logic. Each of these frameworks has its own way of keeping track of time as seen by the processing instance—Spark and Flink use watermarks, and Kafka Streams uses a stream time. I discuss this in more detail in Chapter 6 of my book *Building Event-Driven Microservices*.

When your stream processor windowing operation sees an event with an event time greater than the window cutoff, it starts a new window and closes off the old window, emitting it to the downstream output. Since the input event streams can be temporally out of order, what happens to the next event that should have gone into the initial window? Well, you have a few options:

Discard it
> You can just drop the event as the window is closed, and any time-based aggregations can conceivably be complete. However, this option is much like slamming the airplane door shut when you can see people sprinting to make their connection—perhaps waiting a couple more seconds isn't too bad.

Keep window open and delay output
> You can also delay closing the window until a given amount of time has elapsed. You'll gain a higher likelihood of completeness, but it'll require that your downstream consumers can tolerate the higher latency.

Keep window open and output multiple updates
> You can output the windowed results as soon as the event-time threshold is hit, but then maintain the old window and the new window in parallel. The old window will stick around for the duration of the grace period, and you can merge in late-arriving events up until the the grace period expires. At that point, you finally close the old window and output the results again if they have been updated during the grace period. From then on, any late-arriving events are simply dropped.

There are no hard-and-fast rules for how your consumers should handle out-of-order events—it's really up to each consumer. Because each consumer is independent, you may find that it introduces nonconvergent behavior, *especially when directly comparing data across synchronous boundaries*, such as a query via a synchronous request-response API. If you can't risk nonconvergence, then you should ensure that your application or service is consuming directly from the source data products and computing its own results.

 The SLAs of your upstream data products are extremely important. Make sure that your service consuming services can tolerate an input data product outage for the period of time specified in the SLA. For instance, if it's possible that your source data product may be unavailable (or not producing data) for say, 5-minutes, then you should ensure your consumer service can handle *at the least* a 5-minute outage (though 15 to 20 minutes would be far safer).

Late-arriving data is not strictly a problem in event-driven data products. Batch-computed data sets can be late as well—a processing job may simply take too long due to resource starvation, failures, or greater-than-usual input data volumes. Downstream batch jobs that rely on the upstream data sets will either themselves be delayed or produce incomplete results and need to be rerun later. Event streams simply bring consideration for temporal ordering to the fore.

Summary

Eventual consistency can be a bit tricky to manage, but by and large it's about becoming aware of *how* it can be introduced and figuring out *if* it needs to be mitigated at all. Event streams offer each consumer the means to converge on the same final state. While each consumer must uphold its own end of the bargain by correctly processing and integrating the data into its own domain, this responsibility remains the same regardless of whether the data is sourced by event stream, batches of data at rest, or via a request-response API.

In the event-driven space, a lagging consumer service will often be inconsistent with another service or data set that is fully up to date. Comparing data between them will likely show inconsistencies, which is only to be expected, as both are operating within their own frame of relative time. There are many solutions to deal with this issue. One is to simply source data from other contexts via their own event streams. If this is not possible, then plan for inconsistencies and have retry and mitigation strategies in place to deal with them.

Eventual-consistency issues can also arise when data in one data product references data in another that may not yet have been produced, such as any data product where events would be joined by a primary or foreign key. While the consumers may all be up to date with the latest written events, they have not converged to the same state as the upstream producers of the data.

Finally, out-of-order data can introduce additional complications, particularly when many parallel producers write events to the same stream with slightly skewed timestamps. Consumers can independently handle out-of-order events using late-arrival logic, but they must be cognizant that they may end up interpreting data differently than a neighbor. A best practice is to tie the implementation of late-arrival logic to the SLA of the data product so that your consumers are resilient to any availability or consistency issues within the guarantees of the SLA.

In our next and final chapter, we'll review what we've covered across this book and wrap up with what to look out for in the future of data mesh.

CHAPTER 11

Bringing It All Together

Data mesh is founded on four principles, based on hard-learned lessons of dealing with difficult-to-use data, often provided as no more than a form of exhaust emitted by operational applications. Mechanisms for obtaining and accessing data outside of its original source are typically added as an afterthought, bolted onto the source system in an ad hoc manner.

Data mesh promotes data to a product with the same rigor, ownership, and feature management of any other product in your business. The free-for-all, "figure it out yourself" data access is replaced with purpose-built, maintained, and supported modes. It is as much a social shift as it is a technological shift and requires both top-down and bottom-up buy-in. We reevaluate how we own, create, discover, and access data, and then build out the processes, governance, and technology required to make it work.

Event streams provide the number one option for making data mesh a reality. They provide a singular mechanism for both historical and real-time data communications, forming the data mesh's basic building blocks for consumers to use, mix, and match to their needs.

Data mesh is based on four main principles: domain ownership, data as a product, federated governance, and self-service platform. Together, these principles help us focus on communicating important business data across the entire organization safely, effectively, and at-scale:

Domain ownership

Those who know the data best are charged with the responsibility of making it readily available for their peers and colleagues to use and access as they see fit. Domain owners consult with prospective consumers to source data requirements and ensure that business needs are met. They remain responsible for protecting the internal domain model from overexposure and unacceptable levels of coupling by external parties so that both the internal model and the external data product can independently evolve and change.

Data as a product

Important business data needs to be readily and reliably available as building block primitives for your applications, regardless of the runtime, environment, or codebase of your application. We can accomplish this goal by focusing on creating data as a product, treating data as a first-class citizen, complete with dedicated ownership, minimum quality guarantees, SLAs, and scalable mechanisms for clean and reliable access.

Data products act as the basic building blocks for composing your business services, enabling consumers to access and use the data for their own use cases.

Federated governance

Federated governance concerns itself with maintaining stability and order, balancing individual autonomy and top-down centralized control.

A governance team, drawn from those participating in the data mesh, is empowered with addressing the needs of domain owners, data product creators, data product users, and infrastructure providers. Like any form of effective government, the governance team needs participation, representation, debate, and collaborative action to get meaningful work done. The governance team guides the requirements for the self-service platform, focusing on increasing discoverability, ease of use, and intercompatibility with other data products.

Successful federated governance results in data products that are easy to build, manage, and use. Data product owners should have reasonable options for building and managing their data product in the self-service platform. They should also be provided with guardrails to support necessary nonfunctional business requirements, like encryption, access controls, and automated data retention management.

Self-service platform

Just as every data mesh implementation will be unique unto itself, so will its self-service platform. The main goals of creating a self-service platform include making it easy to:

- Browse, discover, and search through available data products
- Grant, restrict, and manage access controls
- Requisition compute, storage, and serving components, including event streams
- Manage the data product life cycle, including prototyping, publishing, deprecating, and deleting

Building a self-service platform requires working closely with data product owners and the federated governance team. Your best chance for success involves starting with a minimum viable product consisting of technologies and control systems you're already using. Treat your self-service data platform like any other product, iteratively adding and testing new capabilities as usage patterns and requirements become clearer.

Event Streams for Data Mesh

An event is an immutable and self-contained record of something that happened. An event stream is a continuously updating data structure of events, with each stream representing a selection of important business facts.

Event streams are the ideal mechanism for serving data products, as they provide a simple yet powerful way of reliably communicating important business data across an organization. Event streams are fast, scalable, and efficient, letting consumers know when new data is available as it happens and enabling real-time reaction across your business for any use case.

State events form the best option for building data products, though you do have some leeway in your options. You can include information such as *why* the state changed, combining some of the aspects of a delta event with the state event. But remain cautious about overexposing specific business logic transitions from the source domain in your data products because they introduce strong coupling seams.

The Kappa architecture works hand-in-hand with state events. You can source the entire history of the data product from just the event stream instead of splitting historical and real-time data access in two, as with the Lambda architecture. Historical state can be accessed by consuming the event stream from an earlier point in time. You can use compaction to eliminate older, no-longer-relevant state events, making it fast, easy, and inexpensive for consumers to access the data.

Simplicity is key for making a data mesh work, and event streams provide a simple yet powerful solution for making data readily available.

Integrating with Existing Systems

Data mesh implementations are rarely (if ever) greenfield developments. The pains that data mesh resolves are incurred largely by the growth of an organization and the demands for important business data by multiple disparate use cases. Thus, when building a data mesh, you're going to need to contend with all of your existing systems and iteratively work toward improving how data is created, shared, and used across your organization.

Bootstrapping data out of existing databases and systems is an important part of getting started with data mesh. You can get data published to an event stream quickly and easily so that consumers can start trialing it for use in their own domains. It also kick-starts conversations about who owns the connector, and in turn, who owns the data, the domain, and managing feature requests to change what data is available and how it's represented.

Typically, bootstrapped data reflects the internal domain model of the source system. Highly normalized data sourced from relational databases tends to be difficult to use, requiring complex and often expensive denormalizations by downstream users. The frequency of events, the size of events, and the tight internal coupling all remain concerns for bootstrapped data products.

Bootstrapped data products remain a stepping stone on the way to generating first-class data products, with an explicit schema, denormalized data structures, and isolation from the internal data model. But they remain an important part of the iterative growth of a data mesh.

Operations, Analytics, and Everything in Between

Data mesh was originally prescribed for solving the data access and reliability problems inherent in the analytics domain. However, it has proven to be a powerful off-label solution for powering operational systems as well as those that defy categorization as one or the other. Reliable access to clean, well-defined, low-latency data is the bedrock of a strategically flexible architecture. You have the freedom to create, test, and trial new business systems without having to struggle for data access. Your systems will no longer look like Frankenstein's monster, grafted together simply to access the underlying data.

Event streams play a critical role in powering time-sensitive applications. Operational systems, especially those with a human in the loop, benefit heavily from low-latency state events. Analytical systems benefit by drawing their data from the same sources of the operational systems, alleviating the "similar-yet-different" data sources that have historically plagued the data space.

Summary

An event-driven data mesh is an investment in the future. Successfully adopting it requires identifying the data pain points in your organization so you can begin applying the four principles. Obtain buy-in from your colleagues by helping them understand how a data mesh can solve their chronic data problems.

Work iteratively. Your data mesh won't suddenly spring up overnight. Trial new solutions, learn from mistakes, and make iterative improvements. Finding value along the way is essential for keeping people invested and reaping the benefits of your data products.

Finally, celebrate success as you create your data mesh. The road will be winding, and sometimes it may feel like you're going backwards. Share your trials and tribulations with your peers, and work together to find common ground and new ways forward. Good luck in your journey ahead.

Index

About the Author

Adam Bellemare is a staff technologist, office of the CTO at Confluent. Previously, he was a staff engineer, data platform at Shopify, and he was at Flipp from 2014, first as a senior developer, followed by a staff role. He has also held positions in embedded software development and quality assurance. His expertise includes DevOps (Kafka, Spark, Mesos, Zookeeper Clusters; programmatic building, scaling, destroying); technical leadership (bringing Avro formatting to our data end-to-end, championing Kafka as the event-driven microservice bus, prototyping JRuby, Scala, and Java Kafka clients and focusing on removing technical impediments to allow for product delivery); software development (building microservices in Java and Scala using Spark and Kafka libraries); and data engineering (reshaping the way that behavioral data is collected from user devices and shared with machine learning, billing, and analytics teams). He is the author of *Building Event-Driven Microservices* (O'Reilly).

Colophon

The animal on the cover of *Building an Event-Driven Data Mesh* is a red bird-of-paradise (*Paradisaea rubra*). These birds are found on only two islands of Indonesia: Waigeo and Batanta.

Males of the species are known for their bright plumage. They have long red feathers on each side of the breast, a green face with feather pompoms above each eye, and long corkscrew-shaped tail wires. Females are mostly brown, with no ornamentation. The birds have a lek mating system, where males gather to perform competitive courtship rituals while females survey and choose a mate.

The birds' diet predominantly consists of fruit, berries, and insects. The family *Paradisaeidae* is instrumental in dispersing seeds throughout the forests of New Guinea.

Due to habitat loss, the conservation status of the red bird-of-paradise is Near Threatened. Many of the animals on O'Reilly covers are endangered; all of them are important to the world.

The cover illustration is by Karen Montgomery, based on an antique line engraving from *Lydekker's Royal Natural History*. The cover fonts are Gilroy Semibold and Guardian Sans. The text font is Adobe Minion Pro; the heading font is Adobe Myriad Condensed; and the code font is Dalton Maag's Ubuntu Mono.

Milton Keynes UK
Ingram Content Group UK Ltd.
UKHW030712051024
449226UK00004B/8